# The Door
# of No Return

*Text design by Sue Lamble*

Copyright © 2006, 2007 by William St Clair
Published in Great Britain under the title
*The Grand Slave Emporium* by Profile Books Ltd.

LIBRARY OF CONGRESS CATALOGING-IN-PUBLICATION DATA
St. Clair, William.
The door of no return : Cape Coast Castle and the slave trade / William St Clair.
p. cm.
Includes bibliographical references and index.
ISBN-13: 978-1-933346-05-2
ISBN-10: 1-933346-05-1
1. Slave-trade—Ghana—History. 2. Slavery—Ghana—History. 3. Cape Coast
Castle (Cape Coast, Ghana)—History. 4. Cape Coast Castle (Cape Coast,
Ghana)—Sociological aspects. 5. Slave-trade—Great Britain—History. I. Title.

HT1394.G48S73 2007
306.3'6209667—dc22                                                    2006031398

First published in North America in 2007 by
B l u e B r i d g e
An imprint of
United Tribes Media Inc.
Goldens Bridge, New York
www.bluebridgebooks.com

Published in paperback in 2009 (ISBN 9781933346168).

Printed in the United States of America

10 9 8 7 6 5 4

# Contents

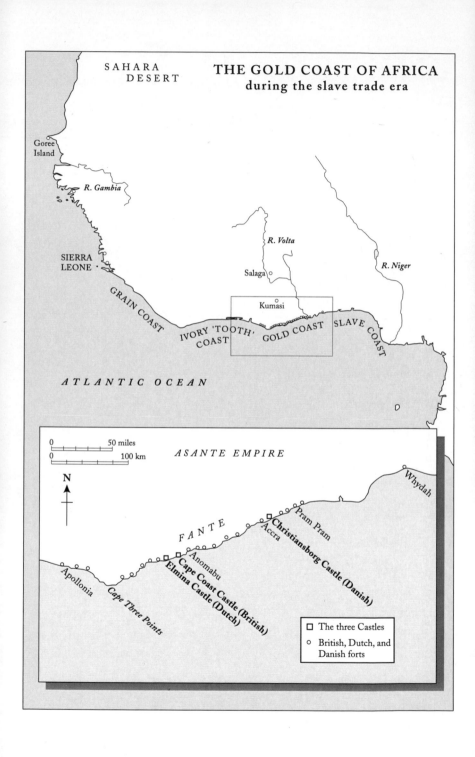

SAHARA
DESERT

THE GOLD COAST OF AFRICA
during the slave trade era

Goree
Island

*R. Gambia*

SIERRA
LEONE

*R. Volta*

Salaga

*R. Niger*

Kumasi

GRAIN COAST

IVORY 'TOOTH'
COAST

GOLD COAST

SLAVE COAST

*ATLANTIC OCEAN*

0        50 miles
0        100 km

*ASANTE EMPIRE*

Whydah

N

FANTE

Pram Pram

Accra

Christiansborg Castle (Danish)

Anomabu

Cape Coast Castle (British)

Elmina Castle (Dutch)

Apollonia

Cape Three Points

□  The three Castles
○  British, Dutch, and
   Danish forts

# Introduction

Along the western coast of Africa, from where the Sahara desert ends in the north to the Cape of Good Hope in the south, are the remains of many castles, forts, and temporary lodges built by the Portuguese, the Spanish, the Dutch, the French, the Germans of the Duchy of Brandenburg, the Danes, the Swedes, and the British. Other countries, notably the United States and Brazil, which had no slaving forts, had fleets of slaving ships. However, nowhere are there such vivid monuments to the transatlantic slave trade as along the coast of Ghana, where about sixty forts were built, some within sight – and even cannon range – of each other. Although that stretch of the African coast was difficult for sailing ships to approach, it was more accessible than either the coast to the west, which was skirted by shallow sandy lagoons, or the coast further to the east, where the deltas of the rivers Volta and Niger caused other problems for mariners. Most of these forts still stand, either adapted for later uses or in various states of ruin.

Cape Coast Castle, which lies almost on the same meridian as London, was the headquarters in Africa of the entire British involvement in the transatlantic slave trade. For 143 years (1664–1807) it was, in the words of one of its British governors, the grand emporium of the British slave trade. From this building perched on the shore of the South Atlantic Ocean, men, women, and children born in Africa were sold to British slave ships and carried to the West Indies, to North and South America, and to destinations elsewhere. Most were then put to work in tropical plantations, growing sugar, tobacco, rice, coffee, cotton, indigo, and other crops, or were employed in mines, in the industrial workshops in which the crops were processed, as soldiers, or as domestic servants.

The British slaving fort at Whydah in Dahomey (modern Ouidah in Benin), nearly 300 miles to the east, was administered from the Castle. Many hundreds of miles from the Castle in the other direction were the British forts in the Gambia and Sierra Leone (and for a time Gorée Island in Senegal), at times formally subordinate to the governor in Cape Coast Castle, but mostly administered directly from London, and all integrated into the same oceanic network of ships and shore settlements that formed the African end of the British slave trade. Henry Meredith, a fort governor, who stayed on after the trade was made illegal in 1807 and who wrote a book recommending that it should be resumed, looked back nostalgically to the days he remembered when 'it was common to see twenty or thirty sailing ships of different nations at one time.'

The Castle today is well preserved, partially restored, and excellently presented, with an informative museum. Along with other castles and forts in Ghana, it is designated a UNESCO World Heritage Site. Although the building has been altered since the slave trade era, much remains the same: the heat and the damp, the unceasing crash and spray of the Atlantic breakers on the rocks, the long canoes by which the local coastal peoples make their living from the sea, and the vultures, which are seldom out of sight. Visitors need no longer fear the malaria, the yellow fever, and the other tropical illnesses that long made West Africa the white man's grave. However, to appreciate the claim of the Castle on the memory of the entire modern world, the journey must take place in the imagination. There is no other way.

ooooo

The transatlantic slave trade was the greatest forced migration in history. From the mid-fifteenth to the late nineteenth century, over 11 million people born in Africa were carried across the ocean. About 3 million were taken by ships belonging to British merchants and those of the British settlers in North America and the West Indies. Nearly a million enslaved Africans went to Jamaica alone. During the 1790s, when the British slave trade was at its height, a slaving ship left London, Bristol, Liverpool, or one of half a dozen other British ports every second day. There was also a huge inter-American slave trade – to, from, within, and between mainland North and South America and the Caribbean. The ancestors of innumerable people living today in the United States, Canada, the English-speaking Caribbean, Britain, and many other countries passed through the 'door of no return' in Cape Coast Castle or in one of its subsidiary forts. Louis Armstrong, for one, believed his family left Africa through the gate of the British fort at Anomabu nearby, although, like others, he only had uncertain traditions to go on.

Thousands of men participated directly, traveling far from their homes in order to do so. But many other men, women, and children, Europeans, Africans, Americans, and Asians, were indirectly employed near where they lived, in making the building materials for the castles and forts, in designing and constructing the specialized sailing vessels, in manufacturing the armaments, chains, and instruments of coercion, in providing the financial capital, the credit, the insurance, the foreign exchange, and the other complex services that were essential to the operation of the trade. Many thousands more were employed in spinning, weaving, dyeing, and packing the fabrics, in casting and forging the metalwares, in distilling the brandy and the rum, and in the manufacture and processing of the many other goods and commodities that were taken to Africa to be exchanged for slaves. Even the peoples of

North America who traded deerskins to the incoming European settlers were drawn into the oceanic economy.

Among those who received dividends from the slave trade were the British royal family, the British aristocracy, the English church, and many institutions, families, and individuals. Plantation owners in North America and the West Indies prospered from the sale of commodities produced by slave labor, as did some of their employees and business partners, and profits remitted to Britain and British settlers overseas supported others who never left home. A similar reckoning could be made for the other slaving nations. But it is scarcely an exaggeration to say that every person in the Europeanized world who put sugar in their tea or coffee, spread jam on their bread, who ate sweets, cakes, or ice cream, who smoked or chewed tobacco, took snuff, drank rum or corn brandy, or wore colored cotton clothes, also benefited from, and participated in, a globalized economy of tropical plantations worked by slaves forcibly brought from Africa.

When in the 1830s Brodie Cruikshank, a governor of Anomabu fort, contemplated the map of West Africa with the European slaving forts dotted along its coast, he saw parasitic leeches that had stuck themselves on to the skin of Africa, ruthlessly sucking its blood and draining away its vitality. At that time illegal slave trading was still rife. But, to others, the same dots on the same maps were already being reimagined as beacons of light, outposts of civilization, and as beachheads for an army of Christian missionaries eager to make the peoples of Africa conform to their own beliefs and customs. As the anonymous author of *West-African Sketches* wrote in 1824, 'The present may be the time decreed by the counsels of the Most High for the ray to go forth which is to enlighten those who sit in darkness, and through the medium of a small British colony on the shores of that vast continent . . . the beam shall pierce the inmost recesses of superstition and idolatry.'

Within a generation of the ending of the legal British slave trade in 1807, the Castle had become one of the advance posts of the sustained and, in human as well as financial terms, costly British policy of ending the slave trade both in West Africa and round the world – an enterprise that can still be seen, even by the most cynical, as among the least ambiguous examples of national altruism in history. The memory of one early-nineteenth-century governor, George Maclean, who promoted peace, schools, and economic development in the locality, is still honored in the Castle, where he is buried. In late Victorian times it was Robert Baden-Powell, who, as a result of his experiences in what had then become the colony of the Gold Coast, founded the Boy Scouts, an organization that aimed to persuade young people to adopt the ideals recommended to Victorian officers and gentlemen. And in the 1950s A. W. Lawrence, a professor of classical archaeology at Cambridge University, then director of the National Museum and Monuments in the Gold Coast, wrote *The Trade Castles and Forts of West Africa.* Inspired by the pioneering researches on the European castles in the Middle East made by his brother T. E. Lawrence (Lawrence of Arabia), A. W. Lawrence and his colleagues ensured that Cape Coast Castle and the other castles and forts were surveyed, photographed, and in many cases preserved and restored, as an enduring testimony to the era of direct British involvement in the government of Ghana that was then drawing to a close.

ooooo

For a century and a half after the legal British slave trade was brought to an end British historians ignored, downplayed, or brushed aside the slaving era as a regrettable preliminary to the glorious British Christian imperialism that followed. It was a small step to suggest that the trade had not been so bad after all. Mary Kingsley, for example, who visited the Castle and its slave dungeons

in late Victorian times, thought abolition had been 'a grave mistake.'
W. Walton Claridge, a colonial medical official, who in 1915 wrote
a two-volume *History of the Gold Coast*, still occasionally referred to
as the standard work, devoted only about 200 pages out of 1,300 to
the slaving era. 'Most of the hysterical nonsense that was written
at the time of the agitation for the abolition of the trade,' Claridge
wrote, 'consisted of gross exaggerations of isolated cases of abuse.'
As recently as 1952 W. E. F. Ward, who had also lived in the country
and was also both knowledgeable and sympathetic, wrote in his
own *History of the Gold Coast* that Claridge's 'great work' could not
be superseded.

Every modern generation rediscovers the horrors of the 'middle
passage,' the five- or six-week voyage of the slaving vessels from
Africa to the Americas during which many enslaved Africans (and
crew members) died. In recent years, however, much careful historical
research has been published on many other aspects of the slave trade,
including the nature and history of indigenous slavery in Africa, the
other oceanic and land slave trades, the impact of the exchange of
pathogens and illnesses among the three continents, the effects of
the migrations out of Africa on African and on American societies,
and the contribution of the slave trade to economic development.
Since 1999 it has been possible to consult an electronic database of
over 27,000 transatlantic slave voyages, thought to include about
75 percent of the total, compiled by a team of scholars from the
archives of many countries. According to Bernard Bailyn, one of
the modern school of historians who study oceanic exchanges, the
impact of the publication of this database, with the opportunities
for research that it has opened up, can be compared to that of the
Hubble telescope on our understanding of the universe.

With the main outlines now established, those who dare to write
face another problem. How can we escape from the assumptions
about the relative value of human lives, European and African,

female and male, non-Christian and Christian, adult and child, and the other hierarchies that permeate the historical writings on which our understanding unavoidably depends? How, if at all, can we cope with the immovable fact that those who were most directly involved in the transatlantic slave trade, the enslaved Africans themselves, are, with only a handful of exceptions, silent? Apart from African oral traditions (see Chapter 8), and what can be learned from occasional archaeological finds, such as utensils and shackles discovered on forest paths inland, the sparse details recorded by Europeans at the first encounter at the coast are, as far as I know, the only eighteenth-century historical records we have of the lives of enslaved individuals before they left the Gold Coast. The chirpy language of the tourist industry tries to take the sting out of history by turning it into heritage – 'Fort Patience . . . this year celebrates the 300th anniversary of its establishment;' 'The castles and forts . . . played an important role in the shaping of Ghana's unique cosmopolitan character.' The dispassionate language of economics, which has been adopted with success by many scholars, is inescapable, but statistics can be chilling unless they can be related to individual lives.

In this book, by telling the story of just one building, and of some of the men, women, and children who spent part of their lives within its walls, I hope to illuminate an immense panorama of history which, in its entirety, is almost impossible to comprehend. As it happens, although there have been excellent books about the Castle as architecture, little has been written, or indeed known, about the people who lived, worked, or were imprisoned there, and about how the African end of the transatlantic slave trade was conducted from day to day. And that gap in knowledge is at its largest during the later eighteenth century, when the British slave trade was at its height.

In my attempt to put the people back into the building, I have used many manuscript and printed sources (see Bibliographical

Note). They include the extensive printed writings of the naturalist Sarah Bowdich, later Lee, who lived in the Castle in 1816 and 1817, and whose vivid descriptions have been overlooked. But my main source has been a vast archive of unpublished, and still mostly unexplored, manuscript records preserved among the British National Archives. When the British government took over direct responsibility for Cape Coast Castle in 1821, following an Act of Parliament of 1820, they arranged for all the papers that had accumulated in the Castle since it was captured by an English fleet in 1664 (see Chapter 2) to be bundled up and sent to London. In the same year the British government took over the papers of the Africa House, the London headquarters from which the Castle had hitherto been managed, so acquiring another huge accumulation of papers, including many letters sent from the Castle. In the nineteenth century the British government deposited all these papers, scarcely sorted, in the Public Record Office, and they are now held at Kew near London.

The bound volumes of journals, letters, ledgers, and accounts that start in the 1660s (many dozens still uncounted from the 1660s to 1750 and about 500 counted from 1750 to 1821) record the life of Cape Coast Castle to an amazing degree of detail – the construction and upkeep of the buildings, the recruitment of the officers and the soldiers, the work of the Castle slaves, the food and drink consumed, the stores imported, the arrivals and departures of ships, the trading of goods and slaves, the correspondence with London and elsewhere, and the negotiations and agreements with local African leaders. There can be few buildings anywhere in the world about which more is knowable. And there was scarcely an event during the century and a half when the Castle was the grand slave emporium that was not recorded in writing, even if, just occasionally, as on two days in 1771 when the weather was set fine, all that the governor could think to write in his log was: 'Ditto weather. Nothing occurred.'

These are the formal and, in human terms, the less revealing part of the archive. Still unsorted in dozens of boxes are thousands of loose papers that contain writings most of which have probably never been read a second time until I began my researches – personal correspondence with colleagues and relatives, letters from home, and, uniquely, hundreds of notes sent between the Castle and the slave ships. Bleached by the sun and slowly crumbling from their salty voyages, these writings offer glimpses of events noted down as they happened, often catching the speech patterns and the regional accents of the men and women who wrote them. Occasionally, too, they preserve tiny pieces of information about individuals among the Africans who, in the slavers' euphemism, were 'sent off the coast,' and who are otherwise nameless statistics. Composed without any thought that they would survive, unmediated by hindsight, and free of any wider agenda, these papers are, as historical documents, not only amazingly full and revealing but are also essentially different from all other writings on the slave trade, plentiful and informative though these are. In telling the story of Cape Coast Castle – moving from the sea, to the building, and then to the people – I will include many quotations from these papers, transcribed with the minimum of editing, to catch the sense of actually being there at the time that their artlessness enables us to share.

# 1

# The sea

## *The coast*

Visitors to Cape Coast Castle nowadays arrive by land. When it was a slave emporium many came by sea. The captains of sailing ships arriving from Europe and the Americas, edging their slow way along the coast of West Africa, past the 'Grain Coast' (pepper) and the 'Tooth Coast' (ivory), discerned through their telescopes the beginning of a line of white forts, each with a brightly colored British or Dutch flag. The captains knew then that after dreary months at sea they had arrived at the fabulous 'Gold Coast.' As they rounded Cape Three Points and turned the bows of their ships towards the land, they suddenly encountered the lush smell of the forest. Soon they could make out what Captain Ellis, a visiting military officer, described as 'the snow white sands, the groves of palms, and the golden haze.' According to Brodie Cruikshank, who made the voyage several times, for every European newly arriving from the north, there was 'a lightness and elasticity in the clear transparent atmosphere, a laughing joyousness in the gentle ripple of the sea, an idea of wild romance about the untried land lying in beauty before him.' The Gold Coast had 'a wild Robinson Crusoe sort of charm.'

To the slave-ship captains of the eighteenth century, these waters were as familiar as any in the world. If Captain Marshall, who gave evidence to a parliamentary inquiry into the slave trade in 1790, was exceptional in having been on nineteen slaving voyages, almost all the others had been here before, either as captains, formally 'masters,' or earlier in their careers as junior officers, 'mates,' or as surgeons.

A typical British slaving voyage, which could take up to two years, involved three sides of an oceanic triangle – the chartering and fitting out of a vessel in a British or British colonial port in mainland North America or the West Indies, freighting her with the goods and commodities to be traded, sailing her to West Africa, where they were bartered for slaves – transactions that might take many months – and then, when the ship was packed with slaves, a direct 'middle passage' voyage to the Americas, to be followed by the landing and sale of the slaves, and the voyage back to the home port.

The captains arriving in the waters off the Castle had charts and maps that gave them excellent information about the winds, the currents, the shallows, the rocks, the underwater reefs, the safest anchorages, the dangerous capes, the possible landing places, and the coastal towns. Many captains were familiar too with the diverse political systems, religions, laws, customs, and languages of the coastal nations and peoples in whose territories the Castle and the forts were located. On what lay beyond the coast, however, they knew little. When they turned their telescopes towards the land, all they could see was an apparently unbroken forest that began near the water's edge and stretched inland towards misty hills in the distance. Although, by the time the slave trade reached its height in the later eighteenth century, Europeans had been settled in this part of the African coast continuously for centuries, the knowledge they had been able to gather about the paths to the interior through the forest was scanty, and direct contact with the inland peoples was infrequent. Richard Miles, twice governor of the Castle, who lived on the coast with only one break for eighteen years, fathered seven children there, and spoke the language of the local Fante people perfectly, told the same inquiry in 1790 that, except once when he went twenty miles inland, he had never been more than five miles from the sea.

Beyond the limits of European exploration, there were many lands that were fabled to be rich in gold, but the name 'the Gold Coast' was more than fantasy. Centuries before the first European ships, those of the Portuguese, appeared off the coast in 1471, gold had been mined near the shore, taken north by land through the forest and savannah to the river Niger, by canoe to Timbuktu, then carried across the Sahara by camel caravans, eventually finding its way into the coinage and jewelry of Morocco, Egypt, Spain, Venice, Florence, and other states of late medieval and Renaissance Europe. When the ships began a regular trade, decades before Columbus reached America, the aim of their captains was to obtain a share of that gold by bringing European goods, mainly cloth, which they offered in exchange. And, centuries later, when the British slaving era was at its height, gold was still much in evidence. Rich African men and women wore gold ornaments. African traders, often naked except for a single cloth, carried gold dust in pouches tied to their legs. At Elmina Castle, headquarters of the Dutch slaving industry, a few miles along the coast from Cape Coast Castle, the slaves who served at the governor's table wore golden chains. The British in the Castle and the forts accumulated gold dust in bottles in heavily locked closets, against the day when they could send it home and translate it into real wealth. According to Paul Isert, a Danish scientist who visited the Gold Coast in 1785, one of the inland kings had a gold nugget so big that it took four men to lift it – just another traveler's tale, some readers thought, but the Asantehene of Asante, or the king of Ashantee as the Europeans called the ruler of the empire 200 miles to the north, had a throne that was carried by four men. Two of its golden decorative vultures, captured in a war of 1874 (see Chapter 9), can now be seen in the Wallace Collection museum in London.

The arriving slave-ship captains knew that beyond the busy British slaving fort at Anomabu – visible on the next cape to the east of Cape Coast Castle – stretched more European forts and the fine Castle of Christiansborg at Accra, from which the Danish government sent slaves to the Danish island colonies in the West Indies, St. Thomas and St. Croix, now the United States Virgin Islands. And beyond the mouth of the Volta river, regarded as the end of the 'Gold Coast,' was the 'Slave Coast,' of the Niger Delta, and the slave markets of Dahomey, Biafra, Benin, Old and New Calabar, the islands of Principe, Sao Tome, and Fernando Po, Angola, and elsewhere south to the Cape of Good Hope, and to the East Indies beyond.

## Riding the roads

On a map, the rocky outcrop on which the Castle stands is little more than a bump on a long, smooth coastline. To the Portuguese, it was the Cabo Corso, the short cape, which the English translated into 'Cape Corso' and the sailors soon called 'Cape Coast.' But for the arriving captains it was a dangerous headland with complex currents and hidden rocks. Although even the biggest British slaving ships were tiny by later standards, displacing only around 300 tons, there was no harbor able to receive them for hundreds of miles. Elmina Castle, built on an island in the estuary of a slow, muddy river, had a dock and crane, but could not be safely approached by any vessel of more than about fifty tons, and even they sometimes stuck on the sandbar at the mouth of the river.

Between the ships and the shore was what the British called 'the surf,' the Atlantic rollers that began as heaving waves far out to sea and broke into white foam and spray as they reached the shallow coastal waters. Ships intending to trade at the Castle, even the smallest oceangoing vessel, had to ride at anchor far offshore in the roadstead, 'the roads,' a stretch of water that was reasonably sheltered from the winds and had been surveyed as deep enough for a laden ship to avoid sticking in the sand or striking a hidden reef. Smaller ships could ride about a mile from shore, where the sea was seven fathoms deep. Others anchored two miles out, and heavy warships needed deep water. When the wind blew, a prudent captain would take his ship further out to sea in case his ship was driven inshore and stuck or was wrecked, as happened from time to time. From May to August, when the wind was strongest, ships lay four miles out. When anchored in the roads, the ships were described as 'under the protection of the Castle,' and any ship that attempted to anchor without exposing its long side to the Castle guns risked being regarded as hostile. Although, at these distances, the Castle guns could not hit such ships, other British ships anchored in the roads could do so, and the Castle could stop traffic with the landing beaches.

For the arriving captains, the guns meant that, for a time at least, their ship was reasonably safe from armed attack. Between 1662 and 1815, a time span that largely coincides with the British slaving era, Britain was at war with France nine times, with the Netherlands twice, with Spain six times, and with the mainland American colonies/United States twice. Every clear day the British governor of Cape Coast Castle and the Dutch governor of Elmina eyed each other's castle through their telescopes, noting which ships came in to anchor, discovering which local leaders and traders were visiting, comparing goods and prices, and generally playing out worldwide European commercial and political rivalries at these distant outposts. One month the British governor could be entertaining the Dutch governor to dinner, the next they could be at war, and sometimes they were at war without either of them knowing.

2. *'Cabo Corso,' from the sea, with canoes and ships on the seaward side of the surf, early eighteenth century.*

In the slaving era, merchant ships were not normally sunk on sight either by warships or by the officially authorized armed merchantmen, 'privateers.' Indeed, wooden ships were not easy to sink at all, except when they had been set on fire or their powder magazines were struck by gunfire and they blew up. In the wars of the eighteenth century many vessels of all types were captured after a chase and sailed to a port where the vessel and its cargo were sold for the benefit of the capturing ship's officers and crew. British ships captured on their way to Africa laden with American, East Indian, and British goods might end up sailing the same seas under another national flag. Some British slaving vessels had originally been French prizes, hence the French names for particular rigs, such as 'sneau.' African slaves on their way to the British plantations in, say, Jamaica might find themselves sent instead to the French or Spanish Caribbean islands, to Dutch or French Guiana, the northern and southern ports of Portuguese Brazil, or the United

States. If captured by the Dutch they might be taken south to the Cape of Good Hope and on to the East Indies. Once the ships were out of sight of the Castle, many months could pass without news. It was reported by the governor in 1796, for example, that of 355 British slave-ship voyages to Africa during the previous three years, 84 vessels were already known to have been lost at sea or captured by the enemy, but also, the governor noted, 'a great number of ships which sailed in 1795 and 1796 have been captured, of which no official account has yet been received.'

It was not only the ships of other countries that interrupted the patterns of the slave trade. From Frederick Marryat and C. S. Forester to Patrick O'Brien, readers have been fed fictional stories, 'yarns,' of dashing young British naval officers 'cutting out' merchant vessels, that is, slashing their cables and seizing them when they drifted. But such exploits, lucrative though they were to the captains and crews of the attacking ships, upset the carefully balanced relationships of the rival castles. During the American revolutionary war the British and Dutch forts at Komenda, situated on opposite sides of a river, bombarded each other with their cannon, and brought all slave trading in the locality to an end. As a result of that experience the governors of Cape Coast and Elmina made a local pact not to attack the other's castle unless specifically instructed to do so by their headquarters in Europe, in which case they promised to give ten days' notice to enable the other side to get ready. When in 1781 Captain Fagan of the *Seccumb*, a privateer of Liverpool, proposed to 'cut out' enemy ships in the roads of Elmina, the governor of Cape Coast Castle was horrified at his disregard of their local treaty. The privateer went ahead, despite being strongly advised not to, and the governor wrote to complain. 'We believe,' he told the *Seccumb*'s owners, 'that Blackbeard the pirate would not have committed such an act of Inhumanity.'

Even if there was no official international war, the seas between

West Africa and the West Indies were seldom free of pirates whose reputation for ruthlessness was fully deserved. For example, Bartholomew Roberts, an officer on board the British slaver *Princess*, captured by pirates in 1720, decided to join them and was soon their captain. Among the 400 or so vessels that he seized, with their gold, goods, and slaves, was a large frigate that he fitted with 40 guns and used to attack shipping on the Gold Coast. When he was eventually hunted down by a British warship and killed in an exchange of fire, his ship was captured and the crew were put on trial. Seventy Africans who had been slaves on board the ships he had captured were returned to slavery, probably put in the dungeons at Cape Coast Castle and later sent to the Americas. Of the crew, fifty-four were hanged from the guns of the Castle, thirty-seven received lesser sentences, and seventy-four were acquitted.

Any ship of any nationality passing through the waters off the Castle was required to lower its topsails, a courtesy that signified peaceful intent: without topsails a ship could not sail fast. British vessels arriving to trade fired a salute of at least nine guns and the salute was returned by the Castle, one of the few places in the world where a British fort routinely exchanged gun salutes with merchant vessels. The Castle welcomed the governors of the two other European castles, Dutch Elmina and Danish Christiansborg, with fifteen salutes when they visited, the governors of the larger British forts with thirteen, and the governors of the lesser British forts with nine. As far as warships were concerned, in 1778 the governor of Komenda fort instructed his deputy to greet any British naval vessel with seventeen salutes on her arrival in the roads and to fire seventeen when she left, with another fifteen if the captain came ashore and fifteen when he returned to his ship. It was the duty of the gunner at Cape Coast Castle to record the expenditure of gunpowder and to prepare a detailed account that was sent to London. From these accounts we learn, to quote just one example, that in 1792 the Castle 'expended returning salute to the ship Vulture, Captain Beecket on his arrival and departure 2/3' (two-thirds of a barrel of gunpowder).

At the Castle a gun was also fired at a set time every morning and evening so that the captains of ships in the roads could synchronize their watches. The ships themselves operated an elaborate system of signals to declare their intentions to the Castle and to other ships. A special flag was run up for weeks before a ship sailed for the Americas, and in the final days the ship fired a gun every morning. All this banging was expensive, but it was an intrinsic part of the infrastructure – and of the cultural superstructure – of the transatlantic slave trade. Everyone living along the coast was reminded every day that the British had heavy guns and the Africans did not.

It was normally only ships flying the British flag, that is, those from Great Britain or from the British colonies in the West Indies and North America, that were permitted to anchor in the roads at Cape Coast Castle. In 1776, the year thirteen American mainland colonies declared independence, almost 40 percent of the British merchant fleet was built in America, and American ships were immediately excluded. Many of the vessels built in British yards to take their place were designed for the transatlantic slave trade, copper-bottomed, fitted out with many expensive specialized features, and operated from enlarged docks and dredged riverways at Liverpool and Bristol. They had a competitive edge over the ships of other slaving nations. In peacetime, however, ships of all nationalities were accorded the courtesies of the sea, helped, for example, if they needed time or planking for emergency repairs or wanted to buy water, and there was a good deal of trading between ships of different nationalities – mostly illegal according to their respective national laws – even in wartime (see Chapter 8). When in 1800 the governor of the Castle ordered that an American schooner should be denied anchorage and water, he had few other remedies. Despite repeated requests to the Admiralty to station a British warship on the West African coast, only occasionally did the Castle receive a visit from the Royal Navy.

Most of the slave ships stayed anchored in the roads at Cape Coast, or in the roads off one of the other British forts, for many months, sometimes for as long as a year. And some ships that left to sail to the slave markets further east came back later. It was easy to sail westward by going far out to sea and catching the prevailing southeasterly trade winds that blew the ship straight to the Americas. Along the coast of the Gold Coast, however, a strong current carried ships to eastward, except for a season beginning in January when it ran in the contrary direction. For centuries the Portuguese had tried to keep their monopoly of the trade by putting about a story that any ship sailing down the West African coast would not be able to sail back, but by the eighteenth century, with patience, European ships could sail almost anywhere provided there was wind.

It was the early Portuguese explorers who discovered that on the Gold Coast a light breeze blew from the landward for a few hours in the early morning before veering round. During the debates about the slave trade of the 1790s, the British Parliament inquired closely about the morning breeze. By leaving silently under cover of darkness or at first light, some people suspected, the captains minimized the risks of the slaves on board attempting a last-minute now-or-never revolt when the African shore was still in sight. That story may have been a landlubber's myth, at any rate during the period of legal slave trading. After the trade was made illegal, however, ships were suspected of taking slaves on board secretly at night and slipping away early with the help of these winds.

News from Europe came slowly and was often inaccurate. 'One of the chiefest lords in England is put in the Tower, the relater not knowing his name,' writes the governor of Komenda fort to the governor of Cape Coast Castle on December 9, 1681, reporting what he had been told by a visiting Dutch captain, and Lord Shaftesbury had indeed been arrested. 'The King of France hath banished out of his Kingdome all Protestants,' he wrote on the same occasion, although the revocation of the Edict of Nantes did not occur until 1685. By contrast local information came fast and was usually accurate. The British in the Castle never ceased to be amazed at how rapidly news could travel by word of mouth and by drum signals along the coast. An early twentieth-century colonial governor, Sir Gordon Guggisberg, recorded a case of a piece of news, the execution of a criminal at Cape Coast Castle, traveling 200 miles along the coast in less than two hours. At the height of the slaving era the Castle ran its own regular postal service between the Castle and forts along the coast. In 1795, for example, the post for Anomabu left at twelve on Sundays, Wednesdays, and Saturdays, with the messenger returning with answers in time for the start of work at ten the following morning.

During the slaving era, whenever a ship was sighted on the horizon, the Castle sent out canoes to find out who she was. Many vessels, especially American, flew false colors, usually Spanish or Portuguese, and changed them frequently. The canoemen, who were highly skilled and, along with the fishermen, among the most influential communities on the coast, could bring back information beyond the reach of a telescope. The canoemen who went to inspect an unidentified vessel in 1804, for example, reported that she 'proved a Portuguese.'

The governors of the Castle spent many hours during the slaving era looking out to sea, observing the canoe traffic to and from the ships, the arrivals, and the departures. 'For the last ten years I was in Africa scarce a ship sailed but I saw her go,' the former governor Richard Miles told the 1790 parliamentary inquiry, and careful records were kept. The Castle diaries note, for example, over a typical four-month period from October 1786 to January

1787, the type of vessel, its professed destination, and often the number of slaves taken on board: the ship *Favourite* for Bonny (on the Slave Coast); the *Olympian Madeleine* for Cape François (Saint-Domingue in the French West Indies) with 50 slaves; a Portuguese smack; the ship *Betty* for leeward; the ship *Wolseley Hall* for Bonny; the barque *Thomas* for Lagoe (modern Lagos); the ship *George* for Jamaica with 500; the ship *Jus* for windward; the brig *Alert* for Jamaica with 321; the ship *Elliott* and the schooner *Dick* for Lagoe; the ship *Venus* for Jamaica with 300; the sneau *John* for Jamaica with 180; the Portuguese schooner for leeward . . . and so on, month after month. Some of the vessels named in these diaries, incidentally, do not appear in the electronic database, and the current estimates of the magnitude of the transatlantic slave trade may need to be revised upwards, as others have suggested for different reasons.

The gun signals that gave notice that a ship was about to sail put pressure on the parties to speed up the final stages of the trade negotiations. During the time when a ship was trading in the roads, there were seldom fewer than half a dozen 'gold takers' on board – the name was a conventional one used for local merchants, dating from the time when the Portuguese sold their goods for gold and then used the gold to buy slaves. The gun signals also alerted the governor of the Castle, with his team of junior officers, known as 'writers,' to finalize and seal the letters that he sent at every opportunity, in multiple copies, in many ships, to London, the slave importers in the Americas, and elsewhere. The distances these letters traveled were vast, many going and coming via the West Indies, and the length of time it took for a reply to arrive could be a year or more, but the gathering, collating, and distributing of information round the Atlantic oceanic world was vital to the whole slaving enterprise. As the British share of the trade grew, more ships, more carefully designed, meant more information carried more quickly, leading to better-informed commercial judgements by an increasing number of participants in three continents.

During the eighteenth century gold was still found by panning in the local rivers and was brought to the coast from the interior of Africa. However, the metal was no longer a commodity but a global international currency, which circulated by sea, east and west, to and from Europe, the Americas, and the West Indies, and by land, north and south, to and from the old world of the Mediterranean, the Middle East, and India. During most of the eighteenth century the price in sterling of buying gold was higher on the Gold Coast than in London. A typical letter from the governor of Cape Coast Castle, dated March 24, 1797, a time of war, contains more than the normal pleas for God's grace:

> Shipped, by the Grace of God, in good order and well conditioned, by Archibald Dalzel, in and upon His Majesty's Ship, the Maidstone whereof is Commander, under God, for the present voyage, John Matthews, Esquire, and now riding at Anchor in the Road of Cape Coast, and by God's Grace bound for the Isle of Princes and the West Indies . . .

The letter reveals that the package numbered 'AC, GR, no 1' contains 123.5 ounces of gold dust, worth about £500 sterling. During the ten-year period before the European peace of 1815, over £250,000 in gold was taken to Portsmouth by the Royal Navy, and then by special coaches to the Africa House in London. But as the demand for slaves, and the price of buying them, rose, the African slave sellers began to require that part of the price should be paid in gold, and it was imported to Africa for that purpose (see Chapter 8). It is impossible to measure the transfers of resources by the flows of gold.

## Coming ashore

It was normally only the ships' officers who came ashore: the captain, who was responsible for all the operations of the ship, including the selling and the buying; and the surgeon, who checked the physical state of the slaves before they were purchased and sent on board. For these officers, there were private apartments in the Castle, a seat at the governor's dinner table, plenty of food and drink, and exchange of news and talk with the officers of the Castle and other visiting captains and surgeons. The junior officers, that is the first and second mates, and the ships' crews, who seldom numbered more than twenty or thirty men, were occasionally sent ashore in parties to help with the unloading, fetching of water, and other duties, but they were needed on board to keep the ship safe, ready at short notice to change the sails or the anchor cables. They also fed and guarded the slaves who had already been embarked. The crews in the slave ships had a reputation for being mutinous when cooped up within sight of a green luxuriant coast, but also for bringing deadly illnesses back on board if a lenient captain allowed them a run ashore.

The larger ships carried their own longboats, some big enough to raise a mast and mount a gun, and they were sailed and rowed long distances along the coast by the ships' crews. Small local sailing vessels could also operate beyond the surf. However, on the Gold Coast, the longboats that linked ship with shore almost everywhere else in the Europeanized oceanic world were normally unable to cross the natural barrier. Accidents were frequent. As the governor of Tantumquerry fort (not far from Winneba) scribbled hurriedly to the Castle governor on August 9, 1775, unhypocritically lamenting the financial consequences to himself more than the loss of life:

Capt King's Boat arrived as far as this on her return at 3 o'clock this morning was overset by a large surf, thinking themself in the proper road, and was too close to the Shore. two White Men and 2 Slaves is drowned, the latter is surely my loss . . .

In 1786 the *Tartar*, commanded by Archibald Dalzel, a former governor of the Castle, lost nine when a longboat capsized, including one slave who had been chained, and then three others in a second accident.

In 1783 the guardroom at the Castle held twelve British seamen who, in three separate incidents, had attempted to desert their slave ships by seizing the longboat, throwing the officer overboard, and deserting. It was to avoid mutinies that some slave-ship captains chained their seamen to the longboats. Since the longboats took up room on board on the return voyage, when every deck space was packed with slaves, the boats were sold or bartered to other ships when the ship was ready to sail. Captain Clement Noble, captain of the *Brookes*, bartered a longboat to Benjamin Cayzneau, captain of another Liverpool slaver, the *Nancy*, when he was about to sail for the West Indies on December 23, 1776. What he gave is noted in Noble's scribbled receipt: 'I accept the Little Boy for the Boat tho he is very small but good.' The engraving of the slave ship *Brookes*, with its decks loaded with hundreds of slaves packed 'spoonwise,' head to toe and toe to head, was to become one of the most potent images of the transatlantic slave trade and it did much to bring about its abolition. (Since it is so well known and so easily accessible, it is not reproduced here. I will, however, quote from other notes that Captain Noble wrote when the *Brookes* lay off Cape Coast Castle – see Chapter 8.)

All contacts between ship and shore, between longboat and shore, and between the Castle and the British forts along the coast, depended on the local canoemen, who either contracted themselves to a visiting ship for the duration of her time in the roads or were paid for every trip. Some canoes, usually described by the number of crew members, for example 'six-hand,' 'eleven-hand,' were long, but all were made from the trunk of a single tree so enabling them to bend in conditions that would cause European boats to break up. To unload the cargo of a single ship on to the beach and into the Castle storerooms could require many round-trip canoe journeys. To unload large items such as guns, it was necessary to build special rafts that could cross the surf when it was particularly low. The canoemen also provided the main communications between ship and shore – a constant exchange of letters, invoices, receipts, bills, sealed packages, and informal notes, carried across the surf of the South Atlantic Ocean.

The canoemen were well paid, always in tradeable goods, mainly cloths, rum, and gunpowder. When a party of local African soldiers brought news that a French frigate had been seen to windward, they were given tobacco and rum valued at £1 and 14 shillings which the soldiers would be able to trade locally for whatever they wanted to buy. As a measure of the value of such payments in the eighteenth century, the annual salary of a skilled British craftsman who voluntarily contracted to spend three years in the Castle and forts was around £30, also paid in tradeable goods (see Chapter 5). (In order to enable comparisons to be easily made among the many payments noted, monetary amounts will be converted into sterling of the time, decimalized.) In 1765 it took three weeks for two 15-hand canoes and one 17-hand canoe to unload the stores brought by the *Royal Charlotte* for Apollonia fort; the canoemen were paid a total of £52 15s 0d (£52.75). The records of Anomabu fort note the payments for typical short journeys in 1804, near the peak of the legal British slave trade: 'paid 11 canoemen who took Dawson [the governor of the fort] to Cape Coast Castle and back 1 romal [cloth] and 1 1/2 gallons of rum valued in total at £1/9/0 [£1.50]'; 'paid canoemen for taking off Captain Crosby of the *Julia*, 2 gallons of rum, valued at 12 shillings [£0.60].' Another payment, from Cape Coast Castle in 1807, is for gathering seashells to make lime for building works: '[p]aid 21 canoemen for 1 trip to Queen Anns Point for shells for this castle 3 gallons of rum' (valued at £1.05).

Although, when crossing the surf, the canoes capsized frequently – in one trip in ten, it was estimated – the canoemen were able to turn them over, climb aboard, bail out the water, and continue the journey. They could do this even if the canoes were carrying cargoes, often barrels lashed to the canoe, and if they were carrying people – including chained slaves – they would make sure that anyone who was thrown into the sea was hauled back onboard. Anyone coming ashore to Cape Coast Castle was certain to be soaked. It was suspected that the canoemen, all good swimmers, liked giving unpopular Europeans an occasional ducking, although only rarely was anyone drowned. For many ships' captains, however, to whom the Bay of Biscay held no terrors, crossing the surf was a voyage too far; as Captain Cayzneau of the *Nancy* explained, in declining an invitation to dinner ashore with the governor of Anomabu fort, 'I am no swimmer.'

The British men who landed at Cape Coast Castle from the ships, most of whom could not swim, were taken across the surf by canoe and then waded ashore. But the inexperienced needed help to avoid being carried back out to sea. Henry Huntley, a naval officer, described the terrifying swell of the waves, the thunderous noise as the breakers hit the beach, the skill of the canoemen in keeping the canoes afloat lengthways on top of an incoming wave, and then having to 'clasp the naked body of his carrier lubricated with palm oil.' Landing ruined his smart white naval trousers, Huntley complained, although 'on this coast alas! there are no fair complexions and dark blue or hazel eyes to gaze upon the well cut and decorated uniforms.' In *Sir Thomas* (1855), Sarah Bowdich's historical novel about the Castle, Sir Thomas FitzOsborne vows

*3. The arrival of Sir Thomas FitzOsborne at Cape Coast Castle.*

never again to endure the terror and humiliation he felt at his
coming ashore. The picture above shows how Sir John Gilbert, the
artist employed to illustrate that event, caught the ambiguity of the
imperial encounter in his own Victorian times. FitzOsborne, sitting

on the shoulders of African porters and entirely dependent on them for his life, points out the way forward in a gesture of leadership, although he has never been in Africa before and the porters are unlikely not to have known the way from the beach to the Castle.

As for the few British women who came ashore at Cape Coast Castle by canoe, the grasp of strong black hands round their thighs was their first experience of Africa. Sarah Bowdich burst into tears.

# 2

# Outside

Cape Coast Castle stands with its back to the land, washed by the tropical ocean on three sides. And it was the view from ships at sea that was the main concern of the many governors who designed, built, adapted, and maintained it during the slaving era. Since it was difficult for an artist to draw the Castle either from a ship anchored out to sea in the roads or from onboard a heaving canoe nearer the shore, most pictures of the Castle before the age of aerial photography are inaccurate and many are misleading. In the 1950s A. W. Lawrence, with his precise archaeologist's eye, was exasperated to discover that hardly any of the beautiful seventeenth- and eighteenth-century engraved prospects and bird's-eye views that he discovered in libraries matched what he found on the ground: one showed the Castle's painted mud brick walls as solid blocks of square-cut masonry, while others included buildings that were never built. The most circulated eighteenth-century engraving, which is also inaccurate, emphasized the frightening rocks (page 39).

It was helpful to the British that the representations of the Castle that were pondered over by the admiralties and chanceries of Europe exaggerated its strength. For Europeans, for most of its active history, the Castle was also wrapped in clouds of romance, not only *Robinson Crusoe*-inspired dreams of adventure and riches (see

*4. The Castle looking like Buckingham Palace, as imagined by a newspaper artist c.1840.*

Chapter 4) but also orientalist visions of luscious, exotic, welcoming lands, ready to be enjoyed. In the nineteenth century, when there were docks, steamships, trained draughtsmen, and little excuse for inaccuracy, the image of the Castle that was offered to stay-at-home travelers was so steeped in presumptions that it bore little relationship to reality. In one engraving (above) the Castle looks like Buckingham Palace. Another (page 122) offers a vague fantasy of a temple on the Nile or the Ganges.

## The building of the castle

The first European settlement on the site took place sometime in the early 1650s, although there are reports of the Portuguese, the Dutch, and the English having been allowed to establish temporary, undefended lodges there in earlier times. In 1652 the African, Asiatic, and American Company of Sweden employed Henrik Carlof, a Polish merchant, who was then working for the Dutch West India Company, to negotiate an agreement with the authorities of Efutu, a small African coastal kingdom, for the building of trading facilities in their territory. The king of Efutu, called by the Europeans Bodema, and his chief adviser Acrosan, known by his title as 'the Dey,' gave their consent on terms that are not recorded but which included the payment of a monthly rent. The commercial aim of the Swedes was to challenge the Dutch, who had established a near monopoly of the trade, while sharing the expected profits with Efutu. The policy of Efutu, whose rulers had given similar concessions to other European companies, was evidently to encourage what today would be called inward investment but without becoming too dependent on just one overseas commercial partner.

In the early 1650s the Swedes constructed a fort that they named Carlusborg in honor of the Swedish king Karl Gustaf X. Its high but thin walls, made from mud bricks, were built by local laborers, under Swedish supervision, and guns that were brought from Europe were landed and mounted. At that time the site appears to have been in use by the local peoples as a fish and provisions market, and it is not recorded whether any families were displaced. However, in 1657, at the urging of Carlof, who had again switched employers, Acrosan, the Dey of Efutu, decided to transfer Fort Carlusborg to the rival Danish West India Company, and the Castle, as it can now be called, was seized after a battle in which the Swedish governor was captured.

The Danish period of occupation was short-lived. With war in northern Europe, and only a few Danish merchant ships able to make the voyage to Africa, the Castle did not pay. In 1659 the Danish Company governor, then a Dutchman called Samuel Schmidt, handed the Castle over to the Dutch, who were both commercially successful and firmly established on land at Elmina nearby. However, the king of Efutu, resisting Dutch dominance, refused to endorse the transfer and Dey Acrosan agreed with the Swedish company that they should resume possession – which the Swedes did in 1660, paying Efutu a large sum in gold and accepting a commitment to employ forty Efutan men in the Castle. However, the Swedes, like the Danes, found they could not send enough ships to Africa to make the venture pay, and in 1663 the Dey again repossessed it, confiscating the gold that was stored there. After a further period of local jostling, and negotiations among the competing countries in Europe, the Dutch West India Company took control of the Castle for a second time, paying compensation to the Swedes, who then abandoned their brief foray into the slave trade.

Then, on May 7, 1664, before the Dutch were securely established in the Castle – they had fewer than twenty men there – an armed English fleet commanded by Captain Robert Holmes captured it after a brief battle in which the Danes and the army of Efutu cooperated with the English in expelling the Dutch. Holmes landed about fifty men, who were set to work to repair its defenses, and he supplied it with enough stores to last six months. On his return to England he was imprisoned for having exceeded his instructions but was pardoned and reemployed in the official wars against the Dutch that broke out soon after. Although the Dutch sent their own fleet under Admiral de Ruyter and recaptured all the other forts that they had recently lost to Holmes, they felt unable to attack the Castle with any hope of success. Thereafter Cape Coast Castle was to remain in English – after 1707 British – hands until Ghana became independent in 1957.

During the later seventeenth century all the European Atlantic trading nations scrambled and jostled for shore facilities in Africa, with many concessions granted by the local rulers, and temporary lodges and permanent forts built, captured, repossessed, abandoned, resettled, pulled down, sold, and exchanged, in a bewildering tumble of events that can only be understood, if at all, as the effects of European geopolitical struggles interacting with local commercial interests. In this competition, as elsewhere in the world, the English were latecomers. Before Holmes's expedition, their main involvement had been three marauding and slaving expeditions in the 1560s under the command of John Hawkins, in the third of which the English queen, Elizabeth, was the principal investor.

By the later seventeenth century, however, the transatlantic slave trade had become a continuous business that needed new and permanent business structures. The competition at that time was mostly between the chartered companies of the European countries, each awarded monopoly trading privileges by its home government, not by the official armed forces of the nations concerned. And the constantly shifting military and commercial alliances were responses to local as well as to wider conditions. For its first thirty years of existence, for example, Cape Coast Castle was within cannon range of a Danish fort that overlooked it from a nearby hill, and until that fort was bought from the Danes in 1685, the English treated them, and their commercial interests, with great respect. The number of Europeans involved in the frequent armed skirmishes was seldom above a hundred, mostly landed from ships. And, although the competing chartered companies of the Dutch, the Swedes, the Danes, the English, the French, the Spanish, the Brandenburgers, and others were named after the country that chartered them, they drew their capital from beyond national borders. The Danish company, for example, was mainly capitalized from Holland and Hamburg. The companies also employed men from many nations who frequently changed employers. The first governor of Cape Coast Castle, when it was Carlusborg, was Isaac Melville, described as a native of Basel in Switzerland, but who sounds more Scottish than Swiss or Swedish; he drowned in the surf in 1654 before the building of the Castle was completed. The Dutch governor who surrendered the Castle to the English was a Frenchman called Tobias Pensado, who may have been Portuguese by birth. And there are references to a Hungarian, a Greek, and men from other lands venturing into the new and booming business of buying slaves in Africa to sell them in the Americas.

However, by the early eighteenth century the initial frantic scramble had come to an end and transfers of shore settlements among the rival European countries became less frequent. And even when they were captured in wartime they were usually restored to the previous occupants by peace treaties. This comparative stability was maintained by informal understandings and truces, and a shared interest among those who were already established in keeping out the French, who had emerged from the seventeenth-century scramble with no land settlements in this part of Africa. The result was that, during the eighteenth century, when the British transatlantic slave trade grew steadily, the whole coastline of present-day Ghana was divided into specific areas of influence among the British, the Dutch, and the Danes. There were three castles, headquarters of the three national enterprises, Cape Coast Castle (British), Elmina (Dutch) nearby, and Christiansborg (Danish) over sixty miles to the east at Accra. Besides its one castle, each of the three European nations maintained a scattering of interspersed forts. There was scarcely a landing beach along the 260 miles of the Gold Coast that had not been let out by the local political leaders to one of these three European transatlantic slaving nations.

## Rebuilt

Cape Coast Castle, in continuous use for over 300 years, is now an agglomeration of many additions, modifications, adaptations, and – recently – restorations to an earlier condition. As can be seen from

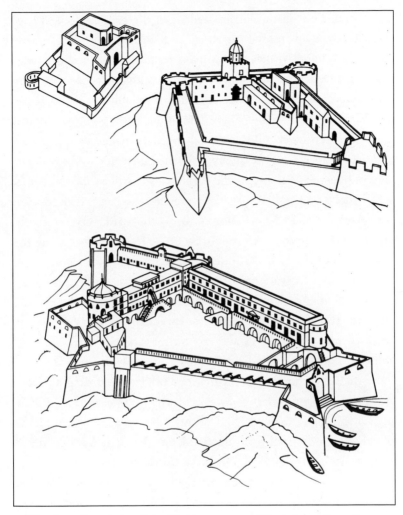

*5. The changing shape of the Castle: seventeenth, eighteenth, and nineteenth centuries.*

the diagram above, it has changed drastically in size, shape, and appearance. The present-day Castle is, to a large extent, an invention of the Victorian period, larger, more regular, more decorated, and more consciously architectural than it was during its days as a slave emporium. The Castle as it existed when the English took it over was already a substantial building, built in the form of a square. Wilhelm Johann Müller, a Lutheran pastor from Hamburg, who joined the Danish company in 1662 and wrote a book about his years on the coast as a slave trader, recorded (probably falsely) that the Castle was built of stone. Then, some time after 1699, the English began an extensive rebuilding that changed its shape and appearance and greatly increased the area within the perimeter walls. It is not certain how much, if any, of the earlier Castle still exists – probably very little. The English, like their predecessors, at first used local materials and paid local laborers to do the work. Oyster shells, always hard to find, were brought by canoe from beaches along the coast and burned to make lime in furnaces fired with wood cut in the forest. Bricks were baked from mud, but, as A. W. Lawrence discovered at Dixcove fort, some were only baked on the outside and had raw clay at their center. Stone was blasted with gunpowder, 'blown,' from the rocks in and around the site, but since the local stone, although hard, is brittle and flakes easily, it provided little more than a strengthening for the mud bricks. According to Sarah Bowdich, reporting what she was told when she lived in the Castle in 1816 and 1817, the outer sides of the walls were built from blocks of cut stone imported from Scotland, but that may have been just another of the stories with which the Castle was buttressed.

During the eighteenth century the Castle was extended further both to landward and seaward, using imported as well as local materials, including bricks baked in Britain specially ordered or carried as ballast by ships. Indeed the British brickmakers were required to carry out scientific tests and to demonstrate that their bricks could withstand salt spray before being given contracts. The archives show London sending out fir and oak timber, kerbstones, steps, and cisterns ready cut. In 1781 they record the sending of '2,000 feet of Bristol Paving Stone.' In 1797 the Castle received

50,000 bricks and 2,000 flat tiles. On the coast, each European nation gradually reproduced its national characteristics. Christiansborg Castle, headquarters of the Danes, was built from stone brought from Denmark. Elmina Castle, with its neat red Dutch bricks, reminds the modern visitor of views of Delft by Vermeer and de Hooch.

Like the other castles and forts on the coast, Cape Coast Castle shows a pattern of development that, within the geographical and climatic constraints, was largely determined by two considerations. The first was the nature of the trade. Until around 1700 the main interest, first of the Portuguese and later of the Dutch and the others, was in obtaining gold and, to a lesser extent, ivory. The ships were small and the goods they brought were unloaded by canoe and exchanged for local products by direct barter. After 1700, by which time about 90 percent of the business was slaves, larger structures were needed, not only to accommodate the captives, but to store the much greater volumes and varieties of imported goods that were required for complex multilateral transactions. Measured by financial value, the ships were always able to bring more goods to Africa than they were able to take away in slaves, and this imbalance encouraged the development of complex intercontinental credit (see Chapter 8).

The other consideration was defense, partly against possible break-in by the local African population, but mainly against armed attack by Europeans arriving by sea. The forts built by the Portuguese around 1500 were essentially medieval keeps with lookout towers, buildings of the pre-gunpowder age. At Elmina Castle, a round tower ninety feet tall that still stands is part of that earliest structure. Later, however, with the arrival in this part of Africa of gunpowder, muskets, and cannon, more substantial defenses were needed. Pointed bastions, unlike round towers, ensured that attackers could not bring up scaling ladders or sap mines under the walls without being exposed to deadly enfilade fire. By the mid-eighteenth century the forts that were then being newly built by the European countries, including the new British fort at Anomabu (see Chapter 7), were – as far as the local topography permitted – regular square structures, with a landward and a seaward gate, diamond-shaped bastions at each corner, and specialized buildings for storage and accommodation that formed an enclosed courtyard within the walls. After the abolition of the legal slave trade, and the end of the threat of attack from the sea, the Castle was adapted further, looking now more to landward than towards the sea, almost turning round on its axis so that the land gate became the main point of entry. For the student of the development of European military architecture, the coastline of Ghana offers a concentration unrivaled in Europe itself.

In the busiest decades of the slaving era Cape Coast Castle presented itself to seaward as a modern European fortress, strong, solid, well positioned, and expertly constructed for its purpose. Dozens of heavy cannon pointed out to sea in three directions from the battlements. Angular bastions jutted on to the frightening rocks at the water's edge that warned of underwater reefs further out. From the sea, a captain could also discern a tall flagstaff, a bell tower, and a lookout post on the highest part of the Castle. The narrow gate to seaward opened directly on to the stony beaches, and on most days canoes could be seen ferrying parties of men, women, and children, as well as barrels of goods and stores, in and out of the Castle, to and from armed British merchant ships anchored offshore. To an eighteenth-century European military or naval officer viewing from the sea, the Castle proclaimed that its British occupants had possessed it for a long time, that they had frequently modernized and extended its defenses, that they were on good terms with the local community with whom they conducted a continuous busy trade, and that they intended to stay.

6. *Cape Coast Castle, as commonly illustrated in the late eighteenth century, exaggerating the frightening rocks.*

## Rented

Cape Coast Castle was built, rebuilt, modified, and maintained with the consent of the local African political and religious leaders in whose territory it was situated. It was not a colony of the British state, nor did the British claim sovereignty over any land inside or outside the walls, or jurisdiction over any of the local population. During the slaving era the Castle's British tenants continued to pay a rent every month to the ruler of Efutu, whose predecessor had given the original concession to the Swedes, and later to the leaders of the Fante confederation who absorbed the kingdom of Efutu around 1720. After 1817 the monthly rent was transferred to the king of Asante in recognition of his (temporary) conquest of the Fante, but they seem to have continued to receive at least some payments. Other regular rents were paid to other local political and military leaders, whom the British called 'caboceers' or 'braffoes,' in whose territories the outlying forts were situated, including fees for the right to take water from local ponds and streams. These rents constituted a substantial part of the costs of maintaining the Castle and the income of the host governments (see Chapter 5). The officers in the Castle and the captains of slave ships also paid customs duties on their slave trading (see Chapter 8). These formal payments were supplemented by a wide range of subsidies, occasional one-off grants, and frequent presents in gold and in goods to local political and religious leaders. Payments were also made to individuals and groups, such as the canoemen, on whose goodwill and cooperation they and their trade depended, in addition to direct payments for services.

Although, during the whole of the slaving era, the extent of British direct military power was not more than one gunshot from the ramparts of the Castle, the governors gradually built up an array of local allies who not only derived their incomes from the work that the Castle provided and from the profits of the trading, but were rewarded for their political cooperation. Relationships occasionally broke down, with strikes, standoffs, rioting, and sometimes shutting of the gates of the Castle with no supplies allowed in or out for many weeks, until the dispute was settled. Occasionally too the British threatened to withdraw from a fort, especially when their local trade monopoly in the vicinity was not being respected, but were usually persuaded to stay on the promise of stricter adherence to the agreements under which the forts had first been established. When, as happened as a result of wars in Europe, the British were at times unable to provision the Castle or the forts by sea, the local allies provisioned them by land. When the British Empire was being rapidly dismantled after the Second World War, it was helpful to both parties in the decolonization process to remember that the long relationship between the Gold Coast and Great Britain had begun as a voluntary, essentially commercial, arrangement.

In the slaving era the local African coastal states and towns maintained their own forces, and when they were in armed conflict with other peoples and towns they were able to field a force of thousands of men armed with muskets provided by, or bought from, the British or other Europeans. Until after 1800 these conflicts were largely unconnected with the presence of the British forts. Indeed, throughout the whole slaving era after 1700, the British maintained a public policy of never interfering or intervening in local wars, except to offer mediation. But if there were incursions by other African peoples, riots, political disturbances, or other dangers, the Castle gates could be opened to give a temporary refuge to the people of Cape Coast town, although only if there were not too many. The local African forces, although unable to withstand military or naval forces armed with European guns, could prevent any hostile European force from landing, even to cut wood or to draw water. In terms of numbers of armed men, the local allies of the British were many hundreds of times stronger than the soldiers, expatriate and locally recruited, that the British maintained in the Castle (see Chapter 5). As the British presence came to look ever more permanent and every year brought a new cohort of young men from Britain to the Castle to live there as officers, soldiers, craftsmen, and traders, the local African allies included a growing number of descendants of unions between British men and African women (see Chapter 6), many of whom regarded themselves as British and maintained close links with the Castle.

Among the papers obtained by William Wilberforce, one of the leaders of the campaign to abolish the slave trade, is a transcript of an agreement made by the British with the people of Komenda, a coastal state where the British had a fort, signed at Cape Coast Castle on December 27, 1749, at which the local political and religious leaders agreed to provide timber, building materials, and labor for the upkeep of the fort on the same terms as those agreed with the people of Dixcove, another coastal town where the British had a fort, up to a total of £800. There survives at Kew the original of a more complex treaty, also unpublished, signed at Cape Coast Castle on February 6, 1753, in which the king, officers, priests, and other leaders of the whole Fante confederation, who at that time controlled a large stretch of the coast, swore not to permit the French to establish a land settlement anywhere on their lands. Its opening declaration, undiplomatically blunt, acknowledges that the Fantes, by accepting arms from the British, had also incurred obligations. For the Fantes to allow the French to establish a settlement, they accepted, would therefore be 'treason' and punishable as such:

> We the Braffoe & Curranteers, the Priests & People of Fantee do declare. That our fathers under the conduct of their Braffoe Imorak were brought by the English from the country now Arcania [not identified] and by them furnished with arms, ammunition, and money not only to take possession of the country now inhabited by us but likewise to conquer all those little states around us at present subject to our dominion . . .

The treaty was signed with a +, in some cases + +, by twenty-four African political and religious leaders, with a similar number on the British side signing their names in full, including the captain of a British naval vessel who signed on behalf of the British king. Some of the titles of the political leaders have been adapted from the Portuguese, whose language was widely spoken as a lingua franca. Other representatives are accorded European titles: 'Aufa, son to Aquanoo, Senator and Treasurer,' 'general,' 'colonel,' 'speaker,' 'herald,' and 'Seki, son to Taky, priest of Bura Bura Wiga.' As a guarantee, the Fante leaders handed over some of their relatives to the British as 'hostages' or 'pledges' – both words were used. They consisted of four boys named in the document as Cudjo Annooma ('sister's son to the Braffoe of Fantee'), Quabino Saki, Quacoo, and Coffee.

The Castle governor, Thomas Melvil, in a secret letter to London dated March 11, 1753, in which he admitted that he had strayed from commercial into political matters, explained the background. His aim was to secure from the local leaders a formal recognition, or 'law,' that would confirm the legitimacy of the British presence. The leaders who signed, he explained, together formed a legislature of all the coastal Fante, a federation comparable to those of Holland and of Switzerland. Anomabu alone remained outside. In order to achieve the agreement, Melvil reported, he had spent £1,000 in presents to the local signatories, paid both before and after the signing of the treaty. The leaders had only undertaken the religious ceremony that accompanied the oath with extreme reluctance, Melvil wrote. As soon as they saw the sacred water:

> . . . their Countenances altered, a sudden Tremor seized
> them, & such a Languor that they had scarcely spirits to
> pronounce the Words of the Oath, & put their hands to the
> Paper: next Morning they told me, they found I would be at
> their Hearts, I had got at their Hearts, now it was over, &
> they were glad of it.

Maybe they appreciated that they had surrendered their independence to the economic power of the British slaving industry?

The boys that were handed over were, to use the words of the agreement, formally 'pawns' who were essentially hostages, but who could be 'redeemed' by the payment of gold, goods, or other human beings of equal monetary value (see Chapter 8). Much of the work of the British in the Castle during the slaving era was negotiation, or as they called it, adopting the Portuguese word, 'palaver,' about obligations that had been entered into in the past, some of which originated in agreements made long before. In the end all palavers, some of which remained unresolved for many years, were settled by payments, some of great multilateral complexity, so that the word 'palaver' came to mean the assortments of gold, goods, or slaves needed to settle a dispute rather than the negotiation itself.

A total of five boys were sent to England in 1753 and 1754 and put into the care of an English priest, Rev. John Moore, son of the future Archbishop of Canterbury of that name, then a curate (junior priest) in St. Sepulchre's church in the City of London. Two of the boys returned home some years later, able to speak and write English, and were given employment in the Castle. Another died of tuberculosis, an illness common in London. Of the other two, Cudjo, renamed William Cudjoe, was described by Moore as having 'no talent for learning' and 'was put out of the Reach of Instruction by a Lunacy which seized him in December 1764.' Cudjo spent more than a year in one of London's bedlams before the money to keep him there ran out and he was sent back to his family. The boy who in the treaty document is named Quacoo, that is, Kweku, was a quick learner. Having spent a total of eleven years in London, first as a pupil at the parish school in Islington and then as a member of Rev. John Moore's household, he returned to Cape Coast Castle in 1765 as Rev. Philip Quaque, the English chaplain. (His experiences there over a long life that included the remaining forty-three years of the legal slaving era are described in Chapters 4 and 6.)

## *The beautiful white castle*

In a report on the state of Cape Coast Castle sent to the British government around 1763, the Governing Committee in London who were responsible for its management, and employed the officers and men of the African Service with which it was staffed (see Chapters 4 and 5), proudly listed its many excellencies, its military might, its strong defenses, its commercial usefulness, its healthy situation, its pleasant climate, its extensive gardens, its orchards, its fish ponds, and its comfortable 'lounging rooms.' Repeating a national stereotype that the English still love to hear, the Committee noted that the Castle's lack of regularity, even its oddly shaped, bumpy parade ground, reflected the English genius for pragmatic adaptation. The Castle, they declared, had 'dignity' and 'magnificence.' The Committee was especially proud of the long white platform with its row of guns pointing out to sea along which visitors can still promenade (see page 81). According to the Committee, this wall, 'for its length, and the beauty of the cannon mounted thereon, challenges a place amongst the most favourite European fortifications.' The outside walls were painted a creamy white, but inside there was color. The annual order for paint, measured by weight, was for 224 pounds each of yellow, white, and lead-color, half that quantity of green, black, and blue, and 56 of red. Today too, visitors often feel the beauty of the Castle, disconcerting for those who, knowing its history, had assumed that it would be grim.

Neither the Castle nor the forts were nearly as strong as they might have appeared to a captain viewing them through a telescope from out at sea. European warships and armed merchantmen were able to bombard buildings on shore if they could get close enough, one of the few types of eighteenth-century warfare in which the attack was superior to the defense. Despite the dangerous rocks in the seas near the Castle, it was reported to Parliament in 1756 that a ship 'may lay before it and soon reduce it to a heap of rubbish.' Although the Castle walls were strengthened and more bastions pushed out to seaward, by the early nineteenth century, as Sir George Collier, an inspecting British naval commodore, noted, a single piece of ordnance would still be enough to knock a hole in them if it could be sailed or rowed close enough or if it could be hauled to the right place on land. The plaster and white paint, which made the Castle look beautiful, clean, fresh, and well-maintained, concealed how flimsy it was. Sarah Bowdich, for one, thought (wrongly) that it was 'a large white stone building.' In fact, as the commodore reported, the walls were mainly built of the small rough stones obtained by blasting, held together by mud and lime – they were built of rubble or, as the commodore said, 'rubbish.' Not only could the walls easily be destroyed by gunfire, but a single barrel of gunpowder set off close by would bring them tumbling down. Two of the Castle's guns were positioned so as to prevent any hostile force from landing on the shore to the west, but since they had been set high up in order to look impressive when seen through a telescope from the sea, and their barrels were set so as to be able to fire to seaward at a high angle, they could not easily be repositioned to fire downwards. Only over the landing beach to the east did the Castle guns have complete command.

On the landward side, outside the land gate, was an area of open ground and the thriving town of Cape Coast, some of whose houses were built near to the Castle walls and even, in some cases, overlooked them. Not far inland, and named after an early eighteenth-century governor, was 'Phipps hill,' fortified with a tower, abandoned most of the time, but which could, if necessary, be reactivated. Another hill, formerly known as 'smallpox hill,' was further back. In 1860, in the confident Victorian colonial era, these outposts of Cape Coast Castle were topped with self-consciously archaic, almost ironic, gothic-revival stone towers, and renamed Fort Victoria and Fort William. They are examples of the fake medievalism, inspired by the universal reading of the novels of Sir Walter Scott, with which the Victorians gave a touch of romance to railway architecture, industrial buildings, and hotels. Fort William was really a lighthouse. But although, to the eye of a modern visitor, these neighboring hills may appear to add strength to the Castle, in the eighteenth century they were a weakness. Any enemy able to haul a gun up these hills would have been able to smash the Castle's land gate and knock down the walls. As Commodore Collier said of the landward side of the Castle after his inspection, 'it is impossible to imagine any thing contrived with less judgement as a defensive post.'

Outside the walls was the spacious Castle garden, where fruits were grown from both sides of the Atlantic tropical world, oranges, lemons, bananas, pineapples, mangos, cherries, but no grapes. The fallen fruit was gathered into barrels, producing a mushy drink that could be sold to slave-ship captains to feed to slaves and crews on their long oceanic journey to the Americas, reducing the risks of scurvy. There was also a bowling green, reseeded every year. The governor had his own garden five miles away with a summer house for picnics, and that was as far as most of the British in the Castle ever promenaded. On the road to the governor's garden, every tree had been taken up by the roots to prevent it reverting to forest. According to Sarah Bowdich, 'it was along this little road that the Europeans used to ride in little phaetons, made in London, and drawn by four black men; the governor had six, by way of distinction, dressed in uniform.' The Castle's house slaves (see Chapter 5), she said, enjoyed this work, which at least took them out of the Castle, but it was hard to maintain the road. One tropical shower and it would be entirely covered in green. Within a few days it would be reclaimed by the forest. On one occasion a ten-mile road to Elmina Castle was cut from the forest to enable visits to be exchanged with the Dutch at Christmas, but by the following Christmas it had disappeared.

Most journeys that the British took beyond the walls of the Castle and its immediate perimeter were made by sea, by canoe. The governor of Anomabu fort, for example, on his frequent, probably weekly, visits to headquarters at the Castle for meetings of the Council, seems invariably to have come by canoe. There were paths along the coast but no horses or draught animals, and walking was regarded as dangerous to Europeans, even when protected with hats and umbrellas, because of the risk of sunstroke. In March 1800, for example, it was reported that 'Mr. Loudon left the Castle in perfect health to join a party that were taking some diversion a little way up the country but was so overcome by the fatigue and heat of the day that he was a corpse two hours after his arrival.'

For some longer journeys the British officers traveled by hammock, although, compared with going by canoe, it was slow. It took over thirty hours to travel from Apollonia, the British fort furthest to the west, to the Castle, and twenty-three hours to come from Accra, the fort furthest to the east on the Gold Coast. Only the richest of local African leaders traveled by hammock. Moreover, traveling by hammock on land along the forest paths, especially on the infrequent diplomatic missions inland to the Asante capital of Kumasi, was extremely uncomfortable – the passenger's feet got snarled in the undergrowth and it was hard to navigate the corners without being bumped by trees. For such journeys the British copied the other custom of local rich men of sitting in baskets carried on the heads of porters. (The picture to the right, drawn by William Hutton, a member of a mission to Asante in 1820, which shows him in a hammock and his colleague Mr. Salmon in a basket, was a rare sight, although highly symbolic of nineteenth-century European imperialism.) Traveling by hammock or basket, with relays of porters, was extremely expensive. Even in Victorian times, when some modern roads had been built, Sir Richard Burton wrote that for the price of a ten-mile hammock ride in the Gold Coast, you could go by train the 600 miles from London to Aberdeen.

Occasionally the governors reported to London that the Castle and its guns were in good order, but such conditions rarely lasted for long. During the two wet seasons, one beginning at the end of May, the second at the end of October, the paint and plaster washed off the walls, and because most of the Castle was still roofed with

7. *Traveling by hammock and by basket. Mr. Hutton and Mr. Salmon leaving the Castle on the 1820 mission to Asante.*

thatch, torrents of rain came into most of the rooms, coursing down through the plaster ceilings and planked floors of three storeys. As Mary Kingsley wrote of the torrential downpours, 'there ought to be some other word than rain for that sort of thing.' After the end of July came a foggy season that lasted for two or three weeks, much feared by Europeans since it was then, they wrongly believed, that they were most likely to catch an illness. But the other extreme brought its own problems. During the hot season – in the winter months – when the dry 'harmattan' winds carrying minute particles of desert sand blew down from the Sahara, crops died, the garden withered, the ponds dried out, the wooden floors shriveled, the barrels and casks leaked, and even ships at sea had to pour water over their decks to prevent them from buckling. A huge workforce was constantly employed just to keep the Castle standing.

Guns mounted in ships could be covered with canvas and enclosed in hatches, and were, to an extent, protected from the salt water. The guns in the Castle, however, which had been brought ashore lashed to catamaran canoes and now stood in the briny open air, subject to extremes of heat and cold, began to deteriorate as soon as they were deployed. The iron hoops of the barrels rusted, as did the gun carriages; without these carriages to absorb the recoil the guns could not be fired. The iron cannonballs, which look impressive when decoratively stacked in neat piles, rusted into unusual and dangerous shapes. The main ammunition was grapeshot, pieces of metal and stones packed into canisters, which could be fired at canoes or at parties of men with deadly effect, but any kind of firing with ammunition – salutes just used gunpowder – required the recoil mechanisms to work.

In many reports the governors described the guns as 'honeycombed with rust,' more dangerous to the gunners than to the enemy, and we find in the muster rolls the names of soldiers killed, blinded, injured, and occasionally repatriated, as a result of accidents. In 1753, when war with France was expected, the governor reported that, although he had eighty guns in the Castle, there were only a few in working order, and none of them could be fired more than four times without blowing up. In 1756, during the war, it was reported that if a hostile ship attacked, Cape Coast Castle 'could not bring above three or four trifling guns to bear upon them.' In 1770, according to Richard Brew, a former member of the African Service who had lived at Anomabu for many years both in the fort and as a private trader in his own house, all the British forts were 'heaps of rubbish' – there was not one that 'may not be taken any day of the year by six men, the capital [the Castle] not excepted.' In 1772 they were described by a Mr. Tweed, who was said to have lived more than fifteen years in

Africa, as 'A disgrace to the nation. They lie like a heap of rubbish – a nest for filth and vermin – without influence, degraded and stigmatised, as mere burlesques on fortification; laughing stocks for Europeans and the derision of the natives.' Mr. Tweed, who is not otherwise recorded, was probably a pseudonym for John Grossle or one of the other governors who came from Scotland.

On occasions the governors bought or borrowed guns and gunpowder from visiting slave ships. Captain Cayzneau of the *Nancy* sold a gun to the governor of Anomabu in 1775. As he explained, he did this partly in his own interest, since the threat of cutting off canoe traffic with the ships was central to the credibility of the trade negotiations. 'I believe few people in the Road would like to Barter without a gun as it must distress them in their canoe, at the Latter end.' Why could Cape Coast Castle not have brass guns that did not rust, like the Dutch in Elmina, the governors constantly demanded. They were, admittedly, more expensive than the iron guns that the British could now mass-produce at low cost. But, of the seventy-five guns listed in the inventory of 1775, only two were of brass. Captain Young of the Royal Navy told the parliamentary inquiry in 1790 that during his four voyages to Africa, three of the British forts were in such a poor state that their governors were unable to fire even one gun salute in case the explosion blew down the walls.

In fact, although bristling with guns, Cape Coast Castle was not really a castle at all. It was not a fortified strongpoint whose military garrison could protect, control, and exact obedience and taxation from a wide area of surrounding country as was the function of a castle in Europe. Cape Coast Castle was, essentially, a defended warehouse within which goods – and people – could be temporarily stored. The ships from Europe brought imports of goods and they took away exports of slaves, but since there were no local facilities, they needed a place on land where both goods and people could be temporarily stored during the long period of time it normally took to complete the transaction. Elmina Castle, when it was built by the Portuguese in the fifteenth century, was the first of such European overseas 'factories' to be built anywhere in the world, and for long afterwards it was the furthest from Europe. But once the other European countries saw how the Portuguese had solved the problem of physically conducting trade thousands of miles from the European manufacturing base, they built factories on the shores of most of the oceans of the world. During the slaving era the British on the coast still often called their smaller forts 'factories' and their officers 'factors.'

## British pluck

The Castle's defenses were put to the test in 1756 during the Seven Years War when the French government sent a naval squadron to the African coast intending to compel the surrender of all the British forts. Since the French squadron, which had powerful guns, was confidently predicted to succeed, some of the local African leaders prepared to change their European business partners. At Anomabu, however, when the local African leader attempted to send a welcoming gift to the French commodore, a gunshot from the British fort destroyed the canoe before it was even launched and the governor threatened to fire on the town if the inhabitants changed sides in defiance of the treaty of 1753. The French commodore then decided to try Cape Coast Castle instead. What happened next was related by Tobias Smollett, who had himself been on the African coast as a naval surgeon, in a style later to become popular as 'deeds that won an empire.' Smollett's *History of England* (1757–58) – a copy is recorded among the books at Anomabu fort – played on a national myth of the British at war: a shameful lack of preparation, official parsimony and incompetence, disaster prevented at the last minute by brilliant makeshift improvisa-

tion, bumbling foreign professionals outwitted by clever British
amateurs, and victory secured by sheer pluck:

> When Mr. Bell, the Governor of this castle, received
> intelligence that [the French squadron] was a few leagues to
> windward, and certainly intended to attack Cape Coast, his
> whole garrison did not exceed thirty white men, exclusive of
> a few Mulatto soldiers; his stock of ammunition was reduced
> to half a barrel of gunpowder; and his fortifications were so
> crazy and inconsiderable, that, in the opinion of the best
> engineers, they could not have sustained for twenty minutes
> the fire of one great ship, had it been properly directed and
> maintained. In these circumstances, few people would have
> dreamed of making any preparation for defence; but Mr.
> Bell entertained other sentiments and acquitted himself
> with equal courage and discretion. He forthwith procured a
> supply of gunpowder and a reinforcement of about fifty men
> from certain trading vessels that happened to be upon that
> part of the coast. He mounted some spare cannon upon an
> occasional battery and assembled a body of twelve hundred
> negroes, well armed, under the command of their chief,
> on whose attachment he could depend, and ordered them
> to take post at the place where he apprehended the enemy
> would attempt a landing. These precautions were hardly
> taken when the French squadron, consisting of two ships
> of the line and a large frigate, appeared, and in a little time
> their attack began, but they met with such a warm reception
> that in less than two hours they desisted, leaving the Castle
> very little damaged, and immediately made sail for the West
> Indies.

Bluff this episode may have been, but among the archives there are other examples that show that it was a sustainable policy. In 1779, when a French frigate appeared off the British fort at Dixcove, George Ogilvie, the factor, who was then in charge, scribbled a note to the governor at Cape Coast Castle: 'This by canoe express. For God's sake send us some four and six pound shot, with cannister of same size and a powder horn or two.' Two days later Ogilvie sent another canoe express to say he did not have a single gun carriage that would be able to withstand the recoil from the firing of its gun. But his bluff was not called. When the captain of the French warship saw a canoe laden with ammunition arriving at Dixcove from Cape Coast Castle, he sailed away. Later too, during the French revolutionary and Napoleonic wars, when the political future of much of the world was decided by sea power, bluff proved sufficient. In January 1800, for example, when a French naval squadron had anchored in Elmina roadstead and was expected to attack, the governor and his council considered their strategy. Their guns, they knew, were of no use and they did not even have enough muskets. But they ostentatiously brought out 221 pikes, most of them rusty, which had been in the Castle store since the days when pikes were weapons of war. No attack occurred.

## Public–private partnership

One reason why bluff was often the only option lay in the way the Castle was financed. Although fortified factories solved the geographical problem of how to conduct a complex trade at long range, they raised another question. Who was to pay for them? The solutions to the financing problem adopted at different times by the different countries determined the architecture of the buildings. When the trade first became a continuous business, the solution normally adopted by the European states was to contract out the national trade to chartered companies. Each company was given a state-conferred national monopoly, financed by subscribed royal, aristocratic, and private commercial capital, with power to raise its own land and sea armed forces and to operate its own shore facilities and ships. In that way the chartered company could decide for itself the mix of ship and shore, armament and personnel, and costs and prices that best suited its trading needs, netting the costs of the shore facilities from its gross profits. The earliest English expeditions to West Africa had been financed individually by groups of 'adventurers,' investors, coming together for particular projects. In 1672, however, soon after the English capture of Cape Coast Castle, the English set up their own chartered company. The Royal African Company of England was given a legal monopoly on English trade 'for a thousand years' along the entire western coast of Africa from the edge of the desert in the north to the Cape of Good Hope in the south, and it was the Royal African Company that rebuilt and enlarged Cape Coast Castle in the following decades. Confident that it would be able to recoup its investment, the well-capitalized Royal African Company built to last.

However, besides losing many of its ships to enemy privateers and pirates, the Royal African Company – which at one time maintained seventeen settlements on shore, far more than were in use during the later eighteenth century when the trade was at its height – found its monopoly difficult to enforce, both against slaving ships from other countries and against free-riding British 'interlopers,' that is, captains of slave ships who were not members of the Company and who, because they paid nothing towards the costs of the Castle and the forts, could undercut the Royal African Company's prices. The Dutch West India Company, faced with the same problem, was given the legal power to put Dutch interlopers to death, but it is hard for trading nations to treat low prices as a crime. In 1750 the British Parliament, after experiments with other mixed solutions, introduced a new way of conducting the British slave trade that was to last until after the end of legal trading in 1807. The Royal African Company was abolished, and with it, the monopoly. Instead, each year Parliament provided a public subsidy to the slaving industry as a whole in the form of a block grant to a private sector body, the Company of Merchants Trading to Africa, who took over the Castle, the forts, and the previous employees. The Governing Committee of the Company of Merchants was drawn from the leaders of the slaving industry in London, Bristol, and Liverpool.

The annual public grant, which was rarely below £15,000 and was sometimes as high as £22,000, was intended to meet the costs of maintaining and staffing the Castle and the forts, that is, the fixed shore-based facilities of the British slave trade in Africa. Under the law of 1750, the Company of Merchants, and the officers of the African Service whom the Company recruited in Britain and employed in Africa, were prohibited from trading or giving credit. Instead the buying and selling of the slaves was to be left entirely to the private slave ships whose owners and captains would compete with one another in the buying, shipping, and selling of slaves. Any British – or British colonial – merchant living anywhere in the world who paid a token annual membership fee of £2 to the Company of Merchants could buy or charter a ship, fill it with goods, sail it to Africa, buy slaves with the goods, and take them to the Americas to be sold, at whatever prices he could negotiate at every stage of the buying and selling.

After 1750 the British slaving industry was officially organized into a mixed public-private commercial system that was intended to exploit the advantages of both sectors. The huge standing costs of maintaining the shore facilities in Africa were regarded as a charge to the public and were paid by the British taxpayer. The day-to-day trading, including the prices, was left to the private sector, that is, the investors in the slave ships and their captains. By this arrangement, it was intended, the disadvantages of monopoly associated with the chartered companies would be avoided, the trade would be thrown open to private enterprise, and the planters in the colonies would pay the lower prices for imported slaves that would be brought about by price competition.

The financing arrangements of the 1750 Act profoundly affected the architecture of Cape Coast Castle. Elmina Castle is decorated with classical pilasters and elegant stone scrolls, glass windows with colored armorial memorials, elaborate wrought iron palings, and other reminders of the fine arts of the European Renaissance, and when Napoleon's brother, Jerome, became the king of the Netherlands, he decorated Elmina in the neoclassical style. Christiansborg Castle in Accra, administered by the kingdom of Denmark, has carved stone crowns and inscriptions celebrating the kings who lived in the other grand Christiansborg Castle in Copenhagen. The old Portuguese fort near Elmina had its decorative coats of arms and its sundial. By contrast, Cape Coast Castle, the smallest of the three castles on the coast, but the emporium of the nation that had, by far, the largest share of the trade, was unornamented. Strictly utilitarian, the Castle did not even have a chapel until the 1820s, although one sometimes appears in engravings. The plain, muddled, no-frills architecture of the Castle not only flaunted its nonroyal status but flattered the self-image of the British as a pragmatic and commercial people. Or, as Napoleon might have sneered, Cape Coast Castle was what you would expect from a nation of shopkeepers.

In another way that is less obvious today, the Castle of the slaving era was a direct result of the financing arrangements of 1750. In early modern Europe, European states normally contracted out not only their overseas trade but the procurement of the armies and the weapons with which their dynastic and religious wars were waged. Count Wallenstein was celebrated in his time as a great prince and soldier, but his real achievement was as a great contractor, able to mobilize credit, buy armaments, and recruit and deploy armies on an international scale. And that contract system invented for chartered monopoly companies such as the Royal African Company was continued by the 1750 Act. During the slave trade era, the governors of Cape Coast Castle had discretion on how to expend the stores that the Governing Committee of the Company of Merchants procured for them from the public subsidy. And, with the possible exception of Governor Hippisley, they found ways of diverting much of this subsidy into their own pockets.

The governors and their accountants in the Castle and their trading partners in Africa and on the slave ships operated an elaborate system of currencies and units of account that few outside the African trade could understand even if they had access to the books. The pound, for example, in which salaries for the African Service were denominated and advertised in London was the 'coastal' pound, which was only worth about 80 percent of the pound sterling – as many British recruits to the Service arriving at the Castle discovered too late – and all salaries and wages were paid not in cash but in tradeable goods allegedly to the stated value in currency. Other transactions were measured in gold ounces, but the 'coastal ounce,' which was roughly equivalent to £4 sterling, varied in value. There were, in addition, other international currencies in common use, for example silver Maria Theresa dollars and cowries, which fluctuated in value in relation to each other and to gold. Many bargains were struck in terms of rolls of tobacco, casks of brandy, and barrels of gunpowder. Governor Miles kept some of his accounts in terms of gallons of rum, paying 180 for men slaves, 160 for women. And the governors used most of the devices that have been used by corrupt military contractors over the centuries, drawing pay for multiple offices held simultaneously, claiming pay for more soldiers than were still alive, employing locally recruited soldiers at low wages while claiming the larger amounts paid to expatriates, overcharging their men for supplies, and overstating the payments made in rents and subsidies, for gun salutes, and for funerals, to name some of the rackets noted at the time.

Once a year – occasionally oftener – the Company's storeship brought out the 'furnishings' ordered for, and intended for, the upkeep of the Castle and the payment of the officers and men. In the accounts the stores were listed in detail – building materials, tools, weapons, gunpowder, uniforms, hats, shirts, shoes – down to the last bag of nails, bottle of purgative, ream of writing paper, and gallon of ink. In addition the storeships brought large quantities of tobacco, brandy, rum, and other commodities that were intended as the means of payment for services provided by the local African communities. It was easy, if complex, for governors and their accountants to sell some of these stores locally and pocket the proceeds. Gunpowder, in particular, was as liquid a currency as gold, and could always be sold and bought at the price of the day, which was sometimes very high. In April 1769, for example, although the storeship had refilled the Castle magazine with gunpowder just three months before, the governor had already embezzled and sold so much of it that he could not fire the morning and evening salutes.

Governor Charles Bell (1756–57 and 1761–63), who had improvised the retreat of the French naval squadron, is said to have taken home £7,000, including profits from slave trading. Richard Brew, who had been a factor, that is, a storekeeper, and was no mean embezzler himself, estimated that Gilbert Petrie, when governor of Cape Coast Castle (1766–69), simply by selling his 'furnishings,' made at least £3,000. Occasionally a governor was so blatant that complaints were made to London and an audit took place. In April 1767 the governor of Accra fort, Thomas Trinder, 'received goods from the public to the amount of £1,812/12/6, all which,' the auditors found, 'he instantly appropriated to his own use.' In August 1770 David Mill, governor of Cape Coast Castle, 'appropriated £6,576 out of

£8,148 by substituting inferior things bought from ships etc.' He had, it was estimated, in five years, stolen goods valued at £46,579 and sixteen shillings, between half and three-quarters of the annual grant for maintaining the entire chain of British forts. Faced with the nuisance of audit, the governors then simply stopped sending even fictionalized accounts. On June 8, 1807, the Audit Office in London reported that out of £337,000 paid by the Treasury to the Company of Merchants between 1785 and 1807, no accounts of any kind had been received, although some were sent later. The governors particularly liked the opportunities for diverting money that arose from new building works. According to Brew, the governors strode about the Castle demanding a spur here, a ravelin there, like Vauban reordering the frontier defenses of France, and Cape Coast Castle is an accumulation of buildings called after slaving era governors – Phipps's Tower, Smith's Tower, Greenhill Point, Grossle's Bastion. According to Brew, the easiest way for a governor to make money was to pull down an old wall.

All this embezzlement, grand larceny conducted on an international industrial scale, was carried out with the tacit consent of the Governing Committee in London, who were complicit in the rackets, benefited personally from them, and connived at the fictions in the accounts. Even when irregularities were officially reported, the governors seldom suffered any penalty unless they were too greedy, too flagrant, or their explanations too implausible. Some governors and officers were dismissed and went back to Britain, where they were often employed writing books and pamphlets in defense of the slave trade, but they were almost always reinstated, if they wished, and in at least two cases dismissed fort governors were promoted to the governorship of Cape Coast Castle, the highest position in the Service. Indeed, from the staff records, it emerges that to have been dismissed and reinstated was almost a requirement on an officer's CV if he was to be considered for promotion to the highest positions.

Corruption was expected and normal, a central part of the elaborate system by which eighteenth-century Britain was governed, and was scarcely regarded as improper by the aristocratic ministers in London, who themselves dug their hands deep into the public purse. And it was expected that men who went to the tropics would make money and then come home. The fortunes to be made by the governors of Cape Coast Castle were, however, different from those amassed by, say, the nabobs of the East India Company. In India the wealth acquired by the British derived from India. In the African Service the pickings were from the British Exchequer. One of the economic roles played by Cape Coast Castle was that of a continuous money-laundering facility, receiving public funds in Africa in the form of goods and sending part of them back to Britain as private gold belonging to the governors.

Grand larceny was one thing, petty larceny another. The governors never felt any compunction at punishing theft from the Castle stores with a severity that can scarcely be comprehended. We might assume that Sarah Bowdich, one of the few educated, expatriate British women to have lived there before Victorian times, was more gentle or merciful than the men. But as she herself records, when she adopted an orphan African boy whom she called Tando, she 'was obliged to send him and another boy to the corporal to receive six lashes' when they were caught stealing sugar. In 1805 a son of Rev. Philip Quaque, who like his father had been taken on to the Company's books as an officer after receiving education in church schools in England, was dismissed 'after receiving seven dozen lashes for thieving.' (I have not found any other instances of officers being punished in this way, although flogging of white soldiers was common.) Canoemen caught pilfering from the stores as they were being landed from the storeships were arrested and, unless they could be redeemed by family or friends, were liable to be enslaved and sold to the slave ships for transportation to the Americas. In 1800, for example, George Torrane, the governor of the Castle, informed the Governing Committee that

> . . . the natives have been so addicted to robbery and theft that harsh measures have become indispensable. Twelve free canoemen are now in irons who were detected in the fact of opening the Company's puncheons of india goods [cloths from Bengal dyed in workshops in London for the African market] per Thames [a storeship] and taking out a considerable quantity of cloth. By threats we have intimidated the townspeople to restore about half of the missing property and we at first signified a determination to send all the culprits whom we apprehended to the West Indies to be sold for the benefit of the Company. We have since however made a gentler proposal, vizt to ship off two by way of example and incorporate ten with the company's slaves; not the offenders but an equal number of young lads to be furnished by the townspeople in their room, as the only way in which the Company can be reimbursed for the depredations committed on the cargoes of the William, Lively, and Thames. They seem to accede to the latter part of the proposal but are exerting all their influence to prevent the two from being shipped.

After a long palaver the two canoemen were freed, the ransom paid for their redemption being young male slaves that their relatives bought from a slave ship whose captain was willing, when the price was right, to sell as well as to buy.

# 3

# Inside

Those arriving in the Castle from the sea for the first time found it smaller inside than they had expected. In some ways it resembled a ship, pointed at both ends, with segregated decks and gangways, and many locked hatches. High on the ramparts were the lookouts scanning the horizons with telescopes. A bell in a tower was rung to mark the hours, and the sentries on their rounds called out 'All's well' in a variety of English accents. Apart from the gun carriages, there were no wheeled vehicles. With the incessant heaving and crashing of the waves, the showers of salt spray, and the sense of being enclosed and isolated, no one who lived in Cape Coast Castle could forget that it was more oceanic than terrestrial.

On the highest floor were the governor's quarters, entered by an outside staircase that had been designed, as at Elmina, to look impressive when seen from the sea. Like the captain of a ship pacing his quarterdeck, the governor was able not only to look outward to the sea but to keep a supervisory eye over his enclosed little empire below. On the floor below the governor's were the private apartments of the officers, and the hall they used for dining, palavers, and infrequent religious services. Apart from the governor's private quarters at the very top of the Castle, those on the first floor were

*8. Inside the Castle: the governor's staircase, with (far right) the graves
of Letitia Landon and Governor George Maclean (see Chapter 6).*

the airiest, coolest, freshest, and most comfortable chambers in the
Castle, with views of the relentless ocean.

What present-day visitors to the Castle can no longer see in
the many chambers on these upper floors are the carved mahogany
furniture, the clocks, the fine Spode china and Georgian silverware,
the Turkish and Indian carpets, the silk wall hangings, the paintings
and prints, the decanters of fine wine, and the billiard table – the
balls perhaps made from ivory, 'teeth,' previously exported from the
coast. Gone too are the many books. In 1780, besides works on law,
surveying, navigation, geography, and other professional matters,
the Castle contained an excellent range of literary, historical,
and philosophical authors, many in large multi-volume editions.
Shakespeare in ten volumes, Plutarch's *Lives*, Rollin's *Ancient
History*, Chesterfield's *Letters to His Son* (four volumes of advice on
how to behave with the manners of a gentleman even when you are

not), the sepulchral religious poetry of Edward Young, the satires of Charles Churchill, celebrations of English rural life by William Shenstone, and Robert Dodsley's *Collection of Poems* were all to be found. The officers read Locke on Human Understanding, Burke on the Sublime. One surgeon had a seventeen-volume encyclopedia. In 1789 the officers formed that quintessential Enlightenment organization, a literary and philosophical society, the 'Torridzonians' – motto on its gold medal 'Friendship Ardent as the Clime' – which met regularly in the Castle to discuss the questions of the day, collecting funds for the basic catechetic books used by Chaplain Quaque in teaching the sons of Castle officers to read and write. (Later the Torridzonians became a Masonic lodge.) In other ways, too, the officers of the slaving era presented themselves as men of the Enlightenment. As 'men of feeling,' they ordered from London contemporary novels in the current fashion of 'sensibility' in which gentlemen choked back tears and ladies swooned at the thought of a sparrow falling from its nest. In 1779 the officers of the Castle were reading the four volumes of *The Mistakes of the Heart*.

Cape Coast Castle was better supplied with books than many a gentleman's country house in England or Scotland. The latest publications arrived on the storeship a few months after they were first published in London and Edinburgh, and others could be bought from visiting slave ships. Many of the same books were to be found in the library of the slave-owning planters of Charleston in South Carolina, and a recently discovered catalogue of the books on sale in Barbados at this time is even fuller. George Maclean, a famous Castle governor in the post-slave-trade era, had prints of scenes from Shakespeare on the walls of his chambers, probably from the same expensive series by Boydell that are also recorded at Charleston. Geographically Cape Coast and Charleston were separated by thousands of miles of ocean, but economically, commercially, and culturally they were conjoined twins, small expatriate, slave trading and slave holding, anglophone communities precariously perched on the coast of a vast, unknown, and frightening continent, populated by human beings about whom they knew little. Both were pieces of 'England' transplanted to the palm-treed edges of the tropical ocean, wealthy, enterprising, and institutionally cruel, but asserting at every opportunity that they were members of a polite, civilized, enlightened European society in the age of sensibility.

In the Castle the rows of soft morocco-bound books, the hard vellum ledgers, the maps, charts, globes, theodolites, and the telescopes were as much part of the political rhetoric of the building as the white of the walls and the banging of the guns. To many African visitors they were probably exotic and potentially threatening but also attractive, a glimpse of the benefits of European modernity which the leaders of local African societies and many of their followers could, literally, buy into by selling slaves to the Castle – although in the slaving era, only those local leaders who were already in regular close contact with the Europeans were likely to have thought of themselves or of the slaves as Africans. When, occasionally, as in 1817, a special mission from Cape Coast Castle went, by invitation, into the interior along the forest paths to establish diplomatic links with the Asante, the gifts specially ordered from London included, besides the usual cloths, guns, and medical supplies, an assortment of wine decanters, silver bowls, snuff boxes, bugles, watches, magic lanterns, microscopes, and compasses. Thomas Bowdich, Sarah's husband, a member of the mission with previous experience, also asked London to send botanical books – these showed that the British, although confined to the coast, already knew which forest trees and plants were valuable. He also asked for works of art, 'two or three landscapes,' portfolios of engravings of English costume – on the coast few local Africans of either sex except the rich wore much – and engravings of famous public London buildings with a set of the original drawings, plus the pencils and the watercolors that showed how the engravings had been derived from originals. The 1820 expedition to Asante (whose setting out from the Castle is illustrated on page 49), carried, as presents for the king, 25 cases of muskets, 100 barrels of rum, 100 kegs of gunpowder – in other words, the staples of European trade that the rulers of Asante wanted, but also many less utilitarian items intended to impress as well as please their hosts, including three dozen tumblers and finger cups, eight decanters, a piano of harmonic glasses, and an aeolian harp – a toy that made music when placed in a breeze, used by Enlightenment philosophers as a metaphor for the human mind reacting to the unrepeatable events of experience.

The forts along the coast, white and impressive though they too appeared from the sea, had even fewer frills than the Castle. The inventories of the possessions of dead officers sold at auction among their colleagues give glimpses of what was once to be seen inside, although only occasionally among the clothes, the hats, the silver buttons, the ornamental dirks, and other paraphernalia of uniformed life, do we see anything personal, such as collections of books, sometimes individually listed (J. G. Zimmerman's *On Solitude*, Johnson's *Journey to the Hebrides*), or pictures (an engraving of the death of Captain Cook, 'an oil painting of Adam and Eve in a carved gilt frame'). When Horatio Smith, fort governor of Anomabu, died in 1783, among the possessions were his gold-topped cane, his gold buckles, and his large library, which included a fourteen-volume history of France. He had about £450 worth of gold dust in his closet. Thomas Trinder, governor of Accra fort, who died in 1775, had '2 prints of king and queen, 1 ditto Britannia,' one pair of silver shoe buckles, one broken silver teaspoon, seventeen knives, nine blue china teacups, one corkscrew, and one comb – essential for fighting the nits. Trinder had nine ruffled shirts, ten plain shirts, twenty-two pairs of silk stockings, one silver-hilted sword, 133 volumes of books, plans, and views, much furniture, plenty of wine, an old print of the heroic death of General Wolfe, and a parrot in a cage. The list goes on for many pages, before noting his main assets: gold and silver coins; gold chains; gold dust kept in bottles; promissory notes awaiting dispatch to London; and slaves, men, women, and children, imprisoned in several forts that now belonged to Trinder's estate and who would shortly be sold in the same sale as his comb.

## Prospero's books

In Shakespeare's fantastical play *The Tempest*, Prospero rules the tropical island on which he has been wrecked not only by direct coercion but by the knowledge he brings from Europe, dramatically represented by the books he keeps by him in his cell. They are, to Prospero, 'volumes that I prize above my Dukedom.' Caliban, who was deprived of his island by Prospero's arrival, believes that the source of Prospero's magic lies in his books, for without them, as Caliban says, Prospero 'hath not one spirit to command.' At the end of the play Prospero inaugurates the new age by destroying both his direct and his indirect power: 'I'll break my staff, / Bury it certain fathoms in the earth, / And deeper than did ever plummet sound / I'll drown my book.'

At Cape Coast Castle, books carried huge symbolic power. Sir George Young, a naval captain who had voyaged to Africa in 1767–68, 1771, and 1772, told the 1790 parliamentary inquiry about an African fable that he had heard from a prominent English-speaking African, who dressed as a European, and with whom he had dined at Tantumquerry fort. Young tried to repeat the story, which reveals the self-image of the European as much as that of the African, as he had heard it verbatim:

That God Almighty made White Man after he had made Black man; that when he made Black man and White man,

he put a great heap of gold upon table, and a great heap of
bookee (by which he meant learning and knowledge) and
when so done, God Almighty said, Black man, which you
like – Black man very great fool come chuse gold; white man
chuse bookee, and in so doing all one come, God himself.

In the slaving era, when agreements such as the 1753 treaty
were made (see Chapter 2), it was customary for the British and
the African leaders to ratify them in the presence of both, each
side in accordance with its own religious customs, which for the
British involved ceremonial oaths while holding a Bible. However,
the books that the Africans most often encountered at that time
were not the printed volumes but the huge manuscript ledgers,
some with gold elephants emblazoned on their ivory-colored vellum
covers, that were brought out for palavers. These were the books in
which the British recorded the agreements, contracts, promises, and
transactions made day by day, year after year, including the records of
customary payments made to local political and religious leaders.

In the Western tradition, literacy has usually been seen as
liberation, a means of taking possession of knowledge, of fixing
it, and of rendering it durable. But, as the anthropologist Claude
Lévi-Strauss pointed out long ago, the power to record is also a
power to control. In a palaver between the men in the Castle and
the men outside, that is, between members of a culture of written
records and one dependent on orality and memory, the men with
books were at an advantage. As some of the reports of long palavers
make clear, in some disputes the local men would bring in witnesses
to confirm the truth of what they claimed. The British could, in
many cases, bring out their ledgers and point to written records
of agreements, maybe only signed with a mark, but attested to as
truthful by 'linguists' who straddled the literacy, language, and skin
color divisions.

If Prospero's books were destroyed, negotiations would become more evenly balanced, may even have tilted in favor of the side with the reliable memories, but this would not necessarily benefit Caliban. The following note records the sale of a slave to Governor James Morgue in 1785, also notable as one of the few records in which the name of a slave being sold is preserved:

> A man named Quodo said to have been given by Amornah to the late T Trinder and from him sold but being claimed by Amoniah and Quashie who pretends that he was never given away, and no evidence can be procured as to the truth, he is now sold at risque of the Buyer who is answerable for all palavers that may hereafter happen.

Price achieved at auction: £34.

## The Company store

The ground level of the Castle was taken up with heavily padlocked warehouses, containing the Company's stores and vast quantities of imports landed from the ships that would gradually be dispersed as payment. On January 14, 1779, for example, the Castle received from the ship *Rumbold* an assortment of goods valued at 2,190 gold ounces (about £10,000), including brandy, rum, tobacco, muskets, gunpowder, a variety of small metal manufactures, scissors, knives, brass basins, pewter vessels, clay pipes, umbrellas, and luxury goods. Materials and cloths originating from all parts of the Europeanized world were among the largest of the imports, with a high proportion from India. Small squares of some of the finest cloths on offer have, incidentally, survived in excellent condition, their many colors quite unfaded, in the sample books that the London cloth merchants gave to the Africa House as part of their advertising. Among the long lists

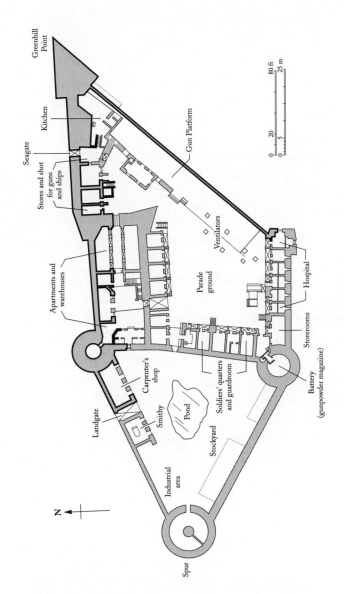

Greenhill Point

Kitchen

Seagate

Stores and shot for guns and ships

Gun Platform

Apartments and warehouses

Ventilators

Parade ground

Hospital

Carpenter's shop

Storerooms

Landgate

Smithy

Pond

Soldiers' quarters and guardroom

Battery (gunpowder magazine)

Industrial area

Stockyard

N

Spur

80 ft

25 m

20

5

0

0

**CAPE COAST CASTLE**

Ground plan, 1756, before the building of the slave prisons, showing the ventilators of the underground 'slave hole.'

9. *Ground plan of the Castle, 1756.*

of cloths with unfamiliar names that are recorded in the barters in Africa – 'says,' 'romauls,' 'chelloes,' 'neganipauls,' 'Glasgow red Danes' – my eye caught the following item, valued at £100, among the goods landed from the ship *Nancy* at Cape Coast Castle on January 12, 1779: '6 jeans, 8 corduroys.' Since most of the fabrics sold through the grand emporium were destined to be made into wearing apparel, the American story that jeans were invented by another Levi Strauss at the time of the Californian Gold Rush of 1848 may need to be revised.

## *Animals*

In Cape Coast Castle there were no dogs or horses, as might have been seen in a castle or country house in Britain. Horses, if they survived the long ocean voyage, found the canoe journey ashore as terrifying as the captains, and the survivors died in agony if they ate the local grass and drank the local water. The young officer who brought the pair of spurs that are recorded among the possessions sold after his funeral was presumably misinformed. Dogs fared little better. There was, however, a motley collection of farm animals standing tethered in the Castle stockyard waiting their turn to be slaughtered and eaten, adding to the noise and the stink. On January 31, 1779, for example, the Castle housed 22 head of cattle, 113 sheep and goats, 7 hogs, 12 turkeys, 8 geese, 10 ducks, 150 fowls, 8 guinea hens, and 13 pigs. At least some of these had come from far away, by ship or canoe. Animals who died before their slaughter time did not escape the pot – for some reason the goats had a high natural mortality rate.

At ground level too were the hospital and the cookhouse and the barracks for the soldiers. In this part of the Castle, according to Sarah Bowdich, 'a number of vultures, called Turkey buzzards, were always to be seen, either hovering about to pick up the offal thrown out, or thoroughly gorged, sitting upon the neighbouring guns, in so stupid a condition that it was easy to knock them over with the hand.' Then, as now, vultures were to be seen everywhere, waiting and watching, and according to William Hutton, who spent many years in the Castle and the forts, they were regarded as sacred. Living at the top of the food chain, the vultures seldom did any killing themselves, but they enjoyed a good and varied diet from the disasters of others – apart from the normal scraps, all remains of an animal or bird not eaten on the day it was killed were thrown away. It was a game among the British to test whether the vultures were really as keen-sighted and keen-scented as they were alleged to be. They would throw out some scrap of meat to see how long it took for the first bird to arrive and then to be joined by others flocking from all over the locality.

The forest nearby was full of wild animals, but the British were not allowed to kill them for amusement as they did in most areas of the world where they lived or settled. It was a constant complaint among the expatriates that there was no 'sport.' When James Swanzy, an officer of the African Service, shot a crocodile, there had to be a long palaver and money paid in compensation. At one time the Castle had its own live leopard called Sai that had been taken as a cub, had its claws and teeth filed, and roamed at will within the Castle walls, playing with the children. Sarah Bowdich reports, with some glee, the alarm of some visiting Dutch officers from Elmina when Sai jumped out from under a sofa. Monkeys and chimpanzees too were occasionally taken live and sold to the ships, as were parrots, although few lived for long. Some of the more exotic birds were extremely expensive, king crown birds being priced at about £4, more than the price of an elderly slave (see Chapter 8). In the exchange of gifts with the Asante, the British gave wonderful works of art, and the Asante gave wonderful works of nature, beasts and birds, some of which survived their journey to London. Sai, the leopard, fell into the sea when being canoed out to a ship but was rescued. During the ship's voyage to London, in which pirates stole all the livestock on board, he was fed solely on parrots, which caused intense stomach pains, and he had to have his jaws held open and purgative poured in. In London he was presented to the royal family, who put him on public exhibition in a zoo, but he died of flu soon after.

Sarah Bowdich spent her months in the Castle in 1816 both in traditional female pastimes – 'my needle and thread were in constant use' – and in observing and classifying the plants and wildlife. She was fascinated by the cats, especially the genet, one of which she tamed as a pet and which helped to keep the rats at bay. Later, when her husband died, she became a well-known author of books about animals and plants, and of a standard book, *Taxidermy*, on how to stuff specimens. She is credited with having identified several species previously unknown to European science. To seaward too, where the local fishing canoes provided a constantly changing panorama, she found strange creatures. As she wrote:

> As I stood one day at a window, looking on to the sea, I saw the dorsal fin of several of these creatures who were proceeding with the utmost rapidity to the spot where five men were swimming and sporting in the water. I immediately sent to warn them of the risk they ran, and four of them returned to the shore, but the fifth scorned all precaution, laughed at my messenger, and said I was too much frightened, because I was a white woman. I then despatched half a bottle of rum, in order to bribe him to come to the beach, but before he could be tempted, I saw the creature seize him, and drag him under the water which was instantaneously covered with blood; he rose again, and a canoe, which put off immediately, brought him to land, with the loss of one leg, the hip-bone having been fairly dragged from the socket; medical aid was instantly summoned, but he died in a few minutes.

The poisonous centipedes that she found in her bed were, Sarah decided, more of a problem than the occasional venomous snake that managed to slide up the governor's grand staircase. The scorpions, she noted in her matter-of-fact scientific way, liked to hide among the books, but their bite, although always severe, was seldom fatal. The Castle house slaves were most afraid of the tarantulas, which Sarah killed by hitting them with a book. As a naturalist, she observed without disgust the lizards, the cockroaches, and the white and red ants. Everyone in the Castle soon got used to them. But as Commodore Collier noted, the ants devoured everything, including clothes packed in chests, and then started on the chests. These had to be put on legs well tarred or placed in water, an arrangement that suited another successful species, the mosquitoes.

## Damp

Perched on its rocks, isolated on its peninsula, and crammed with iron, Cape Coast Castle was frequently struck by lightning, as were the other European buildings on the coast. When Elmina Castle was struck in 1651 the governor reported that all the gold and silver melted but that the bags in which they were stored were not damaged. The swords were broken in their scabbards, which remained untouched. In the British slaving fort at Accra the walls were shattered and pewter vessels melted. In an age that had little or no understanding of electricity, such acts of God were terrifying and nobody knew what He might do next. And although the gunpowder at Cape Coast Castle, stored deep in a corner bastion, never ignited, that was because it was damp, and like everything else, it had to be taken out from time to time and dried in the sun.

Almost everything within the Castle storerooms – even the rats and mice – came from Britain, or from the British colonies in the New World, although much had come to Britain from elsewhere, especially from India. Barrels and casks of various sizes, the only waterproof packaging for most of the goods in the Castle, were carried to and from the ships by canoe, or were 'swum' by local men and boys. Some of these containers had traveled more than once around the North Atlantic oceanic world, one voyage perhaps containing rum, another gunpowder, another salted tripe. Every one was individually numbered and accounted for, with many disputes between the ships' captains, the Castle officers, and the canoemen about lost casks, leaking casks, and casks whose contents had been spoiled, adulterated, or pilfered.

Some things were produced and purchased locally, like the corn that was used to feed the slaves in the slave dungeons and was sold to the slave ships for the transatlantic crossing. In 1779, for example, the Castle's inventory records 60 chests containing 4,200 gallons of corn. Much of the canoe traffic between the Castle, the forts, and the ships was concerned with maintaining stocks of corn for slaves already embarked and with stocking up for the voyage to the Americas. The other local product was the oil made from the nuts of the palm trees that grew wild in profusion all along the coast. Like the olive in ancient Hellas, the palm in West Africa served so many human needs as to require its own deities. The oil was used for seasoning meat or fish, for lighting, and as an ointment for rheumatism. It was also used as a yeast for making bread, although it would only keep for a few hours. According to Decima Moore, wife of a nineteenth-century colonial governor, everything made of leather had to be oiled every day. If a pair of shoes was left for two days without being oiled they would never lose the smell of mould. Without frequent applications of palm oil, keys crumbled, padlocks broke, and even the heavy steel-plated safes in which the Castle's gold was secured soon succumbed to the rust. The soldiers spread palm oil on the guns to cover up the holes. The slave traders rubbed it on their prisoners to make them look younger, more sleek,

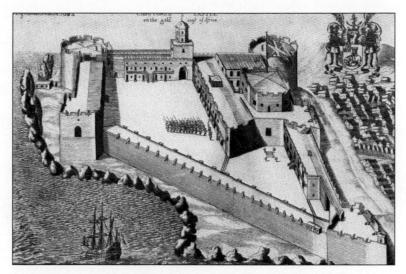

*10. Inside, before the eighteenth century changes to the building, showing the entrance to the 'slave hole' on the lower right.*

and more expensive. The palm trees also gave oblivion. According to Sarah Bowdich, the palm wine when first drawn from the tree was sparkling and sweet, but in two hours it turned sour, and when placed in the sun it fermented; by night-time it had become 'an ardent spirit,' cheaper than the rum and brandy available from the Company store.

After the ending of the British slave trade, palm oil became the main local crop of the Gold Coast, exported from commercial plantations to provide British, and later American, workers with margarine and literally to oil the wheels of the railways and heavy mechanical industry.

## *The prisons*

It was during the Royal African Company's rebuilding of the Castle in the later seventeenth century that a prison was built into the hole in the rock under the parade ground from which the stones for constructing the walls had been quarried. A description by the French traveler Jean Barbot was included in the 1732 *Collection of Voyages*, a magnificent multi-volume work without which no eighteenth-century English gentleman's library was complete, and of which it seems likely that there was a copy in the Castle:

> . . . a very handsome place of arms, well paved; under which is a spacious mansion, or place to keep slaves in, cut out of the rocky ground, arch'd, and divided into several rooms; so that it will conveniently contain a thousand *Blacks*, let down at an opening made for the purpose. The keeping of the slaves thus underground is a good security to the garrison against any insurrection.

The vertical stratification of the Castle ran downward from governor at the top, through the officers on the first floor, to the soldiers and the house slaves on the ground level from where the sea was not visible. The slaves awaiting transportation, the economic foundation of the whole enterprise, were below ground within the architectural foundations, literally walked over by everyone else. One has to look hard at the old engravings to find any sign of this prison, although the gratings are occasionally visible.

Around 1777 specially designed prisons were built at Cape Coast Castle at ground level. A building was demolished, and five vaulted brick chambers were constructed within a bastion. One gate led into the whole dungeon complex, which resembles a suite of connecting rooms that could be divided from one another by internal doors. Some of these spaces were later adapted to hold water tanks, or were used as warehouses for goods, but in recent years they have been restored and can be visited. There were air vents above which let in a little light, but no windows, continuing the tradition that prisoners

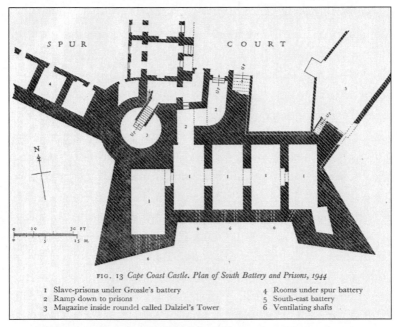

FIG. 13 *Cape Coast Castle. Plan of South Battery and Prisons, 1944*

1 Slave-prisons under Grossle's battery
2 Ramp down to prisons
3 Magazine inside roundel called Dalziel's Tower
4 Rooms under spur battery
5 South-east battery
6 Ventilating shafts

*11. Plan of the eighteenth-century slave prisons.*

*12. The vaulted slave dungeons today.*

should be housed in near darkness as if they were underground or in the hold of a ship. To judge from a gate of the period that survives at Dixcove fort, the single entrance was barred with a heavy iron grille. The carefully laid brick floor included gutters, such as might be found in animal pens, for flushing them clean.

A. B. Ellis, a captain in a British colonial regiment, who spent time in the Castle in the 1870s, described the 'dark and damp ranges of dungeons extending under the Sea Battery, capable of containing two thousand closely-packed human beings, where, in the days of the slave trade, slaves used to be confined before shipment.' Mary Kingsley, who visited the Castle in 1893, was shown what she called 'its commodious accommodation for slaves awaiting shipment, now almost as obsolete as the guns [the Castle] mounts, but not quite so, for these cool and roomy chambers serve to house the native constabulary and their extensive families.' An archaeological excavation in 1972 found evidence of a heavy door securely bolted to the ground, but no fixing points for chains, nor was there confirmation of the conjecture made by A. W. Lawrence during the restorations of the 1950s that bunks might have been arranged along the walls as in the slaving ships.

The new eighteenth-century purpose-built slave prisons kept the older name. A survey of the Castle made in 1797, which reports the state of every wall, room, warehouse, and gun, notes 'Slave hole in good order.' When Captain Norris, who had been on five slaving voyages, was asked by the 1790 parliamentary inquiry, 'Was you ever in an African prison?' he replied, 'I have seen numbers of them – they are not called prisons but slave holes.' When asked, 'Are the slaves closer in those holes than on board the ships?' he replied, 'That must depend on circumstances, there may be but one, or it may be as thronged as the Black Hole of Calcutta.' Anthony How, a botanist, who had been to the coast in 1785 and 1786 on an official British mission to examine the local plants, was asked whether he

*13. The gun platform and tunnel leading to the seaward gate, 'the door of no return.'*

had observed how the slaves were treated. He replied, 'They were chained day and night, and drove down to the sea side twice a day to be washed.'

For many overseas visitors of African descent today, the need physically to enter the prisons in which their ancestors may have spent their last days in Africa is the main reason why they have made the journey, or, as some would say, the pilgrimage, to Cape Coast Castle. For visitors whose ancestral connections are more likely to be to the slavers than to the enslaved individuals, a visit to the Castle without seeing the dungeons would today also be unthinkable. In the slaving era, however, the slave prisons were seldom mentioned. The beautiful white castle by the sea maintained a polite reticence about the sole reason for its existence.

# 4

# The officers

The number of British expatriate officers living on shore in Africa during the slaving era was normally less than fifty. The governor of Cape Coast Castle was governor-in-chief and president of the Council, a formal body responsible for the day-to-day running of all the British settlements. The governors, or 'chiefs,' of the main forts – Anomabu, Accra, Whydah (on the 'Slave Coast'), Winneba (west of Accra), and Tantamkweri (Tantumquerry or Tantam) – were also members of the Council, along with the senior staff in the Castle, but the governors of the other forts – Apollonia, Dixcove, Sekondi, and Komenda – were not. As the scale of trading grew, the British opened, or reopened, other shore facilities elsewhere, notably at Pram Pram east of Accra and Popo in present-day Benin. The governor of Anomabu fort was deputy to the governor-in-chief and normally succeeded him. Besides the governors, the Company of Merchants employed one chaplain, one secretary, one accountant, one surveyor (responsible for the upkeep of the buildings), one 'register' (responsible for pay and personnel), one deputy secretary, one deputy accountant, one deputy surveyor, two officers of the guard (who commanded the Company's soldiers, one officer at Cape Coast Castle, the other at Anomabu), one deputy warehouse keeper, one chief surgeon, five assistant surgeons, seven factors (who recorded the trading in and out of the warehouses), and ten writers (who copied documents while learning the business). During the entire slaving era the number of British expatriate officers employed on the coast was remarkably stable. Even when the trade was at its height in the late eighteenth century, the numbers were much the same as they had been a hundred years earlier in the days of the Royal African Company. Around half the officers were employed in the Castle, the others in the forts.

The Governing Committee of the Company of Merchants in London seldom had any difficulty in finding officer recruits for the African Service. The 1750 Act provided that they should be 'from the middle class of life, young men of respectable connections, and very well educated,' and to judge from the number who wrote books, from the literary allusions that permeate their letters, and from the classical names they imposed on African territories, in that respect they were successful. But, although the Company of Merchants was legally required to recruit by merit, it did not want recruits who, as one governor put it, 'knew Greek' – aristocrats and other young men who had received a humanist university education and might be reluctant to get their hands dirty. As with many public and semi-public offices, there may have been a religious test intended to confine entry to sworn members of the official churches of England and Scotland, but it was not mentioned in any of the hundreds of application letters that have survived. In one letter Chaplain Quaque reports that in the Castle he has found 'no Papists, Quakers, or Anabaptists.' In another, he complains that the English were being supplanted by 'Scotch and Irish peoples, rank Presbyterians.' Members of the official Scottish (Presbyterian) Church were entitled to join English – now British – organizations after the political union of 1707 – but Quaque may just be repeating the common complaint of the time that Scotsmen and Irishmen were taking the best jobs.

The Company offered its officer recruits the possibility of a full career from writer to governor-in-chief, with published tables of salaries for the various grades. A young man would write to the Governing Committee in the Africa House in London offering his services, naming sponsors who would provide 'sureties' – financial guarantees – that were set high enough to confine entry to the richer ranks of British landed, professional, and commercial society. The applicant, who had to be between the ages of eighteen and twenty-five, normally required sureties of £500 to be appointed to the lowest rank of writer, and then had to find more when he was promoted. Before being appointed governor of a fort, an officer had to find sureties of £5,000, and the governor-in-chief £10,000. In many cases, the records show, the officer put up his own sureties, or provided sureties for colleagues in the Service, senior as well as junior, so binding the whole officer cadre of the African Service into mutual dependency. The guarantees were called if an officer died owing money to the Company of Merchants, and dismissed officers had to find new sureties if they wished to be reinstated. Based entirely on credit, these arrangements enabled rich sponsors to start young penniless men in a career without having to spend any money.

Although the cadre of officers on the coast was tiny, the British families from which the officers were drawn were a large and integral part of the political, ecclesiastical, professional, and commercial life of the entire British nation. Indeed this had been true of the British slaving industry from its earliest days. The South Sea Company, set up as a result of an article in the 1713 Treaty of Utrecht, the 'asiento,' by which Great Britain was assigned the commercial monopoly to supply slaves to the mines and plantations of Spanish America, numbered among its stockholders the British king George I, the scientist Sir Isaac Newton, the architect and playwright Sir John Vanbrugh, the poet Alexander Pope, the playwright John Gay, the writers Jonathan Swift and Daniel Defoe, and the publisher Thomas

Guy (who founded Guy's Hospital in London with the money he made in selling his stock before the bursting of the bubble in 1720). Under its charter the South Sea Company was restricted to the Atlantic shores of Spanish possessions in the Americas – the 'South Sea' was the South Atlantic – and between 1714 and 1739 supplied around 75,000 slaves to Cuba and South America, buying them from the British colonies in the West Indies and mainland America. The Royal African Company, chartered to supply slaves direct from Africa to these colonies, was also deeply rooted in British society. The British royal family were among its principal shareholders, with King Charles's brother, the future James II of England and VII of Scotland, also taking a leading personal role in its management. By 1720, a year chosen from the ledgers as a snapshot of the situation shortly before the decades of greatest boom, the list of members (shareholders) included the Duke of Argyll, the Earl of Holderness, the Earl of Lichfield, Lord Londonderry, the Bishop of Oxford, army and navy officers, gentlemen, churchmen, lawyers, merchants, bankers, a few unmarried or widowed women, and members of industries involved in the slave trade, such as cutlers, distillers, goldsmiths, apothecaries, and sail-makers.

After 1750, when the Act of Parliament withdrew the monopolies of the former chartered companies and opened the British slave trade to competition, there are no consolidated lists of investors or of the dividends, but the numbers participating were greater and more widely spread both socially and geographically. In Bristol and Liverpool, the two main ports in addition to London from which the British slave trade was conducted, the leaders of the industry were closely integrated into the structures of political, ecclesiastical, and commercial power. Any London merchant living near Mark Lane, where the Africa House was situated, was probably involved in the slave trade. In Liverpool, for decades, with scarcely a break, all the mayors were members of families involved in the trade. And there were wealthy and influential families, such as the Aspinalls, the Dawsons, the Forsters, the Gascoignes, and the Horatio Smiths, whose names were synonymous with slave-trade money even though only a few family members served in the African Service or in the slave ships.

These families were the 'Africans.' And allied to them was a larger and more influential political constituency, the 'West Indians,' the owners of the sugar plantations in the Caribbean that were worked by slaves brought from Africa and by their descendants. The Victorian prime minister William Gladstone came from such a family, and as a young Member of Parliament frequently voted for the continuation of slavery in British territories – appearing in the lists of those voting to maintain the status quo that were published, in order to shame them, by anti-slavery campaigners.

In the second half of the eighteenth century the British transatlantic slaving industry was a long-established – as economists say, 'mature' – branch of commerce. In its essentials it was little different from what it had been a hundred years earlier, except that the scale of trading was now far higher, the tonnage of some of the slaving vessels was greater, and many more voyages took place. Nor did the industry hesitate to use its political influence. In 1768, for example, when the Company of Merchants heard that measures to regulate the slave trade were being mooted, they immediately advised their colleagues in Bristol and Liverpool to contact their Members of Parliament, so 'that they may be prepared to support the free & Open Trade to Africa, in case any Attack should be made upon it in the House of Commons.' Until the 1780s the slave trade was not only condoned by almost all the country's political and ecclesiastical leaders but actively approved of. In the words of Edmund Burke, the officers of the African Service were 'a body of men trying manfully to carry out a difficult task for the national good on insufficient means.' What right had those who lived comfortably at home, sipping their sugared coffee, to criticize the men who bore the heat of the tropics so that they could continue to do so? Even after the horrors of the middle passage and the cruelty of life in the plantations had been exposed to the British public by parliamentary inquiries, books, and pamphlets, the country's leaders maintained their solidarity. In 1792, for example, John Moore, the long-serving Archbishop of Canterbury and father of Chaplain Quaque's teacher of the same name, a man whom even Church of England apologists now only remember for the grandeur of his lifestyle and the shamelessness of his nepotism, came out in support of the continuation of the slave trade. He was married to the daughter of a Carolina planter.

Recruitment to the African Service was much the same as for the East India Company, the Levant Company, the Hudson's Bay Company, and the other chartered trade companies, but, since patronage and family links were the key to entry, it would be a mistake to think that a young man had an open choice. Some families, such as the Scottish Bannermans, sent young men into both the East Indian and to the African Services, founding dynasties in both. John Thelwall, who debated whether to apply to join the East Indian or the African Service, was appointed to the African in 1794, through the interest of Richard Miles, whose sister, Elizabeth Thelwall, made the approach. Since a Richard Thelwall was a governor of Anomabu fort in the 1680s in the days of the Royal African Company, young John may have had other family connections. (I have not been able to establish whether he was related to the John Thelwall, friend of Godwin, Coleridge, and Wordsworth, who escaped the death penalty in the British Treason Trials of 1794.) Young John died on the voyage without ever seeing the Castle.

The family connections appear from the names of the officers. The Miles family had three brothers on the coast at the same time, one of whom, Richard, became governor of Cape Coast Castle. Of the brothers Mill, David was a governor of the Castle and later a member of the Governing Committee, Richard Mill was a governor of a fort, and Hercules Mill the captain of a slaving ship. At one time there were four members of the Deey family on the coast at the same time, all apparently brothers. These family links stretched across the ocean to the importing end of the business. Robert Norris, described in 1788 as 'a Carolina merchant trading at Liverpool,' was of the same family as the brothers George and Thomas Norris of the African Service, one of whom became governor-in-chief. Some former governors, Archibald Dalzel and David Mill, invested their fortune not only in slave plantations in the West Indies but also in slave ships. On the whole, the names in the lists of officers are English, Scottish, and Irish, but occasionally we find others such as Jerome Bernard Weuves – who became a governor of Cape Coast Castle – and Gustavus Lessler, who may have been officers recruited from the Dutch and Danish services, a regular practice in the previous century. As in many lists, the names sometimes match the men too neatly: Mr. Gold, the accountant; Mr. Bold, who volunteered to fight the Asante; Mr. Corp, guaranteed by Mr. Corp and Mr. Corp, who died immediately on arrival; Governor Mould, whose body and mind rotted like the stores in the Castle until he had to be removed from office; and Governor Morgue, who buried his officers in his Castle.

By the mid-eighteenth century these family connections also extended into Africa. A growing number of the lower officer ranks, such as writers, were sons of expatriate British officers and local women (see Chapter 6), including several sons of governors, although only a few are recorded as having been promoted higher. Richard Brew had two sons in the Service, and established a local commercial dynasty in Anomabu. James Swanzy, who went out in 1789, also placed two sons in the Service, and the Swanzy family remained prominent in the life of the colonial Gold Coast into the twentieth century. The descendants of Adam Bannerman, accountant at the Castle in 1780, or of James Bannerman, governor of Accra fort in the 1790s, are prominent in Ghanaian life to the present day. In 1850 James Bannerman, probably a grandson, was appointed acting governor of Cape Coast Castle and of all the British settlements on the Gold Coast, a symbolic moment but also a turning point. Bannerman was to be the only 'man of color' ever to be entrusted with the highest post. The Victorian colonial service gradually confined the top jobs to white expatriates, replacing the previous hierarchy that was based on ability, education, and family connections with one based on race.

For a young man without family sponsors there was only one way in which he could join the African Service. He could become a surgeon and be sponsored by the Company itself. The Edinburgh and Bristol medical schools turned out numerous surgeons, many of whom found it hard to obtain employment, especially in peace time when the Navy laid off ships and officers, including naval surgeons. The slaving industry, both afloat and ashore, needed medical men to try to ensure that the slaves they purchased in Africa were in good health and that they remained sufficiently well during the long Atlantic crossing to fetch an adequate price when they arrived. To help recruitment, on sea and land, the highest ranks were open to all. 'Every one of you here I will make captains,' Surgeon Alexander Falconbridge was told at the captain's table. Archibald Dalzel, twice governor at Cape Coast Castle, and Henry Meredith, governor of Anomabu and then Winneba forts, started their careers as surgeons. Other governors had been officers of the guard or surveyors. Only Chaplain Quaque was outside the normal open promotion structure, although he took temporary command of a slaving fort on two occasions.

In 1788, in an act named after Sir William Dolben, the British Parliament brought in measures aimed at reducing mortality rates during the middle passage. Besides laying down minimum standards for slaving vessels and limiting the number of slaves who could be carried, the Dolben Act required that every slave ship should carry a surgeon who would be paid a bounty of one shilling (£0.05) for every healthy slave landed. This provision effectively doubled the amount of money a surgeon might earn on a slaving voyage. Captains too were paid a bonus from public funds on each slave landed. As Hugh Crow, a Liverpool slave-ship captain, wrote in his memoirs, 'Many a laugh I and others have had at Mr. Wilberforce and his party [the abolitionists], when we received our hundred pounds bounty.' By the Dolben Act, the parliamentary supporters of the slaving industry obtained a huge new public subsidy at a time when it was booming as never before as an incentive to do what it was strongly in their commercial interest to do anyway.

In the African Service we see early examples of another British stereotype, the embarrassing black sheep of the family who is packed off to the tropics, where few questions are asked and where his true qualities come to the fore. The misfits, the ne'er-do-wells, the alcoholics, the cheats, and the bounders are either never heard of again or they come home rich and triumphant, their mistakes atoned for and their honor redeemed. 'My relations will do nothing for me without I leave this country,' writes John Rutherfoord of Glasgow in 1794, seeking appointment as a writer. He had worked for his father, T. Rutherfoord, who had been secretary of the Governing Committee between 1778 and 1787, and also for his successor, Mr. Schoolbred, but had been dismissed for 'actions which I long have been ashamed of; and for that Misconduct, my Sufferings have been of the most excruciating nature.' Rutherfoord was appointed (but I have not found his name on the lists in Africa). Sarah Bowdich, on her voyage to the Castle in 1816, noted among the other passengers the surgeon whom she described as a 'tall raw-boned Scotchman,' 'well-informed, skilful, and worthy' despite 'his habitual failing' (drink), who died soon after his arrival. Frederick Wootton, appointed writer in 1788, did not even know what had happened. As the Castle register noted in the staff file, 'The Governor and Council kept his appointment secret from him. Being an improper person for the service given to drunkenness.' Even in the late nineteenth century, in the high colonial period, the Gold Coast was a refuge and a repository for the unrespectable. On his voyage out, the Christian missionary Rev. Dennis Kemp noted among the passengers 'a lady of the theatrical profession,' by which he meant a prostitute, 'a gentleman, who has since died, leaving two wives in England to mourn his loss. And a third, a few years ago, was sentenced to two years' imprisonment for embezzlement.' Sir Gordon Guggisberg, one of the most active of all the British colonial governors, was a Canadian who had damaged his prospects in the British army by running off with his commanding officer's wife.

Among the officer recruits to the African Service, it was said, were young men who fled 'the pangs of unrequited passion.' But the Service mainly offered the sense of belonging to a masculine community. Among her fellow passengers, Sarah Bowdich observed, were two Scotsmen, Duncan and Jamie, who vowed never to be separated and shared a secret that neither would divulge. Jamie, who was morose, seldom spoke, and was liable to fits of melancholy that his frequent playing of the bagpipes only partly alleviated. Duncan said that Jamie needed to live in a closed society where others could keep an eye on him. When she lived in the Castle, Sarah was invited to a ball there at which some of the officers, with handkerchiefs on their shoulders, played the women's role, but she felt uncomfortable and declined. She seems not to have appreciated that she was recording a homoerotic element in Castle life, and when her notes were put into book form they were toned down.

## Gold and ivory

How much did the young officers know about what they were letting themselves in for? The slave trade took place thousands of miles away, with only a few slaves and former slaves reaching Britain from the Americas, usually as servants or seamen. Over most of the country the existence of the trade was scarcely known. And it was disguised by euphemisms, none particularly significant in itself, but cumulatively effective. In the eighteenth century the leaders of the British slave trade described themselves as 'adventurers' in the 'African' or the 'Guinea' trade. They associated their business with romantic images, especially with gold and ivory, honey and sugar. The Royal African Company had minted over half a million gold 'guineas,' each stamped with an elephant and castle, and they continued to circulate. One of the first acts of the successor body, the Company of Merchants, was to commission a coat of arms, in modern terms a logo, that showed a ship in full sail, with allegorical personifications of Africa and America, an elephant and a beehive. Of the slave trade, over 90 percent of the business of its members, and the sole reason for the existence of the Company, there was not a hint. Instead the legend on the coat of arms, 'Free Trade to Africa,' celebrated the right of every British citizen to trade in enslaved Africans.

In the Castle and the forts, too, iconic elephants were everywhere, engraved on the guns and muskets and pictured in gold leaf on the accounts ledgers. But it is doubtful whether, during the boom years of the slave trade, many officers of the African Service ever saw a live elephant, and if they did, it was a small forest elephant not at all like the huge elephants of the open country of Africa from which artists made their images. What the officers occasionally saw were 'teeth,' and the ivory trade continued as a sideline alongside slaving. The teeth were mostly found on the forest floor, but, as modern firearms were sold into the African interior, elephants were slaughtered, and their tusks sawn up and carried to the coast on the shoulders of slaves who were being marched to be sold to the slave ships there. Could not Africa yield a harvest of ivory instead of human beings, the British slaving industry representatives were asked at the 1790 parliamentary hearing? No, was their answer. If their partners in the African slaving industry could not transport teeth to the coast for free on the shoulders of the slaves, the elephants would remain unkilled.

## Polite reticence

The reticence is caught by Jane Austen, who had family connections with both Jamaica and Antigua. Austen's sister, Cassandra, was engaged to an English churchman, who died while on a visit to the West Indies and left her his small savings. One of the Austen brothers, who was in the Navy, was opposed to the slave trade. In *Mansfield Park* (1814), Sir Thomas Bertram has just returned from a visit to his slave plantations when the following conversation takes place:

[FANNY:] 'I love to hear my uncle talk of the West Indies. I could listen to him for an hour together ... Did not you hear me ask him about the slave trade last night?'
[EDMUND:] 'I did – and was in hopes the question would be followed up by others. It would have pleased your uncle to be inquired of farther.'
[FANNY:] 'And I longed to do it – but there was such a dead silence! And while my cousins were sitting by without speaking a word, or seeming at all interested in the subject, I did not like – I thought it would appear as if I wanted to set myself off at their expense, by shewing a curiosity and

pleasure in his information which he must wish his own daughters to feel.'

Part of the point is that Sir Thomas Bertram is personally a kind-hearted man. If embarrassment is likely to ensue, the obligation of politeness demands silence. But everyone knows that the family are all financially dependent upon his investments. And, as Austen picks up, it was hard to discuss the transatlantic slave trade without discussing the whole institution of New World slavery.

In *Emma* (1816), Jane Austen offers another example of the embarrassing subject being touched on and hurried over. The conversation is between the penniless young Jane Fairfax (who will soon have to earn her living as a governess) and the officious Mrs. Elton (who is from Bristol and much given to boasting about her rich brother-in-law Mr. Suckling, a merchant in an unspecified business):

[JANE:] 'When I am quite determined as to the time, I
am not at all afraid of being long unemployed. There are
places in town, offices where inquiry would soon produce
something – Offices for the sale – not quite of human flesh
– but of human intellect.'
[MRS ELTON:] 'Oh! my dear, human flesh! You quite shock
me; if you mean a fling at the slave-trade, I assure you Mr.
Suckling was always rather a friend to the abolition.'
[JANE:] 'I did not mean, I was not thinking of the slave-
trade; governess-trade, I assure you, was all that I had in
view; widely different certainly as to the guilt of those who
carry it on; but as to the greater misery of the victims, I do
not know where it lies.'

## *Africa*

The appointment letter from the Governing Committee noted the risks to body and mind that new officers would face on their arrival: 'May you enjoy health and tranquillity till you choose to resign the arduous undertaking in order to enjoy the fruits of your service in this your native land.' Another letter listed what he was required to bring: one coat, two waistcoats, two breeches, one hat and feather, one dirk and belt, one sash, one sofa or tent bed, six chairs, one table, one secretaire 'with the best lock,' one looking glass, one wash hand stand, one 'night chair,' one liquor case 'with the best lock,' one pair of gold scales and weights, 'with as much linen and plain clothing as may be convenient.' For a young man from a genteel but impoverished family, finding the money for the fitting out could be itself a problem, but it was also the young officer's first chance to show his skill at improvisation under pressure. 'When Mr. Gabell was on the point of leaving Portsmouth in the storeship *Penelope*,' the Committee in London reported to the Castle, 'he borrowed £15 of Captain White for which he gave a note on his father but which the latter refuses to pay.' Newly arrived officers were surprised to find how limited was the range of goods to be bought, and how expensive. To judge from a letter from his wife Sarah (discussed in Chapter 6), the factor Daniel O'Keefe had asked for some things he needed to be sent out on the storeship, but Mrs. O'Keefe was unsympathetic. 'Everyone seemed to think it very foolish to send such lumber as mentioned.' In the Company store, according to a list from soon after the end of the slaving era, a pair of shoes cost fourteen shillings (£0.75) and a pair of shoe brushes 2/6 (£0.13), as did a corkscrew.

The officers of the African Service always intended to come home. The British never had a project of settling the coast with British colonists as they did in North America and the West Indies. Neither were the officers of the African Service joining an organization like the British Colonial Service of the nineteenth and twentieth centuries whose members might serve in the Gold Coast as part of a career that might include tours of duty in territories in West, East, Central, and Southern Africa, in the West Indies, the Far East, the Pacific Islands, the Mediterranean, and other British-administered territories and islands round the world. For the officers of the African Service, Africa was not a vast continent of limitless, wide-open spaces. It was not even the Gold Coast of colonial times, but less than a dozen walled buildings perched on rocks on the Atlantic coast, and a narrow strip of coastal land and sea that stretched for 400 miles in between. Once they had arrived in Africa, the officers of the African Service could not ask to be sent to a more congenial posting or grit their teeth until their African tour was over. They had made their life choice, and they lived with, and mostly died from, the consequences.

Although it would be an exaggeration to suggest that they treated the many different African peoples whom they encountered as equals, they were far more closely integrated into the local life than their Colonial Service successors. They mostly knew at least one African language – an ability to speak Fante was a requirement for promotion to the higher ranks. As resident traders, they claimed no right to participate in government, let alone to change how it was conducted, and had no agenda to persuade the local peoples to adopt their social and religious practices. As guests and tenants, the men of the African Service knew and accepted that their whole existence depended, both legally and practically, upon acting in conformity with the laws and customs of their hosts and landlords.

In this respect the attitudes of the British differed markedly from those of their predecessors. The Portuguese, dominant on the coast for more than a century, had attempted to Christianize the African peoples with whom they traded. Although always short of men, money, ships, arms, building materials, and the other resources needed for slave trading, the Portuguese were never short of priests and missionaries. In 1576, for example, a party of six Augustinians performed a rite of baptism over the king of Efutu and his six sons, although in a dispute soon after five of the Augustinians were killed. In 1607 the Portuguese, who by now were so overstretched round the world that they could scarcely afford boots, maintained six priests in Elmina Castle, a ratio of maybe one for every twenty soldiers, and they never gave up on their (largely ineffectual) campaigns. In 1632, for example, in what was to be their last attempt, Pedro Mascarenhas, the newly arriving governor of Elmina, brought three religious images, statues of Mary, St. Antony, and St. Francis. When the face and hands of St. Francis turned black as soon as the ship reached Elmina, this was presented as a miraculous prophecy of what God intended for Africa. The Portuguese were ejected from Elmina by the Dutch five years later.

The Dutch brought another version of Christianity that involved much singing – the Elmina Castle inventories show hundreds of psalm books – but they did not make much attempt to interfere with local beliefs. As for the British, during the eighteenth century they left the various groups who lived within and around the Castle to practice whatever religions they chose, or to not participate at all. The enlarging of the Castle's seaward defenses in the eighteenth century had restricted access to a rock in the sea that was regarded as sacred, but local worshippers continued to conduct their ceremonies, whose celebration of their dependency on the sea and the oil palm, followed by feasting, are reminiscent of those of ancient Athens, inside the walls. It was not until the 1830s that incoming British Christian missionaries made any serious effort to supplant the local religions (see Chapter 9). As part of their campaign, a Danish visitor noted, they destroyed local religious buildings, an action that would have been unthinkable in the slaving era.

And for most of the slaving era the British were largely free of notions of racial superiority. When invited to comment by parliamentary inquiries, even the most hardened British slavers praised the intelligence, commercial acumen, prodigious memories, ability to make complex arithmetical calculations, and skill in languages of the local peoples they knew, regarding any differences from themselves as attributable to their being at an earlier stage in the progress of civilization. Only in the later nineteenth century do we see routine racism – Archer P. Crouch, for example, in his *Glimpses of Feverland* (1889), attributing the misfortunes of the peoples of the Gold Coast to their 'low position on the evolutionary scale.' By that time the missionaries too tended to use notions of essential racial differences as explanations for the mixed welcome that they received. As Rev. Kemp wrote in 1898, listing the many racial characteristics he detected after nine years on the Gold Coast, 'Untruthfulness is transmitted at birth: "they go astray as soon as they are born, speaking lies."' Those, like Sir Richard Burton, who from direct knowledge resisted lazy racial stereotyping – he wrote 'in intellect the black race is palpably superior' – found themselves adopting the vocabulary of their adversaries.

## Seasoning

The first test that British newcomers faced when they scrambled, soaking wet, along the corridor from the sea gate into the Castle was a severe illness. The death rate during the first year, as newcomers were 'seasoned' to the tropical climate, was extraordinarily high, from malaria, yellow fever, dysentery, and other tropical illnesses, few of which were then understood. Believing that disease was carried in the air, the governors paid little attention to the ponds, storage tanks, and water pipes. Nor did they know, as Kwame Nkrumah, the first president of independent Ghana, was to remark, that for the defense of his country, the best soldier was the mosquito. The malaria of West Africa took the form of a single severe attack that was frequently fatal but did not recur, unlike the strain faced by the British in India that could recur throughout a man's lifetime and, in Victorian fiction such as the Sherlock Holmes stories, became a badge, with a touch of romance, of the 'old India hand.' (In the many volumes of ledgers of 'dead men's effects' I have only come across one reference to a mosquito net.)

Some of the early records of Cape Coast Castle are little more than lists of deaths. In 1703, for example, on April 27 died Captain Will Gabbs, chief of Anomabu; on April 29 died Robert Sutton, sergeant at Cape Coast Castle; and on May 1 Peter Marvell, soldier. Did he have any family connection with the poet Andrew Marvell, one wonders, or banter with Edward Shakespear, who is noted as having died in the Castle soon after? The Shakespear family supplied cordage to the Castle for much of the eighteenth century. Of the governors (agents-general) appointed by the Royal African Company, there were seven between 1672 and 1687, including three former slave-ship captains, and some lived to return to England. Of those appointed after 1700, Bagg died soon after his arrival at the Castle, his successor, Boughton, on the voyage out. It has been calculated that in the early eighteenth century life expectancy of officers on the western coast of Africa was about four or five years, and, on average, a funeral took place every ten days. In 1708 Governor Thomas reported 'Mr. Whitefield, chief at Annamaboe, lately dead; he purchased very ordinary slaves,' not the epitaph he might have chosen himself; whereas Thomas, who died in the Castle in 1711, is listed in the *Oxford Dictionary of National Biography*. Nor did the mortality rate improve as the eighteenth century went on. For many new arrivals, death came soon, suddenly, and painfully, the whole disgusting process from first symptoms to fever, dissolution, and funeral being over in a few days.

A typical career was that of Thomas Brice, assistant surveyor, appointed on arrival on February 8, 1792, on a salary of £100, with sureties of £500 each from John Brice and James Burton, and who died November 19, 1792. Charles Locock, assistant surgeon, who arrived at Anomabu fort on March 11, 1797, died 'of a putrid fever' on June 13 of the same year. Christopher Ferrall, assistant surgeon, died so suddenly that another surgeon had to certify that, shortly before his death, he had asked that everything he had owing to him should go to support his sisters. In each letter to London the governors reported the fate of the most recent arrivals: 'Mr. Tosh died suddenly on the 3d inst [October 1799] after having got over his seasoning and appearing to be quite out of danger.' John Gurr was thought to have been unlucky in 1805 – he had almost completed his year's seasoning when he was soaked by an unexpected tornado bursting open the windows of the Castle, and died two days later.

In 1789, a year selected to sample because it had no epidemics, the lists show that eleven officers died. In 1790, another ordinary year, ten died, including one who drowned in the surf coming ashore. Among a total cadre of about forty officers, these casualty levels were higher than in most wars, and were concentrated among new arrivals. Sometimes the Company recruited 'supernumerary writers,' young men for whom there was no vacancy at the time they were accepted in London, but who could, with reasonable confidence, expect that there would be one as soon as they arrived in Africa. But the registers tell their simple story. To take 1782 alone, the supernumerary writers Archibald Dingwall, John Lawrence, Thomas Yare, and William Freebairn all died before their appointments. When we add the officers who died on the voyage out, those who immediately decided to go back but died on the return voyage, several cases of officers suffering a 'sudden derangement of the mind' on their arrival, and other causes of death, the picture that the raw mortality statistics brings to mind is of some proud, stiff-upper-lipped regiment in wartime where the seasoned officers shake their heads wearily at the new arrivals with their trunks full of useless paraphernalia and their heads full of nonsensical romantic ideas of what the future is likely to hold.

Another common illness was 'guinea worms,' not only the intestinal parasites that grew inside but muscular worms that penetrated the legs, arms, and scrotum. With care and patience these worms, whose average length was eighteen inches, could be drawn out, half an inch a day, but if they broke, open sores remained and those afflicted by the disease were lamed. As geneticists have shown, sickle cell anaemia, although a severe illness in itself, has protected some of the peoples of West Africa from succumbing to the fatal illness of malaria; similarly, guinea worms saved some from being sent to the Americas. The British surgeons also noticed that many of the men they examined suffered from swollen testicles, a condition that affected the British as well. The official return of officers at Anomabu fort reports that on February 7, 1804, 'John Dyer departed this life owing to an operation on his testicles made by himself.'

Among the rank and file, the mortality rate was at least as high as among the officers. In 1769, out of forty-eight soldiers who arrived in February in the annual storeship, forty had died by the end of May. The Castle's financial accounts for the soldiers contained a single entry for 'Casualties, sick, and dead,' there being little point in separating out the costs of caring for the sick for a few days from those of burying them. And, apart from the normal risks, there were epidemics, including smallpox. In 1753 twenty people died in the Castle in less than six weeks, including the governor, and the captain of a slave ship. Among the dead listed in 1766 were 'a third part out of five and twenty soldiers,' 'a nephew of the present bishop of Waterford,' a factor, a surveyor, and 'six or seven captains of ships suddenly cut off by a very short illness.' Nor did the other Europeans on the coast fare better. On March 1, 1779, for example, Richard Miles told a colleague, 'They've buried within these last

14 days at Elmina upwards of 120 Europeans, mostly Soldiers.' The
Danish settlements seem to have suffered even more, on at least one
occasion being virtually wiped out, partly because they ventured out
of their coastal forts to attempt agricultural plantations. At Cape
Coast Castle even in normal times, well into the nineteenth century,
after which quinine helped to keep the deadly malaria at bay, the
dead soon outnumbered the living in each arriving generation.

## *Air or water?*

The governors, the surgeons, and the surveyors did what they
could. By the late eighteenth century they had reasonably adequate
precautions against smallpox, and had successfully inoculated
many of the local population as well as themselves. There are many
reports of the dedication, care, and tirelessness of the surgeons
and their African helpers in the Castle hospital. Snail soup was
thought to be a good strengthener. But the British were victims not
only of illnesses but of false theories of why they occurred. They
believed, for example, that illness was carried in the air from the
swamps and ponds of the forest, as 'noxious vapours' or 'pestilential exhalations,' and they retired indoors and closed the shutters
when the wind blew from the landward. They understood correctly
that the human body needed to sweat to keep cool, but in order
to encourage sweating they insisted on heavy woolen clothing
– flannel next to the skin – and ate heavy meals of stew made so
spicy by peppers, mustard, and other 'relishes' that newcomers
could not tolerate them. Moreover, the weekly doses of purgatives
and occasional bleeding recommended for keeping the body 'open'
probably weakened resistance to disease. Daily cold baths were
recommended, but, apart from straining the water through filtering
stones, the governors paid little attention to its quality. For much
of the Castle's history they tolerated a fetid stagnant pond within

the walls that must have pleased the mosquitoes, and when the pond was replaced by enclosed tanks, filled both with rainwater and with water taken from the Efutu river five miles away, they were only emptied, cleaned out, and whitewashed once a year. The last days of Mr. Starland at Anomabu were probably typical. When he was struck by delirious fits, the surgeon cupped 'a considerable quantity of blood from his temples,' gave him a strong purgative, then 'glysters' (emetics), and finally 'blisters' (caustic ointments that caused the skin to burn and break into sores). Starland's fits became intermittent, giving the false impression that he was recovering, but he died on the third day.

Nor, any more than most eighteenth-century gentlemen, did the officers of the African Service pay much attention to personal hygiene. As is shown by the entry in the surveyor's daybook of 1778, when he put his men to work on improving the latrines, it was appearance as much as health that made him act: 'The necessary at the end of the lower platform being a most abominable dirty place, and withal a great eyesore, new seats, doors, frames.' It can be seen in many early views: a little house, on the parade ground near the seaward gate. For most of the people in the Castle, the main washing facility was the sea. In some forts, it was later said, the Europeans had peepholes through which they spied on African women when they stripped naked in order to wash. But it was not until 1819 that a wall was built near the Castle to ensure that local people 'committed their nuisances on the beach and not under the castle walls.' Fresh water was always in short supply, and there are few records of officers swimming in the sea for pleasure – Mr. Herbert, who defied the dangers, was duly drowned. The slave-ship captains were inured to smells, and others had to season themselves. Sarah Bowdich, who arrived in a captured Spanish slave ship that had supposedly been cleaned, noted that the stench of the bilge water was so great that 'the silver spoons could not lie upon the

table without turning perfectly black' – the same as had happened
to the statue of St. Francis. One answer was perfume, which came
annually in the storeship, along with lavender and rose water. At
Elmina the Dutch maintained a 'cat yard' where they kept civets
from which they extracted scent twice a week. Not until the early
nineteenth century could a visitor from a ship expect a hot bath. But
for those who lived outside the walls, the smell of the Castle was
as much part of its meaning as the white of the walls, the raising of
the flags, the banging of the guns, the ringing of the bell, and the
music of the band. During the slaving era the presence of so many
animals in the stockyard must have given the Castle the odours and
sounds of a packed and prosperous farm. And the smells of cooking
meat can seldom have been absent.

In 1770 new health regulations were promulgated by the
Governing Committee. They were to be pinned up both in the
accountant's office and in the guardroom, and read aloud twice
a year, so as to prevent anyone from pleading ignorance: 'All the
inhabited apartments to be smoked with pitch, tar, and a little
tobacco, and sprinkled with lime juice or vinegar at least once in
three months, the barracks and slaves hole oftener especially when
the weather is foggy or damp.' The clothes of the dead were to be
burned, too. But such rules seem never to have been enforced. On the
contrary, as the many records of funeral sales show, the clothes that
arriving officers were required to bring as their fitting out were part
of the economy of the Castle, providing a new supply, scarcely used,
every few weeks. Many young officers and soldiers stepped literally
not only into dead men's shoes, but also into their breeches, their
shirts, their waistcoats, their stockings, and their night gowns. And
in many cases the same clothes would be sold to other colleagues
after their own funeral soon after.

The apartment where an officer died was to be smoked for at
least four hours for seven days, 'and on the seventh day sprinkled

with lime juice or vinegar,' but this was more a purification ritual with falsely reassuring smokes and smells than effective public hygiene. Given the high turnover, and making allowance for the destructive effects of the heat, the damp, and the ants, there must soon, we might guess, have been a superfluity of, say, tea caddies, knee buckles, and night chairs, but everything could be sold – sometimes for extraordinary high prices, such as a bookcase for £33, more than an expatriate sergeant earned in a year. When all the debts had been paid and fees deducted, the money sent back to London for the heirs of dead officers seems seldom to have been more than around £50, for soldiers less, much the same as the costs of their fitting out. But there must have been many soldiers like Anthony Medcalfe, who 'left nothing worth taking notice of but one blew shirt, which those that stript him clame as due to them.'

Henry Meredith, a former surgeon, believed that mental attitudes were as much to blame for the high death rate as the pestilential vapours. Men who allowed themselves to worry, he advised, brought on the problems they most feared. He tells the story of the commander of a British warship who, when he heard that his vessel was ordered to the Gold Coast, believed he was doomed. And sure enough, when his ship anchored off the Castle and he went ashore to dine with the governor, he immediately felt unwell and died a few days later. According to Meredith, who seems to speak from personal knowledge, it was having given way to low spirits that killed the captain – 'a melancholy instance of the force of prejudice. . . . If this unfortunate, and doubtless brave, gentleman had been surrounded by the fury of war, and in the midst of all its horrors, in all probability his mind would have supported itself to the last.'

On all formal occasions the governor-in-chief was required to wear a silk-lined scarlet uniform, with facings, high collar, embroidered waistcoat, and ruffled silk cuffs. His buttons were arranged in threes, and he carried two 'gold bullion epaulettes' on his shoulders.

*14. Governor Archibald Dalzel and another officer of the African Service, with interpreters, visiting the king of Dahomey.*

The other officers were also dressed in scarlet but with buttons in twos and only one epaulette. We have a glimpse of how the officers of the African Service appeared in the 1790s above, which shows Governor Dalzel and another officer visiting the king of Dahomey (and another glimpse on page 49 – the setting off from Cape Coast Castle of the 1820 mission to Asante). To Africans, accustomed to going almost naked, and frequently washing and oiling their bodies, the customs of the men in the Castle were puzzling. Why did being British require a man to sweat all day into heavy clothes in one of the hottest and most humid climates in the known world? According to Sarah Bowdich, the officers' red uniforms turned black after a single evening's partying. Letitia Landon, too, another of the tiny handful of British women who lived in the Castle before Victorian times, was surprised at the uniforms, equivalent to doubling the tropical heat, she remarked. And these heavy clothes added considerably to the risks of drowning when crossing the surf.

But the uniforms were part of the meaning of the Castle. In the era before hierarchy by race became the norm, to be a European was to dress as a European. The black boys who were taught to read and write by Chaplain Quaque in his little school in the Castle wore blue uniforms with red sleeves, and the badge of the Torridzonian Society. The military-style uniforms, which separated the handful of officers from the many others who lived or worked in the Castle, also helped to conceal a contradiction. All officers, including the chaplain, were required to be 'proficient in arms,' ready if called upon to man the guns, or fight men of other European nations with musket and cutlass. Their tricorn hats, gold braid, silver buttons, snuff boxes, canes, and ceremonial swords asserted that they were a military caste, not aristocrats but certainly gentlemen. The officers of the African Service were not, however, commissioned officers of the British armed forces, nor were they, like their Victorian successors, members of a civil service of the 'Crown' with its own ethos of service. They were civilian contractors, servants of a company established by the British state to provide shore facilities for the shipborne British slaving industry. The governor-in-chief had no powers to hold criminal or admiralty prize courts or make agreements with the African authorities except on commercial matters. When any business required British government approval, they had to wait for a naval vessel – the most junior lieutenant of the Royal Navy outranked the governor-in-chief. The officers of the African Service lived among rituals of salutes, marching bands, and pictures of the British king, but their days were spent trading with men whom they disdained, negotiating deals on rolls of cloth, barrels of liquor, and casks of salted pork with African merchants and rough sea captains.

One point seldom noted in histories of the British slave trade is that, for the governors and officers of the African Service, as it had been for the officers of the Royal African Company since 1680, slave trading was illegal – as indeed was trading of any kind. Their task, as laid down in statute, was to provide the shore facilities needed by the slave ships, not to trade themselves. Those who devised the legal framework were determined that the African Service should serve the slave ships, not compete with them. The 1765 British statute, which was more explicit than that of 1750, declared, 'It shall not be lawful for any of the officers or servants employed by the Committee to export negroes upon their own account . . . directly or indirectly.' And in case anyone in the Service claimed he did not know, the Governing Committee issued direct instructions to the governors and the officers to be pinned up in a prominent place in Cape Coast Castle:

> You and each of you have covenanted and are obliged not
> to trade in any sort directly or indirectly, nor be anyways
> interested or concerned in any trade or in any buying or
> selling in the way of trade, nor buy, sell, receive, dispose
> of, nor barter any Negroes, Gold Goods, Merchandise or
> effects for or on your own account, benefit, or advantage . . .

One of the functions performed by the captains of visiting British naval vessels was to obtain sworn statements from governors that they were not involved in slave trading. Captain Irby of the Royal Navy, for example, administered the oath to Governor Edward White of Anomabu fort. But every governor of the Castle and the forts during the slaving era, and every junior officer who wished to progress in his career, was directly involved in slave trading. And this fact too was known to, and silently connived at by, the Governing Committee in London and, to an extent not easy to estimate, the British government and parliament.

In 1766 Governor Mutter was dismissed as governor of Cape Coast Castle for breaching instructions 'in exporting a great number of slaves from the coast on his own account.' But having made an example of him, the Company carried on as before. The governors and officers in Africa knew that inquiries would not be made. They knew, too, that the Governing Committee was able to protect them most of the time. As mentioned, the 1750 Act allowed anyone to join the African trade who paid a nominal £2 to the Company of Merchants – the vaunted 'Free Trade.' But, according to the legislation, anyone 'intending' to trade with Africa could also become a member of the Company for the same modest fee. Of 1,400 freemen of the Company entitled to vote, there were, according to Brew, fewer than fifty real traders, the rest being stooges of the Governing Committee who, by always endorsing what was proposed, enabled it to continue to be both corrupt and self-perpetuating.

One reason why, in its own terms, the 1750 Act was effective in encouraging a thriving British slave trade was that it granted public subsidies. But it also provided the officers of the African Service with two simultaneous justifications, learned from birth in British 'African' families and quickly picked up by the others, stories that could be alternated as occasion required. One was that of the British nation seen as a united community with all ranks of society sharing the burdens and the benefits, a nation that proclaimed its uniqueness with crowns, flags, and other national symbols, and which put war near the center of its identity, with plentiful stories of the heroic hearts of oak fighting those routinely described as their 'traditional' and 'natural' enemies, the French. The slave trade, brutal though it was, trained seamen for the greater brutalities of life in the Royal Navy, 'the great bulwark and glory of the Nation,' as one slaving industry pamphlet claimed. The African Service, according to this narrative, was part of the gallant national armed forces. The officers were, in words often on their lips and in their reports, 'officers' and 'gentlemen,' an elite of the British nation, almost an estate of the realm. And the uniforms and the ethos that they allegedly symbolized was part of the romance that drew many young men to their shivering early death.

In the public debates about the slave trade that began in Britain in the 1780s, during which revelations about institutionalized embezzlement, slave trading, and routine cruelty were frequent, the officers of the African Service affected a lofty aloofness. Why should anyone pay attention to tales put about by their social inferiors, they sneered, 'starving surgeons' and 'parsons convicted of adultery.' They were 'officers,' who to doubt was to insult. Compared with such 'honest, just, and honourable men as Governor Miles and Governor Weuves,' the abolitionists were supporters of Tom Paine, a front for treason, a pro-French Jacobin plot – one of the first actions of the French Revolution had been to outlaw the French slave trade. And the officers of the African Service had little difficulty in rounding up supporters. Among the testimonials is one from the captain of the slave ship *Friendship* in favor of Richard Miles, perhaps the most unscrupulous of all the slaving era governors, assuring London that he 'always found him punctual, honest, and honourable.' (The only visual representation I have found of a governor of the Castle in the slaving era is in a book prepared by the slaving industry as part of their political campaign – the image on page 106 showing Governor Dalzel with the king of Dahomey. In this representation, which is also a self-representation, the British officers are shown as lolling about in attitudes of indifference or superiority, while the subjects of the king are shown – as they had good reason to be – abject and terrified.)

The other justificatory narrative encouraged by the 1750 Act was that of private enterprise, 'free trade,' the words emblazoned on the coat of arms of the Company of Merchants. This was a story of talented individual entrepreneurs, often in later writings praised for 'toughness' (a euphemism for criminality), gaining their just rewards. Out of their scarlet uniforms, the officers presented themselves as 'commercial men,' mere warehouse keepers and merchants. They were simply doing what they were entitled, expected, indeed encouraged to do by the British nation's political and ecclesiastical leaders, who alone had the social position, education, and therefore the responsibility to decide such weighty national matters. The 'honour' that was constantly on their lips when they were performing as officers could be thrown back at their accusers. If the employees of the Company of Merchants embezzled the stores, presented false accounts, condemned themselves to eternal damnation by swearing great oaths that they had no intention of keeping, and if they traded in slaves on a vast scale in direct and deliberate contravention of two recent, unambiguous British statute laws and of Company regulations, what was to be expected from men like themselves? As mere traders to whom there was no morality above the market, no obligations beyond the words of a crafty contract, some quibbled that since the governor-in-chief was not an officer of the 'Crown,' he could not legally administer oaths, and the accounts were not therefore legally 'sworn' at all. Sometimes the accountant had added 'errors excepted' to the sworn accounts. As for breaking the British laws on slave trading, all they could say was that the low salaries paid in goods left them no alternative. And it was indeed true that they were only doing what everyone in the Castle had done, and the government in London had known about, for more than a hundred years. How dare anyone in Britain throw the book at them? And here too, for all their blustering, they had a point. How could a handful of officers in the African Service who had joined the business – the family business – because that was the least bad career option open to men in their unprivileged rank in life accept national responsibility for, let alone change, the economic system of the entire Europeanized oceanic world?

The captains of the slaving ships, rarely gentlemen, as their plain letters show (see Chapter 8), saw the contradictions. Instead of helping their ships with warehousing facilities on shore, the officers of the African Service were stealing their business. The British government, the slave-ship owners argued in one pamphlet, should send out genuine military officers, for 'they are bred to acquire honour not riches by trade.' And it may have been in response to such pressures that the Governing Committee obtained British government approval to give the officers of the African Service nominal military rank. 'Colonel' George Torrane was sent to the Castle as governor-in-chief in 1804, in what was to be the industry's final attempt to clean up the worst abuses of the slave trade in hopes of staving off abolition. Torrane's career had followed the classic pattern of the African Service: writer, deputy accountant, accountant, officer of the guard, governor of a small fort, then of a large one. In an era of almost continuous war, he had never held any military rank in the British army or militia, nor had he had any experience of fighting. In 1807 Torrane was to be responsible for the most dishonorable action in the whole slaving era (see Chapter 7).

## Whited sepulchre

For those who survived their first couple of years, life expectancy rose, and they could live for years on the coast, although only a minority ever returned to Britain. But even if old coasters did not die as soon as new coasters, they were often ill. In August 1801, for example, the governor of the Castle reported that more than two-thirds of the 'gentlemen of the service' were 'laid up.' Survivors were often described as 'pale,' 'wan,' and 'cadaverous,' classic signs of malaria. A Victorian coaster wrote that he could instantly tell another coaster if he saw one in the streets of London: 'a tinge of yellow on the temples, a premature greyness of the hair, a faint blue shadow under the eyes.' But the dice of death also rattled for the seasoned. The note brought by canoe from the captain of the ship *Constantine* to Richard Miles, then governor of Anomabu, literally transcribed to catch the Scottish accent, cannot have been a surprise:

> Saturday morning ½ past nine. Archy Rob's Respectfull Compliments waits on Mr. Miles is sorrie to Aquaint Him with the Death of his Brother Beggs He will Lett Him be Burried in the Spur and that Mr. Miles would be so Obligen as Tell His Canoe men Digg the grave and Bring the Corps from out of the Boat

Everyone who died in the Castle was buried the same day, sometimes after an inquest. The payment made in 1775 to the Castle slaves for burying John Miles was two gallons of rum, equivalent to twelve shillings (£0.60).

Some survivors found their general health and mental abilities deteriorated whether from malaria or drink or both. Governor Mould, after a long career, became so irascible, violent, and unpredictable that he drove his officers to the verge of mutiny, but there was no obvious escape. Going home to northern cold, even if – as was seldom the case – their resignations were accepted and they could renegotiate their sureties, could, or so the officers believed, be as dangerous as staying put. And even if they survived in Africa to reach the top of their profession, and the prospect of going home with a fortune drew closer, the odds did not improve by much. Of the governors of Cape Coast Castle in the second half of the eighteenth century, about 20 percent died in post or on their way back.

For most of its early history, officers were buried in a cemetery outside the Castle walls. Sarah Bowdich, whose two-year-old daughter Florence died in 1817, described the Castle flag flying at half mast, the tiny coffin with its white pall, the Castle soldiers and servants following it in procession through the town as the band played the 'Dead March in Saul.' Most of the mourners were local people and, unlike in Britain, women were present. Since there was seldom a month without a funeral, mourning was routine, and everyone in the Castle knew that he, or occasionally she, could be next. At Mr. Coley's funeral in 1807 the volleys fired over the grave ignited a powder keg, killing a man and 'a bush woman.'

However, it became the custom, around the turn of the eighteenth century, to bury officers within the Castle walls. One reason may have been that, as governors frequently reported, the cemetery was overflowing and often disturbed by scavenging beasts and vultures. The local African custom was to keep the bones of the family beneath the family house. Whatever the reasons, the change in funeral practice can scarcely have improved the salubrious-ness of the Castle. Burials were located here and there, some in the spur, others in tombs built into the walls. In the West Tower was the grave of André, son of Governor Dalzel, who died in 1797. Sir Richard Burton, who visited the Castle in 1860, noticed the grave of a member of the Swanzy family. But most of the burials took place in the parade ground. When the new ground-level slave prisons were built in 1777, the Castle authorities evidently filled in the underground 'slave hole' with 'rubbish,' which formed a layer between the parade ground and the rock. Many British officers left their bones in the former slave dungeons, commingled with mud bricks, broken bottles, rusty nails, and clay pipes. As each generation paid its heavy toll, Cape Coast Castle became one of the most crowded corners of 'England' to be found anywhere in the tropical empire. By the time burials within the Castle ceased in

1872 the entire parade ground, and the floors of the surgery, of the kitchen, and of the hospital store, were paved with tombstones worn illegible by unnumbered boots. The Castle, the whited fortress, was also a whited sepulchre.

## Seasoning the mind

As important as the seasoning of the body, was the seasoning of the mind. As Archibald Dalzel wrote to his family in Scotland in 1763 shortly after his arrival, 'I have at last, come into the Spirit of the Slave trade, & must own (perhaps it ought to be to my Shame) that I can now traffick in that way without remorse.' But others were not so sure. The Castle's chaplains, first reported there in 1697, among whom Rev. Thomas Thompson and Rev. Philip Quaque spanned the decades of greatest boom, by their very presence in the Castle, assured the officers that the British slave trade was consistent not only with the local African religions but with their own. Among the duties of Chaplain Quaque's teacher, Rev. John Moore of St. Sepulchre's church in London, was to wake up condemned prisoners during their last night of life by ringing a handbell in the window of the condemned cell, to perform religious rites over them the following morning, and to give each one a flower to hold to their nose as they made their long journey stinking with fear through the stinking crowds to the scaffold at Tyburn. It was to these ceremonial executions in London that W. Walton Claridge, the monumental-ist colonial historian, who was keenly alert to double standards and sanctimoniousness, referred when he said that 'the sufferings of those unhappy wretches who were stretched upon the rack, broken on the wheel, or otherwise tortured, must have been fully as great, if not greater, than those of any victim of Ashanti. . . . The higher race, indeed, would seem to have used its greater knowledge only to devise more ingeniously cruel torture.' Claridge listed the many crimes, such as clipping the edges of gold guineas, that attracted the death penalty in eighteenth-century England. Women, he noted, were burned alive at Newgate and elsewhere in England until 1789. How far the trainee English priest Philip Quaque assisted his teacher in such death ceremonies is not recorded. But it was probably Moore's father, the archbishop, whose words had most influence in the Castle. Why should the officers of the African Service have qualms when the English chief priest, with whom they had such close, almost familial, connections, assured them that slave trading was a legitimate and honorable occupation for Christian gentlemen?

In a book that the Castle chaplain Rev. Thomas Thompson dedicated to the Company of Merchants, *The African Trade for Negro Slaves Shown to be Consistent with the Principles of Humanity and with the Laws of Revealed Religion* (1772), he assured his readers that the slave trade had full biblical, Christian, and ecclesiastical endorsement – and that it was also part of the famed English national liberty. Like the many other apologists for the slave trade, Thompson had no difficulty in demonstrating that slavery was consistent with the Bible. Both the Old and the New Testament texts had been written in societies in which slavery was normal – in which it was impossible to imagine a society without it. Both testaments are replete with references to slavery and to the buying and selling of slaves, although this was, to an extent, concealed from readers of the Authorised King James English-language version, which uses the word 'bondman.' The Thirty-Nine Articles of the Church of England, to which all its priests were required to swear, and which formed the main staple of the education given to Quaque and the Torridzonian boys in the Castle school, declared that the Old Testament contained nothing contrary to the New. In Leviticus the God of the people of Israel had not only allowed the enslavement of conquered peoples but commanded it: 'Both thy bond-men and thy bond-maids, which thou shalt have, shall be of the heathen that are round about you; of them shall ye buy bond-men and bond-maids.' In the New Testament the apologists could point to the passage in the Gospel of Matthew in which the kingdom of heaven was compared to a lord dealing with a debtor: 'But forasmuch as he had not to pay, his lord commanded him to be sold, and his wife, and children, and all that he had, and payment to be made.' Although it appears from the passage that this was something only to be recommended as a last resort, by describing the norm it appeared to give cover, especially for the enslavement of children. And, of course, some of the central doctrines of the Christian religion employed the language of ancient slavery – pledge, ransom, redemption, and atonement – normal practices in the societies from which the texts emanated.

But the Castle chaplains had an uphill task in getting over their Christian message. There was, Chaplain Thompson wrote, something disagreeable in the notion of human beings, 'even the lowest of such, being treated like mere beasts or cattle.' And, he noted in a reference to his own experience in the Castle, he had known men who had long been involved who 'could never well reconcile themselves to it.' For most of the eighteenth century there were few regular religious services of any kind in the Castle, officers preferring to pay the fine that went to support the Torridzonian school. Gilbert Petrie, one of several Scottish governors, told Quaque that he had no time for prayers when he could be buying slaves. Some of this reluctance may have been due to incipient racism. Chaplain Thompson's book encouraged such attitudes, describing non-Christian Africans as 'of as dark a mind as complexion.' Brew was also blunt, telling Chaplain Quaque that he would never 'sit under the nose of a black boy to hear him pointing or laying out their faults.' But when one officer, Mr. Cohouac, refused 'to attend to hear any blackman whatever,' he was reprimanded by Governor Hippisley for what he called the absurdity and vulgarity of his attitudes. 'As to the colour of the preacher's complexion,' Cohouac was told, 'none but the most illiterate could make objection to that as, under any colour piety and good sense might inhabit.'

In a society that thought of itself as part of the Enlightenment, there was little respect for religion as such. When, in Britain from the 1780s, the morality of the slave trade came increasingly to be questioned, we see the officers in the Castle devising new justifications. One, promoted by Chaplain Thompson and Governor Dalzel, was that transporting African slaves to the Americas was in the best interests of the slaves themselves. For, if they had not been transported, many would have been put to death in accordance with local religions and customs. Thompson drew an elaborate etymological connection between the word 'slave' and 'salvage' that slid into 'salvation.'

Others who disputed that they should live their lives in accordance with texts written in the remote past admitted the cruelty and injustice of the trade but took refuge in a kind of modern economic determinism. 'The impossibility of doing without slaves in the West Indies,' wrote Governor Hippisley, 'will always prevent this traffick being dropped. The necessity, the absolute necessity, then, of carrying it on, must, since there is no other, be its excuse.' And, as the industry declared in one of its pamphlets, it was possible to combine religion, economic determinism, and threats:

> . . . the richest adventurers in it are such men as would scorn
> to be engaged in any pursuit but what the laws of God and
> man would fully sanctify, and were this trade contrary to
> those laws, were it even cruel or inhuman, near a million
> of money might be withdrawn from it in short time, and a
> stagnation of cash at home, and utter ruin in our colonies
> abroad must inevitably ensue.

However, in the Castle Christianity still had a genuine power. Indeed, an outsider might say that the flock in the Castle were more Christian than their shepherds. During the whole 42-year period of Quaque's chaplainship, the boom years of the slaving era, it was impossible for any Castle governor to persuade a single officer of the African Service to participate in the most sacred of all the Christian rites, the communion service. Even at Easter the service was never held. This collective refusal appears to have had little to do with the color of Quaque's skin – he was treated in all respects as an officer and a gentleman, and he performed the rites of baptism, marriage, and burial without anyone demurring. The Christians in the Castle simply felt that, as slave traders, here was a line that they could not – indeed, since they believed in the Last Judgement, dare not – cross. As Quaque explained in a letter to the Society for Propagating the Gospel, his sponsors in London, he:

> . . . found none, of what sect or Denomination soever, that
> was willing or disposed to commence Communicants [the
> following eight words have been obliterated in ink, probably
> by a different hand when the letter was received and
> circulated] or [?] embrace the Rapture of the Lord's Supper,
> and the only plea they offer is that while they are here acting
> against Light & Conscience they dare not come to that
> holy Table, so that while I remain in these remote Soil, that
> branch of Duty will never be exercised in publick, unless it
> be to myself & Spouse.

With the governor's permission, Quaque did, however, perform the communion rite in private at the request of one dying officer whose attitude may have been typical of the unease of the Christians in the Castle at the official Christian line. As Quaque wrote:

The Friday before Xmas Day I was desired to attend Mr. William Lacey late an Accomptant of this Garrison, who was suddenly taken ill sometime before & was Dangerously bad in Cape Coast Town. I went with him and after having prayed with him, he petitioned me to sit up with him. I complied with his Request by the Governor's leave and stayed with him till the Day of his Death and on Xmas Eve finding himself grew worse, desired that I would administer the Sacrament of the Lord's Supper to him before his change came, as he would not think of leaving this Lower Regions without celebrating the same, nor die in Peace with it, since He never partook of it before. Finding him true and sincere a Penitent, his request was instantly fulfilled to his ample Satisfaction and Peace of mind.

Quaque records that Lacey begged him to destroy 'a Book of Copies of Letters' that he did not want anyone to read. What the book contained is not known, but, when the governor demanded that Quaque hand it over, he felt bound to comply.

## Why did they go?

Of all the men and women who lived, worked, or passed through the Castle during the eighteenth century, the expatriate officers of the African Service had the greatest degree of choice. Why were so many eager to go? Why was there a waiting list for officers, but always difficulty in finding soldiers (see Chapter 5)? Part of the answer was the romance of business, or rather of trade. One of the highly inaccurate pictures of the Castle presents it as a multi-storey European warehouse, a fantasy of the riches to be won by trade (see opposite page). Among the best-loved and most read books of the eighteenth century was Daniel Defoe's *The Life and Strange*

*15. The romance of trade: the Castle presented as a bulging warehouse.*

*Surprizing Adventures of Robinson Crusoe . . . written by himself,* first published in 1719, one of the books most commonly read by children as well as by adults all over the English-speaking world. According to William Hazlitt, writing in the early nineteenth century, 'Next to the Holy Scriptures, it may safely be asserted that this delightful romance has ever since it was written excited the first and most powerful influence upon the juvenile mind of England.' *Robinson Crusoe,* believed by many to be a genuine autobiography, was commended as a tale of Christian virtue, hard work, and perseverance eventually rewarded with a large fortune. Rousseau had famously made *Robinson Crusoe* the center of his proposed educational program: 'One book exists which teaches all that books can teach.'

Nowadays it is Robinson Crusoe's adventures on his desert island that are remembered and retold. In the slaving era, readers also appreciated the earlier parts of the book in which Crusoe describes how he made his money by 'adventures,' by which he meant investments, first by going on two slaving voyages and then

*16. The Castle presented as an oriental fantasy.*

by planting tobacco in Brazil. On Crusoe's first slaving voyage, he brought home gold dust worth £300 on an 'adventure' of £40, and he reinvested part of that capital in his next adventure. It is on his third slaving voyage, in which he was due to receive an equity share of the slaves brought to the Americas, that he was wrecked. Crusoe emphasizes that, in his desire to make money, he ignores good advice, runs risks, and breaks the law. Although the word 'God' is always on his lips, he never shows the least discomfort about the slave trade or about slavery. When Crusoe eventually returns to England from his years on his desert island, he finds that his colleagues have invested his money wisely and he is owed a great deal of money, which is immediately paid, a detail that confirms the story's power as a fable of the reliability of financial credit, investment, and payment on which the slave trade depended.

The pre-Enlightenment mind, however, although satisfied that slavery and slave trading had biblical authority, feared other texts, notably the prophecies in the book of Ezekiel. For if, as Ezekiel recorded, the ancient God had deliberately destroyed Tyre, a rich, proud, commercially successful, slave-trading city, was not the same fate providentially ordained for modern Britain? Was not modern Britain as corrupted by luxury as any ancient city that had incurred God's vengeance? Since the whole point of modern oceanic trade, including the slave trade, was to produce riches at home, the contradiction could only be squared by finding some way of validating the institutions of modern commerce. As Rev. Dr. Thomas Newton, the king's chaplain, declared in his *Sermons on the Prophecies* in 1769 – in which he made no criticism of the slave trade – trade had to be tended with 'liberty, sobriety, industry, frugality, modesty, honesty, punctuality, humanity, charity, the love of our country and the fear of God.' Trade, Newton declared, 'will not grow like the palm tree,' without care and cultivation. *Robinson Crusoe*, a permanent presence in Cape Coast Castle, was the imaginative embodiment of that fantasy, the ethical slave trader.

For some officers of the African Service the money did indeed turn out to be good. The death of so many members of the cadre every year meant that promotion was fast. The full career that a young man might aspire to, if he survived, is shown by the case of Richard Miles, who served in the African Service for eighteen and a half years. The staff lists show that he had had a meteoric career, promoted from writer to factor in his first year (1765), in command of his first fort three years later, of five more forts in succession including Accra and Anomabu, and governor of Cape Coast Castle for seven years (1777–84, with one break). He sent enough money to Britain to buy £25,000 worth of stocks. His name then appears with that of another former governor, Jerome Bernard Weuves, as joint owners of at least four slave ships, the *Gambia,* the *Iris,* the *Spy,* and the *Betsey.* Other former members of the African Service invested in slave ships, flaunting their names on the prows. The *Mill* was owned by the Mill family, the *Brew* by Richard Brew. The officers in the Castle probably gave welcoming cheers to Archibald Dalzel, their former governor, when he arrived in 1786 as master of a slave ship, the *Tartar* – although of 360 slaves that he bought, about a third died before the ship reached the West Indies. The *Chalmers* of London, also owned by Dalzel, was at the Castle in 1805 taking slaves for Trinidad, and was back again in 1807, but on this voyage she was lost at sea with all crew and slaves. When the *Governor Dalziel* appeared off the coast, we can imagine an older officer taking the latest newly arrived writer by the arm, passing him the telescope, and asking him to read the name on the bow of the ship anchoring in the roads. 'One day, laddie, you too will have your own fleet of slave ships.'

An economist might explain the eagerness of so many young men to join the African Service in terms of high risk/high reward among those whose grasp of actuarial probability was particularly weak. They took their (miscalculated) chances, and most of them lost. But maybe we should not dismiss out of hand what many of them claimed, that they had gone into the African trade for the sake of their families. Dalzel, for example, said that he had joined the African Service as the only way he could think of to support a large extended family of brothers and sisters who looked to him to put their porridge on the table, and although his brother Andrew became a famous and distinguished professor of Greek at Edinburgh University, Dalzel did pay off a debt of £2,000 for another brother. Since so many officers died young and unmarried, according to the laws of Britain they often bequeathed whatever money they had accumulated to mothers or sisters. George Norris, governor of Winneba fort, who died in 1794, left £300 to his mother, the residue of his estate to be divided among his four sisters, Ann, Amelia, Harriot, and Catherine. Britain had many widowed and unmarried ladies living on small incomes from annuities bought with remitted legacies from men who died in the tropics.

Anthropologists try to explain apparently self-sacrificing behaviour in terms of kinship, putting the needs of the group above that of the members. Although such theories are rarely applied to European societies, is it possible that the 'Africans,' who must have known the risks, accepted some altruistic sense of putting the family's group needs above their own? If two or more brothers joined the African Service, maybe one would survive long enough to come home with some money? But, if so, the code was not always observed. Henry Meredith, who became something of a hero when he assumed the command at Anomabu fort in the Asante invasion of 1806 (see Chapter 7), died in 1811 when he was seized by the people of Winneba. A letter a few years later addressed by his sister to the Governing Committee complains that Richard Meredith, her other brother, took all Henry's money 'to the prejudice of his three sisters.' She begs help from the Governing Committee, 'having a long family of children in embarrassed circumstances.'

How did the officers cope with the contradictions? 'At present we have but two writers on the fort,' one fort governor writes, apologizing for the illegibility of his letter; 'Mr. Johns very capable when sober but continually drunk, Mr. Elliott just the opposite.' In 1765 Mr. Crichton, the accountant, was dismissed for striking Mr. Smith, the surveyor, twice on the head with a stick three inches thick that he had hidden under his coat at a party. Another Mr. Smith was dismissed in 1771 for being in a 'state of stupefaction occasioned by drunkenness ever since his arrival.' If the financial accounts are to be believed, the governor's table for the ten or fifteen officers and their guests was as well supplied with drink and food as any in the world. As Sarah Bowdich wrote of her experience in the Castle, 'Wherever there are Englishmen there are luxuries.' As an example, the summary of expenses of the 'Public Table' at Cape Coast Castle for one month in 1750 (which cost £1,600 at an annual rate) included the following: 124 bottles of Malaga wine,

56 bottles of beer, 11 bottles of red port, 8 bottles of 'Bristol water' (mineral water imported from England?), 52 gallons of rum, 212 bottles of 'government's beer,' 104 bottles of claret, 6 bottles of cider, 12 bottles of small beer, 2 bottles of old stock, and 7 bottles of arrack. The 'provisions expended' consisted of an unspecified amount of chocolate, 3 cheeses, 401 large and 374 small candles, 70 lb. raisins, 89 lb. currants, 3 firkins of butter, 200 fowls, 4 sheep, 15 goats, 4 hogs, 5 ducks, 1 barrel of beef 'and more,' 1 barrel of pork 'and more,' 360 clay pipes, 4 hams, 1 keg of sugar, 120 lb. double refined sugar, 6 lb. common sugar, 646 lb. flour, 2 gallons of palm oil, 1 cask of soap, 2 lb. tea.

But the main drink was spirits: corn-based brandy and sugar-based rum. According to J. J. Crooks, a Victorian colonial official who took a scholarly and sympathetic interest in the earlier history of the Gold Coast settlements, the main drink of officers and men was punch, made from brandy, water, lime juice, and sugar. The archives record that the 1778 storeship brought a normal supply of 20,000 gallons of brandy. Most of this was bartered for slaves, but in the Castle it was drunk round the clock – 'a bowl for every occasion.' In the British West Indian colonies, where the rum was made from the sugar, it was wrongly believed to be a prophylactic against yellow fever, and the officers and men in the Castle probably believed the same. However, it has since been discovered that much of the rum drunk was distilled in ways that produced fusel-oil alcohol, which, in quantity, is a deadly poison. The rum also absorbed lead from the pewter vessels used in the distilling. Many of the deaths that were ascribed to yellow fever, and the jaundiced complexions of old coasters, may have been caused by necrosis of the liver.

For many officers of the African Service, their whole identity from the moment they were born and educated within a British 'African' family until their final malarial shivers in Cape Coast Castle was held together by intertwined strands of institutional silences, hypocrisies, and self-deceptions, manacles that constricted their minds, as they fitted the iron clamps on the arms, legs, and necks of their African captives. But whether from the climate, the loneliness, the hopelessness, the moral contradictions, or sheer despair at where they had found themselves, a steady procession of officers found life in the Castle insupportable. In 1794 Mr. Dinham was found dead after an overdose of opium; verdict: 'died by a visitation of God.' In 1803 Mr. Nixon, who had shown no previous signs of discontent, one evening went alone into the Castle garden and carefully blew his brains out with a pistol. Beside the body of Mr. Salkeld, who shot himself in 1800, was found a suicide note that, naming his father as his heir, included the scrawled words: 'It's my fire next.' What he meant is unexplained, but it may be a premonition of Hell.

# 5

# The soldiers and the workers

## *Soldiers*

The number of soldiers employed by the Company of Merchants in the Castle and the forts was seldom much greater than the number of officers. The soldiers in the Castle lived two to a room; in the forts, probably the same. In the smaller forts the British-born population, officers and other ranks together, was seldom more than half a dozen. For example, in 1754 at Whydah, the fort furthest east from Cape Coast Castle, there were only three expatriate British: the governor, the factor, and the sergeant. To the officers in the forts Cape Coast Castle was a metropolis to which a visit was a rare treat. One of the benefits of promotion was that it entailed frequent canoe journeys to the Castle to attend the governor's Council. As for the soldiers, among the punishments they faced, for example for drunkenness, was transfer to a distant fort.

One muster roll of the total military strength of the African Service, prepared shortly after a new batch of recruits had arrived, lists one sergeant, two corporals, one drum major, ten drummers and fifers, and twenty-six soldiers. A third of the military strength was employed in producing music, another of the means, along with gun salutes, by which the Castle made its presence heard to those who lived nearby. The same limited repertoire of tunes was played, according to more than one visitor to the Castle, from morning to night. The band welcomed visitors arriving ashore from the ships, played at parties in the Castle hall, and paraded at funerals.

The Company frequently pressed the government in London to authorize a larger establishment of soldiers, but the actual numbers do not seem to have varied much, except in wartime when local men were temporarily recruited. Considering the vast scale of the British slave trade in the eighteenth century, the total uniformed expatriate British presence on the coast was tiny, seldom more than a hundred men living in less than a dozen lightly fortified buildings along a 400-mile coast. Although every officer and soldier was expected to be able to fire a musket or wield a cutlass in an emergency, they were scarcely a military force at all, more an armed security guard. In terms of numbers, the expatriate presence had been much the same in the 1680s and 1690s, a hundred years earlier, in the days of the Royal African Company.

Although the muster rolls distinguished between 'Europeans' and the other people who lived or worked in the Service, and sometimes between 'blacks' and 'whites,' it was less of a racial division than a grading convention relating to pay rates and embezzlement opportunities. One of the ways governors made money was to recruit soldiers locally at low pay while claiming expatriate rates. A growing number of the junior officer ranks, such as writers, were sons of expatriate British and local women, including several, such as Petrie and Timewell, whose names suggest they were sons of governors. Only a few rose above the junior grades.

The Company soldiers recruited in Britain enlisted for five years, receiving a gratuity of two months' pay (about £2), bounty money, when they signed on. If, as most did, they signed on for another five years, they were paid another bounty. Each soldier received annually a regimental coat, waistcoat, and breeches, a hat, a cap, two pairs of shoes, two pairs of stockings, and two shirts.

Like the officers, they received no money but only the equivalent in tradeable goods charged at exorbitant Company prices. Since soldiers died in at least as high a proportion as the officers, the sale of their effects provided a welcome supply of second-hand luxuries such as hair combs, empty bottles, and chipped teacups. Since the expatriate soldiers were not permitted to return to Britain in the Company storeship if they had any outstanding debts, and it was easy to lose money by trading (which was formally forbidden), many were trapped for life. The accounts for 1770, for example, record that Shipton, a soldier on a nominal pay of £27, owed the Company over £17. Life was monotonous and discipline harsh, with much drunkenness, brutality, and flogging, as in the British army, but not much risk of having to do any fighting.

Although the Governing Committee in London had waiting lists for men wishing to be officers in the African Service, they were always short of recruits for the rank and file of their little private contract army. The advertised pay rates were much higher than those of a soldier in the British army, who in 1800 received a shilling a day or about £18.30 a year, and there was a penny a day more for the drummers and fifers. But, unless the soldiers could make money by trading – formally forbidden, although permitted in practice – their standard of living was lower than the advertised rates implied. For men with some knowledge of cannon, the Committee paid an agent, known as a crimp, nine guineas (£9.50) a head to hang about Woolwich Arsenal, the headquarters of the Royal Artillery in London, offering part of his fee as a signing-on bonus. For crimping rank and file without military skills, the Committee paid half a guinea (£0.60) for every recruit delivered – only a third of the amount paid for recruits to the East India Company, who were more choosy. Indeed most of the men who became soldiers in Africa can scarcely be regarded as having volunteered at all. Some were disgraced former officers. On her voyage out, Sarah Bowdich met a former officer of a British infantry regiment who was reprieved from the death penalty on condition that he enlisted as a private soldier in the Sierra Leone Regiment; since he continued to steal useless things at every opportunity on the voyage, she concluded that he was not so much a thief as a pathological kleptomaniac in need of help. Some soldiers were convicted criminals and deserters who were offered the African Service as an alternative to death. John Morris, who, with his brother, was arrested in London in 1780, at the age of seventeen, for being a member of the mob in the government-inspired Gordon riots, was pardoned on condition that he joined the African Service. In 1795, after fifteen years in Africa, his petition to be allowed to go home was rejected, but it did go all the way to the secretary of state in London.

Creating an army for Africa from British-born misfits and criminals, even in small numbers, was, however, not cheap. In 1777, during the American revolutionary war, knowing that the African Company's garrison was mainly a bluff, the British government estimated the cost of transporting 200 convicts to the Gambia and maintaining them for one year. The total came to over £7,000, about £350 for each man, or £700, taking account of the expected initial death rate. Instead, in 1782 the government sent the British army to the Castle for the first time. Two companies recruited from the prisons and hulks of London were sent out under the command of regular officers. The intention was to mount land and sea attacks on the Dutch forts, but although some forts were taken, the assault on Elmina failed when the warships could not get close enough to bombard it and the soldiers broke ranks and ran away. As Richard Miles, then the governor of the Castle, wrote to the Governing Committee in November 1782, the British army was not a success:

We surmize Government will be disposed again to send out some of the convicts – in such case for God's sake send us good Locks, for we have already experienced that those we now have here are not proof against the Villainy of these Wretches . . . indeed unless a power is sent out to try the most notorious of them and to hang them, they must be kept always in Irons, for how in the name of God can it be thought the Lives of 8 or 10 Officers are safe among such a crew of felons.

Of the two hundred men who landed, only sixty were fit for duty six months later. One officer killed another in a duel. Among the soldiers, some sold their weapons, many disappeared – perhaps being accepted on to slave ships, which were always short of men – many died of disease, and a party who had been put on board a captured ship are thought to have killed their officers and become sea pirates. One officer who, in a futile attempt to restore discipline, ordered a sergeant to receive 800 lashes, from which he died, was tried for murder and hanged. The commander, Captain Mackenzie, who ordered an insubordinate soldier to be put to death – by strapping him over a cannon mouth which was then fired – was also found guilty of murder and sentenced to death, but received a royal pardon – perhaps allowed to enlist as a private soldier in some other tropical colonial force. The remnants of the force were disbanded soon after. However, the garrison ledgers of Cape Coast Castle show that British jails continued to be a main source of men for the expatriate contract army, and that soldiers recruited that way kept their status. The ledger for 1790, for example, lists 'John Prime, Convict,' his nominal salary £27.

## Workers

By the time the slave trade approached its height in the late eighteenth century, the largest group of people in the Castle and the forts were the so-called 'public' or 'Castle' slaves – men, women, and children all born in Africa, who were 'owned' by the Company and who did most of the manual work. The Castle slaves seem mainly to have lived outside the Castle and came in through the land gate every morning to report for work and left before it closed in the afternoon. But many, particularly personal servants, lived in the Castle itself. According to a fascinating aside about gender differences noted by Sarah Bowdich, the male servants slept on the bare floor but the women were allowed upstairs and slept upon matting.

Like the soldiers, the Castle slaves received no pay in cash, but frequent rations of tradeable tobacco, brandy, rum, cloths, plus many occasional gratuities. The white bricklayers could only endure five hours in the heat; the black slave bricklayers worked seven. They were all paid for working overtime outside the regular working hours sounded by the Castle bell. 'Please let the Company's slaves dig a grave to bury one of my mates,' writes the captain of a slave ship to the governor of Anomabu in 1776, 'and I'll pay them for the trouble.' The accounts record numerous other extra payments to Castle slaves, although not on the scale of those paid to the canoemen. Some extras were paid in gunpowder, always readily tradeable, including the annual Christmas bonus.

Some of the Castle slaves were born to women who were themselves Castle slaves, and they took their places in a hereditary matrilinear slave community. Others were 'pawns' who had been surrendered as security for credit and had not yet been redeemed (see Chapter 8). There are records of Castle slaves being bought in the Gambia, over 1,000 miles away, another practice already common a hundred years earlier. Although in modern terms the Gambians were black and African, Cape Coast Castle was as far from home as Jamaica, and the Gambians had little in common with the local peoples among whom they were settled.

As far as the British in the Castle were concerned, employing Company slaves was cheaper than free laborers, but men always had to be brought in when new building works were in progress. In 1770, for example, Governor Mill was contemplating hiring thirty or forty laborers to carry stones. In the Castle office a list was kept of the names of the Castle slaves – men, women, and children – and of their various specialities. As with the officers and soldiers, every one is a named individual whose age and state of health is also recorded. Both men and women did heavy work, but only men had formally recognized technical skills. The women washed the clothes and served as orderlies in the hospital and the kitchens, but the starching and ironing of the shirts were occupations reserved for men. Many of the girls were employed in the Castle garden. Like the 'wenches' (described in Chapter 6), the children could go almost anywhere in the Castle, and the younger slave women looked after them. And since an increasing number could speak and read English, governors had to remind their officers to keep their papers locked up and to avoid chatting about palavers. Governor Miles demanded that the Council 'meet in a retired room that we may not be overheard by boys or interrupted by wenches.'

In 1749, according to an inventory that may have been exaggerated for purposes of embezzlement, the Company's workforce at the Castle consisted of the following, all of whose names were listed, of whom the majority were Castle slaves:

| | |
|---|---|
| carpenters | 10 |
| blacksmiths | 7 |
| armorers | 3 |
| brickmakers | 3 |
| bricklayers | 9 |
| gunner | 1 |
| goldsmiths | 3 |

| | |
|---|---|
| slave cooks | 2 |
| chief cooks | 3 |
| doctor's servant | 2 |
| coopers | 3 |
| chapel servants | 7 (although there was no chapel) |
| gold takers | 2 |
| men | 137 |
| canoemen | 29 |
| women | 79 |
| children | 76 |
| | |
| Total | 376 |

The Castle canoemen were not slaves, and may have been included in this list because they had a regular contract. Their work was dangerous not only because of the daily perils of crossing the surf, but because, in delivering stores or slaves to ships about to sail, they were themselves occasionally seized and carried off the coast, a serious crime that always involved the Castle taking severe measures against the captains and the ship owners (see Chapter 8). But the canoemen were involved in many disputes about other matters, including pay rates, losses from the goods being carried, and the stealing of fish from local nets by the crews of slave ships. Since the whole transatlantic slave trade depended upon the canoemen, they had enormous negotiating power. If a captain displeased them, they would refuse to supply his ship even with water, and any captain who thought that his crimes would be forgotten once he left the coast could find himself in severe trouble if he ever returned. Sometimes, too, the canoemen went on general strike. In December 1770, for example, they refused to deliver provisions or water to any of the ships in the roads for six or seven weeks, while other local people blockaded the land gate of the Castle, causing hardship to all those concerned, especially the slaves already embarked, until the dispute was palavered and settled by the making of a payment.

The Castle slaves, who had lifetime security, were supported if they became ill, and retired at the age of 55 with small pensions. A list of 1796 notes few male slaves over the age of 40, but of the 'unserviceable' slaves, two were aged 79. The four 'superannuated and unserviceable' women were aged 66, 67, 73, and 76. The life expectancy rates for locally-born workers were far better than for expatriates. When a Company slave died, a formal death certificate was signed by the surgeon and the surveyor. On April 11, 1753, 'at Cape Coast Castle died Dough, a Negro Man slave, Superannuated, aged 70 years.' On June 11, 1753, 'died Kainoch, negro slave Boy aged one year.' The Castle slaves were as integrated into the life of the masters as servants in a British country house.

The list of Company slaves at Winneba fort in 1799, which is unusually full, gives a glimpse of a group of named people whose lives are seldom recorded in even the sparsest terms:

**Men**
Yeow, 42, cooper, healthy
Akassie, 25, carpenter, healthy
Aduamah, 18, carpenter, healthy
Tom, 62, bricklayer, nearly blind
Branja, 64, laborer, very infirm
Sheetah, 66, laborer, very infirm
Quacoe Owan, smith, healthy

**Women**
Eccoah, 58, washerwoman, infirm
Abrawah, 27, laboress, healthy
Amonenewa, 25, laboress, healthy, one child
Eccoah Berichey, 25, laboress, healthy, two children

Quacoah, 22, laboress, healthy, one child
Effuah, 10, pra pra girl
Aquishebah, 8, garden girl, healthy

A 'pra pra girl' was mentioned by Sarah Bowdich – 'a woman who swept the floor of the Great Hall every day before dinner was laid, with a little hand-broom called a prah-prah.'

The list of staff changes below reveals that the two girls mentioned in the preceding list are daughters of one of the laboresses:

**January 1, 1799**
Cockaboe, carpenter, sent to C coast [Cape Coast Castle] to commence there this day
Awishie succeeds Coffee, as Big river Bomboy
Quashie succeeds Qua as free cook
Akassie, carpenter, commences here this day from C Coast
Effuah and Aquishebah, daughters of Amonewah, received notes this day [taken on to the payroll]

January 31, Eccoah Bouchie delivered of a male child this day.

A list of 1805 for the same fort shows quite a rapid turnover, but some members of the workforce are still there. Of the men, Akassie and Quacoe Owan remain healthy and at work; Tom, the retired bricklayer, has gone blind. The list now includes Aduam, 65, bricklayer, infirm; Sam, 23, carpenter, worms; Jen, 32, cooper, healthy; and Aduamah, 21, carpenter's apprentice, mad. Of the women, Quacoah, the laboress, remains healthy and at work; Eccoah, the washerwoman, has been superannuated. Aquishebah, the young garden girl, is now a pra pra girl. The newcomers are Acoah, 37, laboress, worms; Quacoah, 27, laboress, healthy; Effwah,

24, laboress, healthy; Mary, 10, mulatto, healthy; and Abrawah, 19, pra pra girl, healthy.

In the mid-nineteenth century, when the British Navy was deployed off West Africa to intercept the continuing slave trade, releasing and resettling the freed slaves in Sierra Leone, a German Christian missionary, S. W. Koelle, discovered a great deal about the origins of the slaves whom the British admiralty courts released by investigating their languages – confirming that many came from far inland. If the names of the Castle slaves recorded in the archives were collected, it might be possible for an expert in African languages to discover something of the origins of the Castle slaves, including those brought from the Gambia. Many follow the local Fante custom of being named after the day of the week on which they were born; for example boys called Kofi, often at the time spelled Coffee, were born on a Friday, and girls born on that day were called Effuah. But there appear to be names, apart from those that have been anglicized, that were not used among the coastal peoples.

A modern visitor looking only at the architecture might assume that the white British lived within the Castle walls, the black Africans outside. In fact only around 10 percent of those who worked in the Castle were expatriate, and it was the social as well as commercial integration of the Castle into local life that enabled it to function. As the Governing Committee in London wrote indignantly in 1769 to a British investor who had suggested cutting the workforce and selling some surplus slaves, he had been confused by the word 'slave,' and misunderstood the real situation:

> . . . the castle Slaves are so closely connected with the
> People of the country by Marriage and other social Ties,
> that an attempt to remove any of the former would
> infallibly occasion very great Disturbance and Insurrections
> among the Natives; and render the Safety of the Forts and

Settlements highly precarious, as their Defence depends
more on the Attachment of the Slaves, than on their feeble
Force in Civil and Military Servants.

British expatriates might come and go; for hundreds of families,
Cape Coast, castle and town, was not only their place of employment
but their home.

From accounts of the total payments made over representative
periods that I have extracted from the archives, we can see the extent
to which the Castle made a huge contribution to the local economy,
quite apart from the profits made in trading. We also see a growth in
expenditure, and therefore in its contribution to the economy, even
though the numbers employed were little different:

**Expenditure other than on buildings, 1734,
Royal African Company**

|  | £000 *(rounded)* | *percent* |
|---|---|---|
| 'Salaries and diet' of 228 officers, soldiers, and artificers, plus pay to Castle slaves and 'free Blacks' | 10 | 66 |
| Canoes and boats | 1 | 7 |
| Rents to 'the neighbouring kings and Great men, in whose countries the said forts are situate' | 4 | 27 |
| Total | 16 | 100 |

**Expenditure other than on buildings, 1770–76,**
**Company of Merchants**

|  | £000 (rounded) | percent |
|---|---|---|
| 'White men's salaries' | 59 | 56 |
| 'Black men's pay' | 7 | 7 |
| Castle slaves | 20 | 19 |
| Free canoemen and laborers | 7 | 7 |
| Other local payments | 11 | 11 |
| Total | 104 | 100 |

The status of Castle slave continued long after the abolition of the slave trade. And, even when slavery was formally abolished by law throughout British territories, it was argued that British law did not apply to the Castle and forts, as they were buildings rented from African rulers.

It was often said both at that time and later that the Castle slaves were content with their status, and preferred working as slaves to the British to any alternative available to them. 'Domestic' slavery in the Castle, it was said, was little different from domestic service in the large extended households of local African society, a role that gave status, customary rights, security, the prospect of promotion, of marriage out of slave status, and of being declared free at the master's death. How far there was mobility of this kind among the Castle slaves I have not been able to judge, although the reference to 'free cook' suggests that it happened. However, another common comment, that the life of, say, a Castle slave carpenter was as satisfactory as that of an expatriate British soldier, even though the soldier was formally free, has at least some validity.

A consensus of scholars, following pioneering work by Suzanne Miers and Igor Kopytoff in 1977 and by Paul Lovejoy in 1986, has identified the characteristics that distinguish the slavery practiced in the transatlantic slave trade from the innumerable other forms of exploitation found throughout history. First, slaves were 'property,' commodities that could be owned, bought, and sold. Second, slaves were, by origin, outsiders who lacked kinship ties and who had been denied their heritage through judicial or other sanctions. Third, slaves were entirely at the disposal of their master. In her recent *History of Indigenous Slavery in Ghana*, which is based on years of study among a wide variety of written records, and on the collecting of oral traditions in all parts of Ghana, Akosua Adoma Perbi has identified five broad types of servitude as existing independently of, and prior to, the arrival of Europeans on the Gold Coast. But in none of these indigenous traditions was a slave an owned chattel entirely without rights, as the Europeans may have mistakenly assumed or asserted. To some extent the Castle slaves in Cape Coast Castle were inheritors of traditions of what the later British colonial administrators called 'domestic slavery,' and they were not without bargaining power or potential remedies. However, as regards the slaves in the dungeons, as Perbi comments, in discussing the European ideology of slaves as property, 'The labor power of slaves could be used however desired; even their sexuality, and by extension, their reproductive capacities were not theirs by right; for children who were born to slaves inherited slave status unless specific provisions were made to ameliorate their status.' This was the slavery that was taken to the Americas and practiced more or less legally for centuries in the anglophone plantation societies in the West Indies and southern parts of North America. One of the most striking manifestations of the difference between Castle slaves and those sold to slave ships, as far as the British were concerned, is that the Castle slaves were all named individuals, whereas the slaves to be sold were nameless, treated not only as having no rights, except possibly a right to life and food, but as entirely interchangeable.

Occasionally Castle slaves ran away, either individually or in groups, but they were generally caught or brought back just as runaway indigenous slaves were returned to their local owners. In 1778 one of the Castle gardeners, who had been caught stealing corn, ran away and was taken in by the people of Saltpond far along the coast. Governor Miles, who prided himself on his knowledge of local customs, was so perplexed that he had to seek advice from the Fante on what should be done in such unusual circumstances. Their answer: pay the people of Saltpond an equivalent slave to get him back. When it was reported that the runaway had been seen on board a slave ship, an officer went on board to buy him back, with the following reported result:

> Mr. Collins saw the Co[mpany]'s Slave on B[oar]d the
> Portugueze at Elmina, and offered a Prime man [slave]
> for him, w[hi]ch the Capt[ai]n. agreed to accept, but the
> fellow himself swore that if he was taken out of the Ship he
> w[oul]d Embrace the 1st opportunity of killing himself for
> he was determined to go off.

However, the governor, knowing the man's age and health, and the normal choosiness of the Portuguese buyers, immediately suspected what he called a 'snack.' The whole episode, it emerged, was an agreement between the man, the people of Saltpond, and the Portuguese to share the proceeds (about £25 split three ways). The gardener was returned to the Castle and a counterclaim made against the people of Saltpond. It may be significant that this episode, one of the rare cases in which we have the actual reported words of a Castle slave, shows him trying to work the system rather than resist it, one of the few options open to the powerless.

Only very rarely did the Castle governors sell any Company slaves, and in accordance with local custom they only did so in cases of crime or debt. In 1780 Governor Roberts received at

Cape Coast Castle 'a Company's slave cook named Affancon, belonging to Apollonia fort, delivered in double chains, as he is a very troublesome fellow who has repeatedly deserted the said fort.' In 1792 an armorer caught stealing was sold off the coast 'in order that this Instance of exemplary Severity might deter others in being concerned in like Practices.' In 1805 a woman was sold off the coast because she had an unpayable debt of £4 in order, as it was noted, 'to deter Company's slaves from contracting debts.' Although in these, as in other matters, the governors appear to have followed local practice, they were frequently reprimanded by the Governing Committee in London for doing so.

I have been unable to discover how far, if at all, the Castle slaves had dealings with the quite different group of slaves, those held in the dungeons waiting to be taken to the slave ships. Architecturally the slave dungeons were out of sight and hearing for the governor and officers, except when they came downstairs. But they were not so easily ignorable by those living and working on the ground level. Was it, as seems likely, the Castle slaves who gave the prisoners their food and water, escorted them to and from the beach twice daily, and cleaned out the dungeons? Were the slaves who came blinking out of the dungeons and then made their way down the dark tunnel to the sea door, the beaches, and the canoes escorted by the soldiers or by Castle slaves? I have found no record of the Castle slaves cooperating with the imprisoned slaves, let alone of helping them to revolt (see Chapter 8), but it is possible, indeed likely, that in some cases where the imprisoned slaves came from the coastal areas, the Castle slaves may have been able to pass messages back to families and arrange for some of them to be palavered for and redeemed.

## Daily routines

Most of the people in Cape Coast Castle were employed simply in keeping it standing. A 1777 daybook of the surveyor's department records how his Castle slaves were employed day by day. In July, for example, the department workforce consisted of '11 bricklayers, 7 carpenters, 4 sawyers, 5 smiths, 3 armorers, 4 coopers, 9 artificer boys, 17 laborers, 32 laboresses, and 6 stoneblowers.' The bricklayers are building a new bastion and repairing a parapet that fell down when the saluting gun was fired. The 'laborers and laboresses' are filling the new bastion with rubbish. The carpenters are laying a new roof on the gallery, the old one having fallen in during the rains. The sawyers are cutting 3-inch planks 'for sundry uses.' The smiths are making ironwork for the Anomabu gun carriages. The coopers are making tubs for carrying mortar and building rubbish (rubble). The armorers are cleaning the muskets and making sets of keys for the gentlemen's necessary. On another day part of the workforce are taking up pavements to destroy red ants 'that have appeared in incredible numbers about the Castle.' The garden girls are reseeding the bowling green. A party of twenty goes into the forest to cut two pieces of timber for the ship *Hen*, 'she having carried away her gallows in a gale of wind coming out.' When there is nothing more urgent to do, the coopers make nails, the bricklayers whitewash the walls, and the others are employed on 'sundry tasks about the Castle.'

In 1786, shells were discovered on the seashore six miles from the Castle in the direction of Elmina, a valuable resource from which lime could be made. However, since it took so long for the laboresses to make the journey to and fro with their basins, the surveyor instituted a shift system. Twelve laboresses with their children would stay near the beach in temporary accommodation, to be relieved after a week by another detachment. However, when the Castle men heard about the plan, they arranged a mass down-tools and exit of all the Castle slaves. At a meeting the Castle slaves contributed to buying arms and gunpowder, and on November 19 a total of forty left the Castle, leaving only 'the bomboy, the coopers, one carpenter, one smith [the foreman and some skilled workers] and a number of old and infirm.' Whether the Castle slaves regarded themselves as taking part in a revolt, a desertion, or a strike cannot be easily judged, but they threatened violence. Five attempts were made to kill the surveyor, and he had to stay within the Castle while other officers were sent to try to negotiate a return to work. The local coastal African leaders declined to help either side, and there was nowhere for the little community to go. After a month of standoff, they agreed to go back, having received promises of shorter hours, more pay, and an amnesty. The governor spluttered to London about his difficulties in controling the Castle slaves, but as far as I can ascertain, no reprisals were taken and the Castle returned to normal working. Cape Coast Castle was Prospero and Caliban. It was also Robinson Crusoe and Man Friday on their island, the European manager and the local laborer called after a day of the week, together running a busy and productive economy, largely self-sufficient except for the materials and arms that Crusoe had rafted ashore from a European ship.

Most of the day-to-day work of Cape Coast Castle was only indirectly related to the transatlantic slave trade. The garden girls, who were all very young, can scarcely have appreciated that the fallen fruit they gathered provided food for slaves on the middle passage. Nor can we attribute much personal responsibility to the pra pra women who swept the floors, the men who painted the walls, or even to the soldiers who oiled, but seldom fired, the Castle guns. But even many of the senior British expatriate officers only occasionally encountered the slave trade in their daily lives. The surveyor was busy just keeping the Castle standing, the officer of the guard was practicing his band and parading his men at funerals, the register was selling the clothes of dead colleagues, the surgeon was conscientiously tending the sick, the chaplain was teaching the Castle children, and so on. The accountant, one of the highest officers in the African Service, kept a daybook of all the transactions of the Castle: stores received, stores traded, stores issued, payments received, payments made. Only occasionally, as when a man, woman, or child was sold into the Castle or out to a ship, is there any indication of what all this activity was designed to achieve.

## *The House that Jack Built*

For the Castle was also the House that Jack Built. To get the sugar to put in his tea, Jack set up tropical plantations. To work the fields, he needed men able to withstand the climate and the illnesses. To obtain the workers, he built castles with walls in Africa. To keep the walls from falling down, he needed lime. To make the lime, he needed shells. To gather the shells, he needed basins. To make the basins to carry the shells to make the lime to build the walls to lock up the men to work in the fields to grow the sugar to put in the tea, Jack built metal furnaces. To cut the wood to fire the furnaces, he needed saws. To sharpen the saws, he needed coopers, and to prevent the saws being pilfered, he needed locks and hinges for which he needed carpenters and blacksmiths. To find the coopers, the carpenters, the blacksmiths, and the clerks to keep the records of the work, he set up training programs, apprenticeships, career structures, elementary schools, and arrangements for negotiating pay, pensions, and working conditions. He even set up rudimentary crèches for the children of the women among the Castle workforce. Cape Coast Castle, on the edge of the South Atlantic Ocean, was a microcosm of the British industrial economy.

# 6

# The women

## 'Wenches'

One of the attractions of the African Service was the prospect of plentiful sex. When Archibald Dalzel was a young and unemployed surgeon in Scotland, he told his brother that he had decided to apply after meeting John Grossle, a future governor of Cape Coast Castle. The risks from the tropical climate, Grossle assured him, were much exaggerated. After five years on the coast, he had always been in perfect health, except when, as Dalzel explained in the style that the officers of the African Service felt obliged to adopt when discussing women, 'he is a little given to gratifying a particular sensual desire. . . .'

It was part of the welcome for a young officer arriving in the Castle to be supplied with a local sexual partner, one of the ways in which the British embraced local laws and customs without attempting to change them. Such unions with 'wenches' were not regarded as marriages under British laws and conventions, and for officers who returned to Britain, the option of a British marriage remained open. In 1764, for example, John Hippisley, who had been dismissed and had gone back to England to await his expected reinstatement, was married in an English church to an English woman. Ten years earlier Hippisley had had a son by his African wench, both of whom had remained in Africa during his visit to England. When, in 1766,

Hippisley returned to the Castle as governor, his African son was baptized by Chaplain Quaque into membership of the Anglican Church, but that did not change his status as regards the disposal of property. It was a son born in England, whom Hippisley probably never saw, who inherited his father's fortune when Hippisley died in the Castle a few months later.

The unions with wenches were not informal casual sexual encounters, although these were available too, but marriages conducted in accordance with local African conventions that included polygamy. The provision of a wench was primarily a matter for the wench's mother, with whom the officer made the contract, and the mother played a prominent part in the ceremony of union. Essentially, the officer made a gift, paid like all transactions in tradeable goods, normally equivalent to £15 or £20. In addition he made over a 'note' that the wench's mother could encash for about 15 shillings (£0.75) in tradeable goods every month, a regular maintenance payment of about £9 a year. Whereas in Britain it was normally the family of the woman who had to pay a dowry to secure a suitable marriage for their daughter, on the Gold Coast the man paid a bride price. For a newly arriving writer or factor, the amount required was equivalent to about a third of his salary and taking a wench put him immediately in debt to the Company store at Cape Coast Castle, yet another of the bonds within which his choices were constrained.

The wench notes took the form of a standing order from the officer to the governor to make a monthly payment on presentation of the letter. For example:

Mr. Miles will much oblige A Bold by Paying Jamah, a Mullattoe Girl, at the rate of Five Ackies Gold p[e]r Month [about £1.25], from 1st May 1776 on my Account until I may write him to discontinue it.

Jamah was paid every month for at least three and a half years. Since her note has not survived in its entirety, it is impossible to say how long the arrangement lasted, but in the circumstances of the time the amounts are considerable and the union was evidently a stable one.

How far the arriving officers chose their wenches and on what grounds, I have been unable to discover except that, as in the marriages contracted in Britain under British laws and customs, the cementing of commercial and political connections with leading local families was a consideration in at least some cases. Wenches seem to have normally been free, not slaves, and are recorded, for example, as owning their own house slaves, and having slaves bequeathed to them in officers' wills. In the eighteenth century the local girls went entirely naked until they reached their menarche – which, according to European writers, they reached at around the age of ten – after which they covered the lower part of their body and were regarded as of marriageable age. By the standards of Europe, some wenches were evidently very young. And, as with tropical illnesses, the officers of the African Service suffered from errors about the effects of the hot climate on their bodies, believing that the heat stimulated sexual desire but also that those who succumbed to desire lost strength. As Dalzel wrote proudly to his family in cold Scotland, 'I have been able as yet, notwithstanding the heat of the Climate to abstain from Amours with the black fair sex (if I may so speak) tho' most of the Gentlemen here, have got wives.' In the event Dalzel's resolution soon yielded to the heat and he fathered at least three children, of whom two sons were put into the African Service.

If an officer could afford to make the payments, he might have more than one wench. Indeed, in accordance with local custom, the taking on of more wives was an indication of rising status and wealth. Since by the later eighteenth century the Gold Coast had hosted a rapidly changing population of around forty young expatriate British officers for more than a hundred years, many of the wenches were British Africans born in or near the Castle. Sarah Bowdich's chance remark that the gradations of skin color were 'mulatoo, mustee, mustafee, after which people were regarded as white,' tends to confirm that many of the local unions were with women who were daughters of previous wench unions. (As regards divorce, I have not been able to discover the details of local law and custom as they were understood and applied by the British in the Castle during the slaving era.)

Under local law and custom, a wife could separate from a husband by repaying the bride price. According to some travelers, an officer was able to bring the wench relationship to an end by ceasing to pay the monthly 'note' (but I have not come across any reclaiming of the bride price). Since many officers died within a year or two of their arrival, the archives contain many examples of the posthumous settling of accounts. It was the duty of the Castle register (sometimes doubling as the accountant) to wind up the estate of a dead officer, paying off his liabilities, selling his assets, and sending the balance to London to be paid, in due course and after deductions, to his heirs. The register's accounts suggest that, when an officer died, wenches may normally have received a lump sum equivalent to about a year's maintenance payments.

The following extract from the accounts of the winding up of the estate of William Caldwell, who died in the Castle in 1787, is typical:

| | |
|---|---|
| paid his mulatto wench her note in full | £5/17/9 |
| paid his black wench her note in full | £3/12/6 |
| paid his boy Quey in full | £3/10/0 |
| gave his mulatto wench and child as a present [goods worth] | £5/12/6 |
| gave his black wench and child [goods worth] | £2 |

In these accounts, the register emphasizes that the second group of payments are made 'as a present,' so simultaneously denying that the property and inheritance obligations of British marriage customs applied, and disowning any liability to make further payments.

What was exchanged in these local marriages? Did, for example, the partners normally share a language? Was it from their wenches that so many officers learned to speak the Fante language? And if they were posted to another locality, did they take their wench with them or start again and learn another language? Did wenches live in the officer's apartments in the Castle? Was that why women were allowed upstairs in the Castle? Or, as is also recorded, did the wench live in the town nearby? Did they take meals together? Or did the officer normally dine at the governor's table and spend his evenings in the Castle hall with his fellow officers and the visiting captains? And was life different in the forts, where the number of expatriate officers was often less than three? And how far did fathers participate in the bringing up of the children? There is little among the records to enable such questions to be answered with much certainty. Of all the people who lived in and around the Castle, the wenches were those that the later colonial histories found most embarrassing. To the Victorian missionaries, the wench custom was a constant reminder that the British, after a century and a half, had not only not attempted to change the local marriage customs but had themselves, as they would say, 'gone native.'

Governor Hippisley, one of the few during the slaving era who survived long enough to be able to afford both types of marriage, evidently preferred the African. As he wrote in a book that may not have pleased the British Mrs. Hippisley, in Africa there was no 'coquetry, platonism, inappetency and whim among the women.' Indeed, he argued, European marriage customs risked bringing about depopulation:

How many Men abstain from marriage from humour, a
contemplative and philosophical turn, love of retirement, an
indolent or a pleasurable disposition! How many Women
from coldness, caprice, coquetry, and the not being asked!
The increase in luxury has always been a hindrance to
marriage. The vain are unwilling to abridge any part of the
sumptuousness of their appearance in the world, and if they
cannot figure as much after matrimony as before, give up
all thoughts of marrying at all. The inconveniences from
indigent circumstances, and the certainty of multiplying
them by having children, prevent vast numbers of both sexes
from entering into wedlock, and many others till very late
in life. The long absence of husbands on account of trade,
to say nothing of war, prevents the latter from breeding as
often as they otherwise would . . .

Occasionally, as in the following exchange of letters between
the governors of two forts, we find affection, dynastic interest, and
coarseness. These letters too catch the arch, and self-consciously
literary, style that the officers of the African Service believed was
a mark of their gentility, so different from the plain, phonetically
spelled letters of most slave-ship captains:

**Richard Miles at Anomabu fort to Thomas Westgate at
Winneba fort, Sunday, December 13 (1770s)**

My Lady is in general pretty good Natur'd; but the loss
of her son and Heir the other day has made me quite
melancholy and has deprived her of her Days of Jollity; I
suppose tho only for a little while – Apropos you're very
secret in <u>your</u> amour with a certain Lady who I hear has

the honor of napping in your room of late; though from the Branch she springs from I dare say she's useful in her way.

**Westgate to Miles (no date)**

I am sorry for your Lady's Loss – but she ought to be comforted when she considers that you can at any time cast a New Heir in the same Forge

Tis true I have taken a great Strong back'd W—e, rather surreptitiously. but it is only to tickle me when I happen to be in the humour – I find however its impossible for an old fellow to do a foolish thing on <u>this here coast</u> without its flying (as Pope says) on poetic wings.

Robert Collins, governor of Accra fort, kept in touch with his wench families in his previous fort in Apollonia where the language and customs were different. The canoe journey was dangerous and expensive, and took many days in both directions:

I expect my Appolonia Wenches & Children down [the coast] soon so beg you will give them a Canoe down if they arrive before you come away. If not, desire you'll order your Second [deputy] to give them a Canoe . . .

Most wenches remain nameless. However, occasionally, the officers' wills specify legacies to named women and children: 'I leave my slave boy Atchaken to my wench Eccoah.' Occasionally, too, a will makes a substantial provision, and even in these most formal of documents we glimpse actual lived lives. Thomas Mitchell, who died on May 24, 1795, wrote in his will:

I give and bequeath to my wench Nance, in consideration
of her strict attention and attendance on me during the
three years we have lived together the sum of twenty pounds
sterling to be paid her in gold dust at the rate of four pounds
sterling per ounce ... together with two gold rings which
belong to me as a token of remembrance.

As a factor, Mitchell knew that he had to spell out the amount in
explicit detail to avoid the artificial prices by which the dead as well
as the living were routinely robbed.

Occasionally, too, the wills record a father's concern for his
children. James Phipps, governor of Cape Coast Castle in the early
eighteenth century in the days of the Royal African Company, had a
local wife whom he is said to have deeply loved, and whose father had
come from the Netherlands. Phipps begged her to go to England with
him and, although she refused, he extracted her reluctant consent to
send their four children there to be educated (what happened I have
not discovered). Phipps died at the Castle, leaving 'all my goods in
Africa to my beloved friend William Dodging, Carpenter in Cabo
Corso.' Like others, he may have being trying to avoid the rule that
local wives and children could not inherit property by setting up
some kind of trusteeship arrangement, and it is notable too that
the friendship between a governor and a carpenter, which in later
British military and colonial history would have been forbidden, did
not stand in the way. James Smyth of Belfast, governor of Winneba
fort, who died on April 5, 1790, left a quarter of his estate to his sister
and the other three-quarters to his father, mother, and brother, but
only on condition that they took care of his infant daughter Rachel
Smyth, who was to be sent to Europe for education when she was
older. He makes other legacies to 'each of my wenches' and 'each of
my boys,' Cudjo, Mulatto Joe, and Affrey. In such wills, we can see
the men in the Castle attempting to negotiate a personal solution

across the deep divide between the customs of the two societies to which they belonged.

And what of the others with an interest in the encounter? In a long letter to her husband Dan in Africa (undated, *c.* 1785) Sarah O'Keefe, who lived near Dublin in Ireland, tells him she has been to see her uncle, who was evidently Dan's guarantor. He had reminded her that appointments in the African Service were difficult to get, that Dan would be foolish to resign, that fortunes were not made in a hurry, and that he would emphatically not lend the £50 or £60 that he had asked for. 'Last time I dined at forthfield,' she writes, 'he hardly spoke. . . . But I am told that there was a Leady at my uncles the day he received your letter that said if she was the chief Barron and had £50 or £60 to throw away she would much rather give it to Mr. Okeefes poor wife and children than to seind it hop of the Vinter [phrase not understood] to Mr. Okeefe, who is well able to take care of himself.' Sarah pours out her despair, the impossibility of her going out to join him, or of his coming back, her humiliation at being so absolutely dependent on her uncle and at having to ask her grandmother even for the money to release his letters from the post office. 'I send you a lock of poor Dickson and of my little darling Barry Dans hair [their children; Dickson has presumably died] with a lock of my own as the ownly preasant I can give you.' She is sure that neither she nor their two boys will ever see Dan again. And she was right. The Castle register records that Daniel O'Keefe, factor, died on May 15, 1786, less than a year after his arrival, and he never saw the letter.

The two men who had given sureties of £500 each were named as Felix McCarthy and Dennis Mahony, one of whom was presumably Sarah's uncle. If Factor O'Keefe had saved as much as half his salary, say, as seems unlikely, Sarah would eventually have received about £30, not much different from what Dan may have had to lodge in advance for his wench, plus whatever his second-hand clothes were able to fetch – they were so scanty as not to require an auction in the Castle. It is, however, more likely that O'Keefe had nothing to leave her, except a debt that would be deducted from her uncle's surety.

The African wench contract was unequal and exploitative, but for the women as well as for the men, and in some cases for the children too, it had some advantages over the British marriage contract. The woman had some money and income of her own, at any rate when her man was alive and content, whereas under British law the man took complete control of all assets. And, with the local wench contract, as was not the case with the British marriage contract, the man and the woman actually spent time together. The eighteenth-century British/African encounter produced 'wenches' who lived with their men day by day, year after year, in some cases at least, in sexual, caring, and affectionate unions, who looked after them when they were sick, brought up their children, and grieved at their funerals, but were paid off the moment the men died; and 'wives' such as Mrs. Hippisley and Mrs. O'Keefe, who lived thousands of miles from husbands whom in some cases they scarcely knew, without even a letter for years on end, with no property of their own but utterly dependent on the charity of relatives, awaiting their widowhood. With widowhood came the right to own property and the freedom to be married again – perhaps to another African officer temporarily home in Britain with almost no adult experience outside the walls of an African slaving fort, impatient to be reinstated in the Service and to return to the life, including the women and children, he had left behind.

## Sexual slavery

Whether, during the slaving era, the officers or other men in the Castle exploited the Castle slaves or the imprisoned slaves for sexual purposes is hard to judge. Most of the printed sources of the colonial period, influenced by a Victorian agenda, tended to lump together all sexual activity outside monogamous marriage, including formal wench unions, as 'debauchery,' and few made any attempt to understand them except to condemn and mock. That sexual exploitation of slaves did, or could, happen was denied, and in the case of the Castle slaves, who had a clear status, it seems unlikely, but with so many institutionalized half truths and hypocrisies, it is difficult to know. Stories of drunken officers shouting 'get me wench' after a good dinner suggest commercial prostitution or worse. But, as often, the Castle records give us actual cases.

At the sale held after the death of a governor of Accra fort in 1775, Miles bought a girl noted as 'T[homas] T[rinder's] Shantee Beauty' for goods worth about £21. On March 4, 1777, he noted that, for the same price, he 'Bartered for a Girl (D.M's Lady)' that probably was not a wench with rights, but a young female slave who, like the Asante beauty, was to be 'sent off the coast' when her male owner, perhaps in this case Governor David Mill, either died, left the coast, or brought the relationship to an end. But in the following letter, sent to another governor, which concerns girls who were not slaves but 'pawns' handed over as security for debts (see Chapter 8), the false delicacy that marks such writings encourages us to decode what is implied:

Take as many good Women Girl Pawns as you can. by yr letter it would seem you expected to get more than the 17 indeed the whole 34; but mind at takg. the Girls for Pawns for to make a positive Agreement that there is to be no Palaver should any of those Ladys be — by any Body here – such a Law must be made or we will have no Peace. Shall keep the 16 in Irons till the Palaver is settled then let them loose. The Irons you shall have by Yr Canoe . . .

The girls, like other pawns, could hope to be redeemed by their families. But women and girls who had, like the Asante beauty, come from the interior of Africa, had no protector. In their journey through the forest paths they had lost their residual rights, including their names, and were perhaps already as available to their European masters in Africa as they would be on the slave ships and when they reached the new world across the ocean.

## Crossing the divides

The arrival of the first British-born white women in Cape Coast Castle threatened the whole sexual, marriage, and property economy. Both the Royal African Company and the Company of Merchants prohibited officers and men from bringing their British wives. In 1766, however, the Governing Committee suddenly changed its policy, announcing the appointment, as chaplain, of Rev. Philip Quaque, who would be accompanied by the wife he had met and married when in England. Quaque, the letter from London announced, was to be paid '£60 per annum in gold, his wife and another woman by way of companion attends him and are to be paid after the rate of £13 per annum each as the usual encouragement given to White women who reside on the coast.' When the decision, which seems to have come as a surprise, reached the Castle, the governor and officers lodged an immediate protest – or as immediate as it could be when letters took three months in either direction. The tenor of their protest (not found) can be guessed from the Committee's reply – it was evidently not about the fact of a black officer marrying a white wife. The Governing Committee agreed, they wrote, with the 'objections you make to the sending out of white women to the coast, as well with respect to the public as the many disagreeable circumstances there women must be subject to, but the reasons you assign of the impropriety of separating man and wife are what had weight with us . . . she must be given every comfort.' The point of sending Quaque to England in the first place was so that he could return, and his appointment seems to have been fast-tracked to catch the storeship – his induction as deacon, then as priest, and his British marriage all occurring within a month.

Along the coast at Elmina Castle the Dutch had employed as a pastor Jacobus Elisa Johannes Capitein, who had also been born locally, as an even more direct instrument of legitimation of the slave trade. Capitein, who had been taken to Elmina as a boy slave, had been freed by his master – as Dutch law required – when he arrived in the Netherlands, and had been instructed in the doctrines of the Dutch Church. As part of his degree, he had composed a dissertation in Latin, *Dissertatio politico-theologica, qua disquitur, Num libertati Christianae servitus adversetur, nec ne?* (1742), confirming the view of his teachers and paymasters that slavery was entirely compatible with Christianity. (The dissertation does not mention slave trading.) When Capitein returned to Elmina and wanted to take an African wife, a white Dutch woman was specially sent from the Netherlands so as to prevent him from taking an unbaptized wench, another indication that racial origin was less important than religious affiliation. However, Capitein was not regarded as a success by the authorities in the Dutch castle, it being said, in almost the same words as were later to be used of Quaque, that his 'craving for trade had dampened his zeal for religion.' Capitein died within two years of his return to Africa.

The first Mrs. Quaque, born Catherine Blunt, about whom nothing is known beyond her name, did not survive her seasoning, after which Quaque took up with the lady companion whose name is unrecorded, and who was also probably white. But, as he reported to London, 'I have frequently suffered the jealous lashes of many scandalous tongues,' and in order to silence those reproaches he had 'once more entered the Holy State of Matrimony, with my

Spouses waiting maid.' The ceremony took place publicly before the governor, the officers of the Castle, and the leading local men, but with no Christian priest present except himself. However, when not long after, the second Mrs. Quaque also died, Quaque adopted the custom of his fellow countrymen and of his Company colleagues of living with a wench. With his pay, and profits from trading, he moved out of his quarters in the Castle to his own house in the town, only visiting the Castle when required.

But the property aspects of the differing marriage customs raised new problems. Quaque adopted the notion of personal private property disposable at will that was practiced in the Castle, and quarrelled with his children, who demanded that he maintain the local custom of property as a family trust. When, after an unusually long life, having survived the whole range of Castle illnesses, fluxes, fevers, and worms, Quaque felt the end approaching and he reverted to his ancestral religion, the news caused consternation among the English missionaries, who were inordinately proud of having produced their first black English priest. Although Quaque's return to his African religion is well attested, it was denied, or attributed to senile dementia, and is not mentioned on his tombstone, which can still be read in the Castle. Having been forcibly straddled across the cultural divide from the day in 1753 when, for reasons of state policy, his relatives had pledged their boy to the British, Quaque opted at the end for the customs of his childhood. A sale of his effects among his colleagues on July 29, 1817, raised £178 11s 8d. Among the usual lists of clothes and furniture, only his books, unnamed, his fiddle, and his spectacles (an item I have not noticed in other lists) suggest anything personal. His total assets were valued at over £469, a substantial sum for his heirs to quarrel over.

## *Children*

The boys born from unions with wenches seem mainly to have become part of local society, forming a growing and influential middle class, with increasing levels of literacy, education, and commercial success. As for the girls, only a few are more than names. Elizabeth Dalzel, who appears to have been born in the Castle in 1793 when her father was governor for a second time, visited her brother Edward in Algiers when she was a teenager; Edward was probably also born in the Castle and had settled in Algiers in 1812 as a merchant agent and Portuguese vice-consul. She saw there the plight of white Christians who had been captured and enslaved by Barbary pirates. In Algiers alone in 1816 there were more than 1,500 of these slaves – men, women, and children from France, Spain, Portugal, and Britain. Other Christian slaves, mainly captured from ships, were held in captivity in Tunis and Tripoli. By leading a campaign in the British press, Elizabeth Dalzel helped to promote a movement in Britain that resulted in a naval expedition to Algiers in 1816 and the release of 3,000 Christian slaves. Married to John Dickson, a naval surgeon – a profession that provided one of the few sources of educated men to be met on the coast – she later settled in Tripoli, where Dickson was surgeon to the local ruler. She died there as a widow in 1862, leaving four sons and two daughters.

A different fate awaited Sally Abson, daughter of Lionel Abson, governor of Whydah fort in the slaving era. John McLeod, a ship's surgeon who, after reductions in the Royal Navy, was, as he records, 'fortunate to be appointed to a slave ship,' told her story. His ship, after calling at Cape Coast Castle, went on to Whydah, which was famous for supplying slave women with particularly glossy skin, whom he calls 'black Circassians,' hinting at their suitability for oriental harems. At Whydah he met Sally, who was looking after her dying father, but when he died she was left with no male protector. McLeod, whom she helped through his seasoning, agreed to take

*17. Sally Abson, daughter of fort governor Lionel Abson by his African wench.*

her with him on the ship, but one day she disappeared, seized, it was revealed locally, by agents of the ruler who wanted her for his harem. Attempts to free her failed, and as McLeod records in the literary language picked up from reading sentimental novels such as *Paul and Virginia* (1788) – the Europe-wide bestseller about love and innocence set in the uncorrupted paradise of the the Indies, in which one of the partners is black – 'from the moment of her seizure she had become a prey to grief, and after lingering some years in this state of despondency, sunk at last broken-hearted to the grave.'

## De mortuis nil nisi bonum

Another tombstone in the Castle that can still be read is, like Philip Quaque's, made of black marble specially ordered from England.

Set on the highest part of the Castle furthest back from the sea spray, it has the following inscription:

> Sacred to the Memory of / Mrs. Eliza Fountaine / and two infant female children / Wife of Mr. John Fountaine / many years an officer / in the service of / the African Committee. This stone / was inscribed and laid down / by her sincere and afflicted friends / the Governor and Gentlemen / of this Settlement / as a just tribute / to her manifold virtues / and in testimony / of their unfeigned sorrow and regard / at the loss / they have sustained / by her death / which happened at / Cape Coast Castle / on the 26th August 1803 / in the 38th year / of her age.

Such memorials are found in many places in the former British tropical empire. To the British visitor who happens upon them, they conjure up a poignant story that already seems familiar – that of a promising, adventurous young man, his hopes of a brilliant career and a splendid fortune, the kindness of a well-placed relative who makes the personal introduction and secures the appointment, the enthusiastic letters home describing the exotic life, the childhood sweetheart who becomes his wife and decides to join him, and then the letter with the sad news. It is an imagined narrative of empire as settled in Britain's national memory as that of the young soldier who lies in some corner of a foreign field that is forever England. Only occasionally do we know anything personal of the lives of the people whose names appear on these memorials. In this case, because of the chance survival of records, we can draw back the curtain of cliché.

John Fountaine, Eliza's husband, was the son of Rev. John Fountaine of the parish church in Islington into whose household in London Quaque's son was sent, although he too was also taught by Rev. John Moore of St. Sepulchre's in London. Fountaine, was, therefore, a member of one of the British 'African' ecclesiastical families involved in the slave trade, and in 1778, after some years in Jamaica, he was duly appointed to Cape Coast Castle. It was on a brief visit to England in 1783 that he married Eliza, and she became pregnant, but he was soon back 'on the coast' without her, being appointed governor of a small and then a larger fort, with a seat on the Council. At that time he had sureties of £5,000.

Fountaine never showed any discomfort about his involvement in the slave trade, except to regret his lack of financial success. He was, however, ostentatiously religious in ways which his colleagues found tiresome: he lectured them on their swearing and playing billiards on Sundays, and he publicly criticized Governor Norris for allowing an infant child by his African wench to die without having received the Christian rite of baptism, particularly as the child had been taken ill and there had been time before she had died. One governor described his behaviour as 'rather strange, his companions always the young gentlemen in the Castle.' He also thought Fountaine was 'too friendly in his conversations with the blacks,' another phrase that may be potentially decoded. At some point, after some quarrel at which the governor struck him in the face, Fountaine was dismissed and returned to England for a second time.

But, with little money, and a wife and children to support, Fountaine's misfortunes multiplied and he spent eleven months in a British debtors' prison. However, it was bad publicity for the slaving industry to have one of their senior officers in financial difficulties, especially one who had been a supportive witness at the parliamentary inquiry in 1790, and who had helped Governor Dalzel with the researches among the Castle records for his *History of Dahomy* (he appears as J. F. in that defense of the slave trade). A subscription was raised to pay his debts by his friends – in Castle terms he was 'redeemed' – and he was reinstated and sent back to

Cape Coast Castle. The financial package Fountaine received was generous: a salary for himself, with the stipulation that he had no duties; a salaried appointment for his son, John Fountaine Junior; and a salary – not carried on the books – for Eliza; plus free passage for the whole family of husband, wife, three children, and an English woman companion, Elizabeth (Betty) Fawcett, with full accommodation, and dining rights for the men in the Castle hall. Since both John Fountaines, father and son, were outside the normal age limits – the father at sixty being too old, the son at sixteen too young – the regulations were waived, but given the life expectancy rates, the family was unlikely to be a financial burden for long.

The party arrived at Cape Coast Castle on September 4, 1802. One daughter died the following May. Eliza died in August 1803; it was remembered that in her final fevered delirium she kept singing the old song 'The Air of Marlborough.' Fountaine, left to look after the second daughter with Betty's help, withdrew from Castle life, never going up to dinner, and scarcely leaving his room for months except to visit the grave of Eliza and the child. It was then that Samuel Ellis and Nathaniel Deey, two younger officers in the Castle, started to torment him. 'Orestes and Pylades' Fountaine called them, showing off his education and hinting at a homoerotic relationship. They poured water through the floorboards of the hall into his room below and stamped up and down all night to stop the family from sleeping. They threw corn in his door to encourage the rats, pissed from the balcony into his flour barrel, and peeped through the lattices at night to see what he was up to with Betty. One night when in desperation he went up to the hall where they were drinking, carrying his ceremonial sword drawn, but they knocked him down and he was arrested and locked up. When his second daughter died in November 1804, Fountaine suffered a breakdown, blaming Governor Mould for refusing him food so that the sick child had to be fed on wine and ship's biscuit. He also said that the same governor who had 'turned on the waterworks' when he visited the bedside of the dying Eliza, later repeatedly ordered the Castle band to play 'The Air of Marlborough' as a deliberate cruelty. A few months later, when a new governor arrived, Fountaine faced a disciplinary hearing, but in the circumstances, on the advice of former surgeon Meredith, was only given a reprimand.

Deey wanted to resign, and when his request was refused he stole a boat and attempted to run away. As for accountant Ellis, he had been financing the speculations of Governor Mould, 'borrowing' not only from goods in the warehouses, but from the gold due to the legatees of dead officers and soldiers that, as register, he had in his trust in his safe. All was lost. Ellis, bankrupt and 'a prey to despair,' died in 1807, leaving his guarantors to pick up the bill. Fountaine died of dysentery in 1808. And what of Eliza, Mrs. Fountaine? Who was she? Her unmarried name is unknown. Why did she, at the age of nineteen, marry a man briefly home from Africa twenty years her senior whom she had scarcely met? A man whose adult life had been confined, as he told a parliamentary inquiry, 'entirely to the forts, except in passing from the one to another.' Was she a woman her relatives wanted to be rid of?

## *Butterfly and Pinkerton*

It was not until the arrival of Christian missionaries in substantial numbers in the post-slave-era nineteenth century when the Castle had an entirely different purpose (see Chapter 9) that the British began to attempt to change local sexual and marriage laws and customs instead of living in conformity with them. The missionaries offered education, literacy, and a share in the power conferred by Prospero's books, and they had no trouble in explaining their doctrines of ransom, redemption, atonement, and the other terms from slavery that were part of daily life in West Africa. But, as the Victorian missionary Rev. Dennis Kemp wrote, as soon as he arrived at Cape Coast he was faced with 'one of the gravest difficulties with which the missionary has to deal . . . the local marriage laws.' Women did not see why they should have to give up receiving money on marriage, which provided at least a modicum of financial security, on the grounds that, as Kemp wrote indignantly, 'the bride is *purchased*.' Nor was Kemp impressed with the argument put to him by an African Christian, that the local marriage customs gave an opportunity 'for ascertaining if the parties suited one another.' 'Fancy taking a wife,' Kemp wrote, 'like a sewing machine, on a month's free trial!'

If an officer survived to rise high in the Service, his daughters could cross the divide between wench and wife, at least in local British-African terms. Part of a broken tombstone, recently dug up in the Castle, records the death in 1839, after a long life, of 'Mrs. Sarah Dawson/Late Sarah Mould.' She was the daughter of Governor Miles – who had left forever in 1784, when she was a child – and the widow of two governors: Mould was dismissed in 1804 and died onboard ship on the way back to England, and Dawson went home to Liverpool without her in 1816. Sarah may have been unusual in being accorded the rank of 'Mrs.' on her tomb, but not in remaining in the Castle when her men left.

An American sea captain, Edward Harrington, who came ashore at Dixcove fort in 1840, was one of the many exponents of the fake-genteel, consciously literary, apologetic, and mincing style that expatriate men felt obliged to adopt when local marriage customs were discussed, especially when writing to their women at home:

> At tea . . . we were favored with Mrs. Swanzy company
> or Mr. Swanzys Lady 'pro tempore' or for a time a young
> molatto Girl of considerable attraction. Such a distinction

and indulgence to a Lady by their Lords I have never witnessed on the coast. Probably Mr. Swanzys greater liberality of sentiment and his lonely situation prompted him to admit his Lady to his board as to his b — d.

In the slaving era only a minority of the officers of the African Service who sailed from Britain ever returned to their homeland. And of those who did – a few were given home leave on health grounds, for example – only a minority came back to Africa. In 1770 Mr. Dunn, who was leaving the coast, arranged for his wench Nancy to be paid £0.75 a month during his absence, but when he had been gone for two and a half years without news, the Castle governor stopped the payments, recording on her note: 'I gave her free Liberty to look for an[othe]r Husband.'

As steamships made visits to Britain more affordable, as quinine improved life expectancy among expatriates, as British-born wives began to expect to accompany their husbands, and as the Christian missionaries attempted to impose Victorian bourgeois domesticity, the balance that had existed in the male-dominated world of the Castle during the slaving era was rapidly tilted towards a more racially divided set of customs. However, some of the essentials of the wench marriage contract remained in place. According to Harrington, if an officer said he intended to return to Africa, the wench would remain 'faithful and inviolate.' If he said he did not intend to come back, he gave her money and she was at liberty to accept another offer. On the Gold Coast the drama of Madam Butterfly and Lieutenant Pinkerton could be seen whenever the steamship arrived or was ready to leave. Harrington witnessed the scene when 'Mr. G' was about to board the canoe, his young wench and their baby on the beach, begging him to come back as soon as possible. Harrington attempted to catch her speech and choking sobs, one of the few records that, however inadequately, gives a wench's voice. 'William William see see little little Mary Ch. William come quick.'

When the Castle and forts were taken over by the British government in 1821, and a policy of education adopted (see Chapter 9), a few women were recruited to join the establishment. The first woman whose name I have found on the payroll of officers was a 'Mrs. Jarvis, Teacher of Needlework, £200,' recorded in 1822. Whether she was locally born or expatriate I do not know.

## Robinson Crusoe again

The most visited tombs in Cape Coast Castle, now roped off to protect them from visitors' feet, lie flat on the parade ground at the foot of the grand staircase. The English poet Letitia Elizabeth Landon, known as L. E. L., and George Maclean, her husband, governor of Cape Coast Castle from 1830 until 1847, except for 1836–38 when he returned to Britain on business, lie – or 'sleep' as the Victorians liked to say – side by side in death as they did in life. One stone bears the initials L. E. L. in large letters, the other G. M. and the St. Andrew's cross of Scotland laid like a flag on the body of a soldier. They are, as one could almost guess, memorials of the Victorian age, built by Governor Connor in 1850 as part of the Victorianizing of the Castle. A tablet ordered from London by Maclean some years earlier, whose Latin inscription emphasizes Landon's married status as Letitia Maclean, is set into a wall under the grand staircase.

From the moment in 1820 when her first verses began to appear under the genderless three initials in the *Literary Gazette*, it was realized that the world had a new genius, a new Byron. When it emerged that the unknown writer was an unmarried woman, of less than twenty years of age, who wore extravagant hats and pink dresses, she became the darling of what Disraeli called silver fork society. Although Landon wrote profusely, skillfully, and confidently in both verse and prose, she had, however, essentially only one voice, which can be loosely characterized as feminine romantic despair. Her heroines are victims of hopeless love, and if they are betrayed by unworthy and faithless men, that is their fate. The passions that L. E. L. romanticized occur far from the false and superficial workaday world of modern London – in Italy, Spain, India, Arabia, Africa, islands in the tropical oceans, and in exotic imagined lands amalgamated from childhood readings of *The Arabian Nights*, *Paul and Virginia*, and Byronic orientalism. *Robinson Crusoe* had been a special favorite. As she wrote:

> For weeks after reading that book, I lived as if in a dream; indeed I scarcely dreamt of anything else at night. I went to sleep with the cave, its parrots and goats, floating before my closed eyes. I awakened in some rapid flight from the savages landing in their canoes. The elms in our hedges were not more familiar than the prickly shrubs which formed his palisades, and the grapes whose drooping branches made fertile the wide savannahs.

Like Byron, to whom she was constantly compared, Landon protested that she was herself not at all the same as her female literary characters, but readers did not believe her. Like Byron, Landon was invited to grand parties, fawned over by adoring admirers, and courted with offers of love. Byron had discovered that the waters of celebrity concealed underwater reefs that wrecked his reputation, and had only escaped by leaving England. Landon too suddenly became the victim of a whispering campaign. In 1826 a society satirical magazine called *The Wasp* suggested that she had had a child by William Jerdan, the editor of the *Literary Gazette* who had first discovered her and put her name on the map:

This young lady is a most useful and indefatigable
contributor, and the salubrious air of Sloane-street and
Brompton-row (between which places she passes her
time), has been of peculiar advantage both to her *mental*
and *bodily* health. With respect to the latter, it is a singular
circumstance, that altho' she was a short time since as thin
and aereal as one of her own sylphs, she in the course of a
few months acquired so perceptible a degree of *embonpoint*,
as to induce her kind friend Jerdan to recommend a change
of air, lest her health and strength should be affected. She
followed his advice, and strange to say, such was the effect of
even two months absence from Brompton, that she returned
as thin and poetical as ever . . .

The story was indignantly denied, but when Landon, more than
once, became engaged to be married, the men broke off the
engagement without public explanation. When, on her return from
a visit to Paris, she was found by the French customs to be wearing
a man's bulky waistcoat, Jerdan explained in his newspaper that she
was just attempting to avoid paying duty. (Landon, incidentally,
is commemorated in the short and inconspicuous Landon Street
at the back entrance to the Harrods department store, where she
lived in a single room in a girls' school.) Although the story that
Landon had had a child was dismissed as a slander by all her
friends and by her biographers – the most recent being Germaine
Greer in 1995 – the finding by Cynthia Lawford of a London
parish record for 'Laura, daughter of William Jerdan and Letitia
Elizabeth Landon' proves that she had had at least one child by
Jerdan, and other evidence suggests that she may have had two
others, one of whom went to Australia, and another to Trinidad,
bundled off to far distant parts of the British oceanic empire.
Landon's father, a military contractor, long dead, who left her

with scarcely any money, is said to have been to Africa. And many of Landon's friends in literary London had business connections in Africa, notably John Forster, who would write a life of Dickens and who was a Member of Parliament and a member of the Governing Committee, and his brother to whom she was briefly engaged. It was Forster who in 1836 arranged an introduction to George Maclean, governor of Cape Coast Castle, a real-life romantic hero – or so it seemed to many people. Landon almost certainly also knew Sarah Bowdich, whose husband Thomas, now dead, had written a famous book about the 1817 mission to Asante and was something of a hero. At the time of Landon's greatest popularity – in the 1830s – Sarah Bowdich had become a published writer, providing a series of tales about her experiences in Africa in the ladies' annuals, sometimes appearing in the same volume as Landon. Maybe Landon thought that she would be able to do the same or better? To a romanticist like Landon, Bowdich's plain stories must have seemed like lost opportunities.

In June 1838 Maclean and Landon were hurriedly and quietly married in an English church, shortly after Lieutenant Maclean had been promoted to captain, and they set out for Africa immediately afterwards. An application by her brother to secure a position with the Royal Literary Fund, which had been set up to help indigent authors, was turned down – on account of her reputation. The British government, however, granted Landon a pension of £15 a year, although under British marriage laws this would belong to her husband. It was also arranged that she would continue her literary career while in the Castle, writing and editing the ladies' annual *Fishers' Drawing Room Scrapbook* at an annual fee of £100, although that too would legally belong to her husband. The plan was that Landon would stay in the Castle for three years; however, whether this was part of the understanding with Maclean or was regarded as a sufficient period for quarantining her reputation is not certain.

*18. Letitia Elizabeth Landon (L. E. L.).*

On the voyage Landon was almost continuously sick, although it is not suggested that she was pregnant.

Except for his visit 'home' during which he met Landon, Maclean had lived in Africa since 1826. Indeed, apart from two years between the ages of fifteen and seventeen when he had been in the army, he had spent his whole adult life in the Castle and along the coast. His acknowledged wench was the half sister of James Bannerman of Accra, one of the most highly educated and the most powerful men on the Gold Coast, not excluding the British governors and officers, and he was also rich. Maclean had lived with her in the Castle, presumably in the governor's private quarters at the top, and they had more than one child; one was called Ellen, a common forename at a time when everyone admired the romances of Sir Walter Scott.

What arrangement Maclean had made with Miss Bannerman – her first name is not recorded – before his visit to Britain in 1836 is not known, but he always intended to return. Nor is it known how far he might have been able to inform the acting governor of the Castle of his changed situation by letter before he arrived back. What is certain is that, when the ship reached the roads off Cape Coast Castle, Maclean insisted on going ashore alone and at once – although it was two o'clock in the morning, when landing through the surf and rocks was particularly dangerous. It was said later that he had done so in order to make sure that Miss Bannerman was not in the Castle. Maclean was taken ill shortly afterwards with a severe fever that, in accordance with the medical understanding of the time, was attributed to the soaking and chilling he had suffered in his night ride through the surf.

Landon, who came ashore next day, appears for a time to have enjoyed the romance of her life in the Castle. In one letter she says she has become 'a sort of female Robinson Crusoe.' 'I am very well and very happy,' she writes, adding, unable to let go the style she had made her own, 'my only regret – the emerald ring that I fling into the dark sea of life to propitiate fate – is the constant sorrow I feel whenever I think of those whose kindness is so deeply treasured. . . . The castle is a fine building, with excellent rooms, on three sides surrounded by the sea. I like the perpetual dash on the rocks; one wave comes up after another, and is for ever dashed to pieces, like human hopes, that only swell to be disappointed.'

Every evening Landon walked round the Castle walls for an hour before dinner. She had plenty of occasions to read the inscriptions on tombs, something that she had always found fascinating, including those of an increasing number of expatriate missionaries, their wives, and children, such as the following:

Sacred to the memory of Elizabeth Anne / Daughter of
Robert and Catherine Jackson / Who died on 9th of July
1837 / Aged one year two months / And three days

Whether Maclean had been pressurized by his bosses to marry Landon – as seems likely – or had other motivations, is now irrecoverable. Nor can we know much about how he regarded Landon and her writings. What seems clear is that Maclean was a prototype of a new type of colonialist, a son of the manse, a man of parts with no social connections, a man deeply interested in his mission, respected by the African communities, and more at home among his friends and employees in the Castle than he had ever been in London or Scotland. During his governorship many local disputes were voluntarily brought to him for adjudication so that gradually a de facto British sovereignty was extended deeper inland. After a day of palavers with the people among whom he had made his life, much of it conducted in the local languages, he preferred to retire to his private quarters at the top of the Castle, to which no one was admitted, to his astronomical telescope through which he contemplated the wonders of the heavens in a clear sky, to his books, including his Bible, and to his violin. He was Prospero in his cell.

The nineteenth century was to produce many Macleans. A high official in the later nineteenth century who toured extensively through what is now Ghana, met British expatriate teachers, doctors, magistrates, engineers, and forestry advisers living self-sufficient lives and seldom meeting other expatriates, their only link with their home country a handful of favored books. In this new colonial world, as in the slaving era, there was little role for a British expatriate woman. During her weeks in Cape Coast Castle Landon busied herself with her writing and made one trip into the country by hammock. She talked with Brodie Cruikshank, governor of Anomabu fort, another of the new-style governors, about the task of bringing European modernity to the interior of Africa that they regarded not as an 'atonement' for the recently ended slaving era but as a worthy – or as Victorians would say a 'manly' – enterprise in its own right.

One morning, two months after arriving, Landon was found dead, having apparently taken her own life with prussic acid. Perhaps she knew the story of the famous aesthete and social misfit Richard Payne Knight, who had stylishly dipped his pen in prussic acid, 'and drawing it through his lips closed the account.' Maybe the poet of despair contrived her own stylish exit? Maybe she would follow Byron, who had famously died after completing his thirty-sixth year? Maybe, like many others, she realized too late the gap between the romance of the warm south that had shaped and driven her life and the lonely, friendless, formal, humdrum English reality of life within the walls. Maclean, as was normal, held an immediate inquest in the Castle – verdict: accidental overdose – and Landon's body was buried in the parade ground the same afternoon. In the evening Maclean sailed to Accra, another unusual and dangerous

19. *Outside Letitia Landon's room in the Castle where she was found dead.*

night voyage, for what purpose the private, self-contained man kept to himself.

In 1841 a petition was sent from the Castle to Lord John Russell, the British secretary of state for war and the colonies, by 'The Principal Mulatoo Females of the Gold Coast' asking that indigenous slavery should not be outlawed. It contains seven names, each one a descendant of a wench union with a governor or high-ranking officer of the African Service, 'Fanny Smith, Mary Jackson, Elizabeth Swanzy, Mary Hutton, Sarah Crosby, Catherine Bannerman, Helen Colliver.' Each one is signed only with a mark, the women having not yet benefited from the recent educational initiatives. Catherine Bannerman is likely to have been, to use the language of the Victorian sentimentalists, the African mistress who had had to make way for the English bride. Whether Maclean reinstated her is not known.

The grave of L. E. L. soon became the most famous spot in the Castle, and it is hard to think of a more fitting resting place for her type of exotic romance. In 1860, the American Rev. Charles Thomas, echoing her own style, predicted that 'deep-voiced moans shall chant her wild sad requiem until the earth and the sea shall give up their dead.' To Sir Garnet Wolseley, another victim of literary cliché, who was there in 1874, the Atlantic breakers had:

> ... the remorselessness of fate ... Those who on that hateful
> coast have tossed through the long hours of a night made
> sleepless and horrible by fever, can never forget that sound.
> It falls on the over-wrought, misery-stricken brain, much as
> the ticking of Time's pendulum must on the ear of the man
> condemned to die next morning. But it also reminds you of
> how often in the fresh cool air of the rising summer tide at
> home ...

Below are a few stanzas from one of Landon's poems, entitled 'Night at Sea,' set to the rhythms of the rolling ocean, in the roads of Cape Coast Castle. It echoes Byron's 'Night at Sea,' a favorite in the commonplace books of the wives and daughters of empire who stayed at home. It can stand for all the myths and romances of Africa that carried so many British men, women, and children to Cape Coast Castle:

> By each dark wave around the vessel sweeping,
> Farther am I from old dear friends removed,

Till the lone vigil that I now am keeping,
I did not know how much you were beloved.
How many acts of kindness little heeded,
Kind looks, kind words, rise half reproachful now!
Hurried and anxious, my vexed life has speeded,
And memory wears a soft accusing brow.
    My friends, my absent friends!
    Do you think of me, as I think of you?

Yesterday has a charm, to-day could never
Fling o'er the mind, which knows not till it parts
How it turns back with tenderest endeavour
To fix the past within the heart of hearts.
Absence is full of memory, it teaches
The value of all old familiar things;
The strengthener of affection, while it reaches
O'er the dark parting, with an angel's wings.
    My friends, my absent friends!
    Do you think of me, as I think of you?

A dusk line in the moonlight I discover,
What all day long vainly I sought to catch;
Or is it but the varying clouds that hover
Thick in the air, to mock the eyes that watch?
No! well the sailor knows each speck appearing,
Upon the tossing waves, the far-off strand
    To that dusk line our eager ship is steering.
    Her voyage done – to-morrow we shall land.

In 'L. E. L.'s Last Question,' Elizabeth Barrett Browning, another
woman who had suffered from a lack of role at home, attempted a
reply that also caught the lure of the palm trees:

Could she not wait to catch their answering breath?
Was she content, content with ocean's sound
Which dashed its mocking infinite around
One thirsty for a little love?
… … … … … … … … … … … … … …


None smile and none are crowned where lieth she,
With all her visions unfulfilled save one,
Her childhood's, of the palm-trees in the sun –
And lo! their shadow on her sepulchre!

In our own time Kwadwo Opoku-Agyemang, a Ghanaian who
grew up in sight of the Castle, has written a series of poems, one
of which catches the spirit of its sepulchral commemoration of the
named and the nameless:

And the sea cackled, foaming at the mouth
Till dry cracks ploughed the waves back;
Hope, said the sea, is not a method
There are too many sad stories
Carved in indifferent stones:

There is always another story
After this is told

# 7

# The fort

## Oceanic rivalries

In the middle of the eighteenth century the French government, which had no land facilities on the Gold Coast, made a series of determined efforts to establish their own slaving fort. France had the largest population of any country in western Europe and access to immense resources, but French merchants seemed to be losing out commercially to the British wherever they clashed, in India, in Canada, and in the Caribbean. French efforts to settle French-born colonists in Guiana had resulted in catastrophe, and they rightly suspected that the British, the Dutch, and the Danes had informal understandings aimed at keeping them out of the best sources of African slaves. The site the French chose was Anomabu, a few miles down the coast from Cape Coast Castle, where one of the main trading paths from Asante reached the sea.

Near Anomabu was the slave market of Kormantse, known to the British as Cormantine, where the Dutch had a fort. Slaves obtained from this market, 'Cormantees,' were believed by the British and American planters to be physically the strongest available to be bought in Africa, the most suited to withstand the harsh working conditions in the plantations, and therefore, commercially, the most efficient at producing the tropical crops that their owners exported across the oceans. Although 'Cormantees' also had a reputation for being more rebellious than slaves obtained from elsewhere, they commanded a premium price.

At Anomabu, the landing beaches, although rocky and always dangerous, were better than anywhere nearby. A lodge had been built by the Dutch around 1640, captured in turn by the Swedes, the Danes, the Dutch again, the English, the Dutch again, and then the English, who built a fort there in the days of the Royal African Company. That fort, Fort Charles, matched Fort James at Accra – the two sons of King Charles I being major shareholders and promoters. However, by the mid-eighteenth century, when Fort Charles had become ruinous, the French government calculated that if they could obtain permission to build a new fort in the vicinity, not only would they have a source of supply of strong slaves for their own plantations but they could oust the British. For a time it seemed to the political leaders in London and Paris that the rocky headland of Anomabu on the Gold Coast was the key to commercial dominance in the whole Atlantic basin, if not the whole Europeanized oceanic world.

The local political leader, Eno Basi Korante, known to the British as 'John Corrantee,' kept his options open. In 1751, when the decision point seemed near, the British made what they thought was a clever preemptive move. As Richard Brew, the governor of the British fort, wrote, 'I sent a secret message to their priests offering oz 20 [about £80] to them to make their God declare in our favour. But to my great mortification had this answer – John Currantee has offered oz 60 [about £240] to speak for the French.'

The contest seemed to be over. However, when two French naval warships arrived off Anomabu with materials to build the French fort, they found that they could not complete their bargain. The lieutenant they sent ashore to announce their arrival declared that they had been sent by the king of France to build the fort as agreed.

When John Corrantee said they could not do so unless they had a letter from the king of England, the result was reported to Cape Coast Castle by the gleeful British governor:

> John Corantee moved to indignation told him that if he
> ever catched any of them ashore he would cut off their
> heads. The men of war lay in the roads until they had sold
> their brandy to the English ships for very bad gold, during
> which time they buried a great part of their ship's crews and
> will not in all probability attempt any more Annamaboe
> expeditions in a hurry.

French warships returned two years later. In August 1753 the British governor reported that the French had promised £40,000 to buy the land for a new fort, equivalent to twice or three times the British annual budget for the Castle and all the British forts combined, and an indication of their eagerness to seize a share of the trade. All three parties knew, however, that even if the British outbribed the French, they could still lose. John Corrantee, who had not signed the 1753 treaty under which the leaders of the Fante agreed to give the British exclusive rights, sent one of his sons to France, and a daughter was married to Richard Brew. As Brew wrote with a frankness seldom encountered in a business normally smothered in hypocrisies about mutual esteem, friendship, and loyalty, 'And how should it be otherwise? The nature of the trade excludes what we call affection. The negroes know we would buy every one of them if we could sell them again, and reckon it is as fair trade to sell our interest as we do to sell their persons.'

Occasionally, in the records of the negotiations for Anomabu, the British preserve an individual African voice. One local leader and trader, Abbrah Acriphy, who favored keeping the Anomabu concession in the hands of the British, is reported as emphasizing that he too acted in his own interests, and it is striking that, in protecting himself from the charge that he was a British puppet, it was by their costume that he distinguished them: 'I am no Englishman's servant. I have no silver-headed cane nor fine cloth, yet I am here waiting for Annamaboe [to be built].' Acriphy may be teasing the British, perhaps even sharing a literary allusion with them. It was only twenty years before that John Atkins, a naval surgeon, in his published account of his voyage to Guinea, had commented that at Anomabu the pale and thin British officers were so slovenly in their dress that they wore no cane and carried no snuff box.

It was in these circumstances that the Company of Merchants persuaded the British government to pay for the building of a new state-of-the-art British slaving fort at Anomabu. The result was the only British fort in Africa specially designed by the British for the slave trade. Unlike Cape Coast Castle, to whose construction several European nations contributed, Anomabu is, as a piece of architectural design, as British as Buckingham Palace. The building was designed by John Apperley, the military engineer who had built Plymouth dockyard in England; he went to Anomabu to supervise the construction, and became the first governor. It is often referred to in the secondary literature as Fort William, one of several Fort Williams built around this time by the British in India, North America, and in the Scottish highlands. However, this 'Fort William' was a renaming in Victorian colonial times. The Royal African Company had called its forts after its royal investors, but to the Company of Merchants, representing the nation of free-trading shopkeepers, it was always just 'Annamaboe fort.'

The foundations of the new fort were laid in August 1753. The fort consists of a regular square with pointed diamond-shaped bastions at each corner, and small gates to seaward and landward. Since the British were not allowed to close a right of way linking two parts of the town of Anomabu that ran along the shore, the fort was built

20. *The British purpose-built slaving fort at Anomabu with the private 'Castle Brew' fort nearby.*

further back from the beaches than they would have preferred. Like the other forts it seems to have been designed to look impressive when seen from the sea, and that may have been the reason why it has unusually high walls and no defensive ditch. These walls were, as Lawrence discovered when he undertook his restorations in the 1950s, built to an unusually strong standard, being brick all through and not just faced with brick as at Cape Coast Castle. As elsewhere, the fort was painted white. Apperley blasted at the rocks in hopes of finding a freshwater spring but without success. Unlike the Castle, therefore, Anomabu fort could be approached by land from all sides, although all the ground nearby was exposed to deadly enfilade fire from the bastions. If it were besieged, it would be dependent on whatever food, water, and armaments it had stocked up.

Architecturally, the fort at Anomabu was as plain and utilitarian as the Castle. Inside were private chambers for the governor and a handful of officers, a hall, living quarters for a small military garrison and for the Company's house slaves, and warehouses. The gunpowder magazine was located in the northwest bastion, and a vaulted slave prison was built into the northeast bastion. As at the Castle, the dungeon was divided into narrow compartments, presumably to keep the slaves segregated from one another, and to distinguish and control them more easily. Although the dungeon was above ground with small overhead gratings to let in some light and air, Apperley called it the 'slave hole,' as they did at the Castle.

Most of the building materials were brought from England, the Governing Committee calling for tenders in the three main ports from which the slaving ships sailed, London, Bristol, and Liverpool; and over 2 million crimson bricks, specially baked for hardness, arrived from various ports, usually in chartered vessels carrying 20,000 bricks a voyage. The lime was the finest from Portland on the English south coast. The stones used to filter the water came from Barbados. The shipping contracts were also put out to tender – materials could be sent from Britain to the roads at Anomabu for £4 a ton, plus tools, planking, and forty wheelbarrows. Everything was brought ashore by the local canoemen, the heaviest items in rafts lashed across more than one canoe to make catamarans. The order for 100,000 'iron canoe staples' may have been for building these craft. Among a full range of artillery sent out, were six 'twenty four pounders,' the heaviest guns anywhere on the Gold Coast. The total number of guns mounted was fifty, not including those that were lost when they were being brought ashore.

Trading continued while the construction work was going on. The Liverpool slavers listed the following vessels as sent to Anomabu in the year January 1754 to January 1755 alone, with a rounded estimate of how many slaves they might take:

*Juno*, Captain Eagles, 150 tons, 300 slaves, *Swallow*, Captain

Nelson, 100 tons, 200 slaves, *Marquis of Rockingham*,
Captain Charles, 200 tons, 400 slaves, *Britannia*, Captain
Hughes, 100 tons, 240 slaves, *Benin*, Captain Blunden,
200 tons, 400 slaves, *Ingram*, Captain Paisley, 150 tons, 260
slaves, *Will*, Captain Taylor, 100 tons, 250 slaves, *Nancy*,
Captain Cazneaux, 120 tons, 300 slaves.

Apperley sent streams of letters to London demanding ever larger
quantities and complaining of the quality of what was being sent.
He demands 'ten hundred thousand bricks' and, since no seashells
were available locally, 'four hundred tun of lime.' Of 25,000 tiles
landed, he complains, 5,000 were useless. Detailed accounts were
kept both in physical and financial terms, and sent to London. It is
recorded, for example, that the slave prison required 74,880 bricks.
The fort was operational, although not finished, by 1760. The cost
was put at £13,419, roughly the same as the British government's
annual grant for maintaining the Castle and existing forts.

The supervisory and skilled building work was done by a handful
of expatriate British craftsmen whom Apperley brought with him
from Britain. Other skilled workers were borrowed from the Castle
and the forts. But the main work of building Anomabu was done by
slaves, brought there for the purpose and specially trained on the spot.
The governor of the British fort in the Gambia, over a thousand miles
to the north, was directed to 'provide 60 of the best male slaves you
can procure from 14 to 20 years of age and not older.' (I have not been
able to discover whether, after their years in Anomabu, they were ever
returned to the Gambia, or – as seems more likely – they and their
descendents remained as Company slaves in the fort that they had
helped to build, or were added to the pool of skilled men at Cape
Coast Castle.) Apperley, as the first governor, was proud that he had
survived his seasoning, and that all the men had 'sickness and guinea
worms' except himself, but he died in the fort soon afterwards.

It was about the time that the new fort was being built that questions were raised by the British slaving industry at home about the role of the African Service. Had the 1750 Act simply produced the monopoly of the Royal African Company in a new guise? What was the purpose of building and maintaining these expensive forts, the slave-ship owners asked? Were they not, in essence, grand houses that enabled a spoiled group of uniformed officers to live at public expense in fine style and illegally take over the business that ought to belong to the ships? Brew's own solution, having resigned from the African Service and established himself at Anomabu as a private slave trader, was to build his own fort – Castle Brew, as he called it – with the approval of the local African political and religious authorities. Completed in 1764, it took the form of an enclosed quadrangle whose tall, inward-looking brick buildings, without a single outward-facing window, were designed primarily for physical security against break-ins by the local population. Inside, as in the fort, it had living quarters and warehouses, and there were a few guns, but Castle Brew made no pretensions to be other than a 'factory' in the original sense, a walled building in which goods could be temporarily housed. As can be seen from the aerial photograph on page 185, taken when it was less ruinous than it has since become, Castle Brew, the 'Little Fort,' was defiantly situated a few dozen yards from the official fort. According to the Dutch governor of Elmina Castle, who saw it when it was in use, it covered a larger ground area. I have not been able to find out whether it had slave dungeons – I think not. Brew preferred to keep his slaves in the dungeons at the official fort, paying the costs of lodging and feeding them until they were sent to the ships. Where the building materials for Castle Brew came from I do not know for certain, but it looks probable that some of the millions of bricks that Apperley had persuaded the British government to send were diverted. I would guess that he used the fort's slaves as his labor force.

The French, meanwhile, having failed to establish a shore facility at Anomabu, turned their attention to another site not far away, this time at Amoku, where they obtained the approval of the local leaders. Although the site was a quarter of a mile from the sea, with a more dangerous surf than at Anomabu, and the nearest source of reasonably fresh water two miles away, it was the best on the coast that had not already been occupied by the British, the Dutch, or the Danes. The flotilla of French warships and transports that arrived in 1786 landed 850 men, who were then accommodated in tents on shore. Within six weeks, however, 49 had died, 120 were sick, and 20 more were falling ill every day. Work was abandoned, and the flotilla sailed away. In later years other expeditions were sent from France, and a fort was eventually built from which small numbers of slaves were exported to the plantations in the French West Indies. By January 1788, however, the governor of Cape Coast Castle reported that 'only a few invalids remain there to hoist a flag as a mark of possession and fire a morning and evening gun.' With the outbreak of the French Revolution and the European wars that followed, and the French government's decision to ban the French slave trade, the soldiers in the fort were left isolated. They hung on for several years, their numbers steadily depleting by death, disease, and desertion, until – against the express wishes of the governor of Cape Coast Castle – the fort was bombarded and destroyed from the sea by a British warship. The remains of Amoku are still to be seen: a few overgrown ditches, broken bricks, and rusty cannon.

Anomabu soon became the main center of the British slave trade on the Gold Coast, with tens of thousands of men, women, and children held within its walls before being led through the 'door of no return' to the beach, the canoes, and the slave ships in the roads. In a letter of 1778, copies of which he sent to London by every ship sailing west, Governor Miles wrote to the secretary of the Governing Committee, a London underwriter who financed and took an equity share in many slaving voyages, telling his colleagues in Britain of a sudden influx of slaves, a resulting fall in prices, and the flocking of the rival vultures:

Mr. John Shoolbred
I am a little at a loss how to begin! What in God's name are you about; where is Martin & Clieland [captains of slave ships], or either of them? In this six weeks from the 7th August that they were to sail? Since my last, no less than a Dutch Storeship, a Danish Do. & three Portuguese are arrived, and all very lately. What is Clieland to do now with his Tobacco and Provisions? Surely they are not waiting for Convoy? & yet something seems to tell me they are. The Lord George Germain is to Wind[war]d & not yet come down. Cazneau sails with 540 Slaves; they do not stand him in more than £12 on an average; indeed not so much. You are certainly very unlucky in not having had your ships down e'er this. All I fear is, they'll stay so long, that they will have somebody upon their heels. Consider what great Voyages have been made lately

| Nelson at £17 | 337 |
| King at 15 | 303 |
| Rhein not quite 11 | 370 |
| Norris say 12 | 510 |
| Cazneau not 12 | 540 |

2060 Slaves on an average at £13:8 p[e]r Head.

No sooner this gets wind but out they flock 8 or 10 sail and then up goes Slaves again to £20 p[e]r H[ea]d. The Danes have now three Ships on the Coast ... I do not

believe I ever saw so large a lott of fine ones [slaves] in
my life in one ship.

According to former Governor Weuves when he was questioned
in 1789, Anomabu was 'the best built fort in Africa without any
exception.' And it gave its British masters a sense of invulnerability.
In 1791, when an attempt was made to kidnap fort governor Richard
Miles and two other officers, George Torrane and Edward White,
as part of a property dispute (see 'Panyarring' in Chapter 8), Miles
in 'atonement' fired one of his new guns on the town, set it on fire,
and it was burned down. For a time the whole Fante community
stopped all trade until a palaver brought the standoff to an end.
However, although modern, solid, and built for permanence, the
fort at Anomabu was soon as defenseless as all the others against
the wind, the rain, and the brine. Within a few years one bastion
collapsed, and the gun carriages rotted or rusted, as did the gates.
The floors buckled and the roofs leaked. Substantial repairs and
new works were authorized but the finest slaving fort in Africa was
still not fully completed when, after a series of political campaigns,
the British slave trade was declared illegal. The aspirations that it
was designed to embody, to display, and to render permanent in the
minds of the British, the local populations, and other nations, had
already passed into history.

From May 1, 1807, the Act of Parliament declared:

The African Slave Trade, and all manner of dealing and
trading in the Purchase, Sale, Barter, or Transfer of Slaves,
or of Persons intended to be sold, transferred, used or dealt
with as Slaves, practised or carried on, in, at, to or from any
Port of the Coast or Countries of Africa, shall be, and the
same is hereby abolished, prohibited, and declared to be
unlawful.

## 'A civil and well-bred people'

In that year came the first major invasion of the coastal states by the Asante, whose empire lay less than 200 miles to the north of Cape Coast Castle. That invasion was to be followed by others during the nineteenth century (see Chapter 9). The Asantes had a long history of conquering neighboring peoples, not least in order to acquire slaves to sell to slave merchants who took many of them to the coast to be sold to the ships. Among the motives behind the invasion was a wish to have direct trading links with the British and the other Europeans to whom the slaves were sold, so cutting out the middlemen in the coastal states. During the whole slaving era the Fante on the coast, with whom the Asante were ethnically and linguistically akin, tried to prevent the principals from direct contact. Other coastal peoples did the same, keeping the Asante landlocked. By the end of the eighteenth century the Fante were conspicuously richer, in terms of the European goods they took for granted, than the interior peoples.

The Asante army consisted of some tens of thousands of men, according to the British accounts. When they reached Cormantine, the Dutch surrendered the fort, and the Asante commander took possession, the first occasion ever in which an African army had possessed a European fort and European guns. As proof that he had reached the sea, the commander sent baskets of sea water to the king in Kumasi. Turning to the British, he sent a message to the governor of Anomabu, Edward White, demanding to be given twenty barrels of gunpowder and a hundred muskets; when he had received those indications of British submission, he declared, he would tell him what the king of Asante had decided to do. It was the biggest crisis ever to have occurred in relationships between the British and the peoples of this region of Africa. White sent a message offering a palaver about any grievances but declared that if the Asante attacked the people of Anomabu he would use the guns of the fort to defend them. He was honoring the guarantee to the local community that, here as elsewhere, was part of the bargain permitting the building of the Castle and the forts.

On June 14, 1807, the army of the people of Anomabu attacked a detached force of Asantes, but they had misjudged their strength and the Asante army entered the town of Anomabu and began to kill and capture the inhabitants. White took about 2,000 women, children, and older men into the fort, the maximum it could accommodate, and barred the gates. Other Anomabu townspeople huddled round the foot of the walls in the areas of ground that had been designed by Apperley to provide protection in such circumstances; enemies could not approach the walls without being exposed to deadly fire from the heavy guns of the fort's four carefully angled bastions. But the rhetoric of the fort had no power against men unable to read it. On June 15, for the first time ever, a British fort in Africa faced a hostile attack by an African army. The defenders consisted of five expatriate British officers of the African Service, four 'free mulattoes,' and twenty men described as 'soldiers, artificers and servants.' They did, however, have a state-of-the-art European military fort, specially designed for the site, with a wide range of modern artillery. On the other side was an army of men who outnumbered them by about fifty to one armed with flintlock muskets and iron-tipped arrows fired from bows.

In the first exchanges the Asante proved to be skilled marksmen, killing two men and wounding Governor White when they showed themselves on the ramparts. Former surgeon Meredith took command. But the defenders were unable to fire a single one of the heavy guns that bristled from the fort on all sides. No explanation was ever offered, but members of the African Service would not need to be reminded of rotted gun carriages, rusty wheels, honeycombed barrels, and embezzled ammunition. To the landward, with no firearms but muskets, the defenders were unable to prevent many of the women who had huddled under the useless guns from being seized and carried off into slavery. However, on the seaward side, the defenders did manage to fire two small 'three pounders' armed with canisters of deadly grapeshot. Since the Asante were pursuing the terrified people of Anomabu on to the beaches, that was where most of the killing took place.

The Asante army, which had never previously encountered European artillery, tried to attack the gates. Every blast struck down about twenty or thirty men, but others immediately took their place, to be slaughtered in turn. Meanwhile other Asante were engaged in killing the townspeople of Anomabu. On June 16, with the fort surrounded by thousands of decomposing bodies and flocks of vultures, a truce was agreed. Two British slave ships that had been in Cape Coast Castle roads arrived in the roads at Anomabu and, under cover of a smokescreen, three volunteering officers of the African Service, including Mr. Bold, together with a corporal and twelve soldiers, were landed by canoe. The remnants of the Asante army retreated inland, but the violence continued in the coastal regions for months afterwards.

Among the African peoples involved in the conflicts it was estimated that out of 15,000 inhabitants of Anomabu, about 10,000 died, as well as about 8,000 Fantes and at least 3,000 Asantes. Among the British the dead appear to have numbered four. And it was carefully recorded that White, the governor, suffered an arm wound and lost four teeth, and Meredith suffered pain in his shoulder from the recoil of a musket for some weeks, as did Francis Swanzy. It was another stirring tale of British pluck triumphing over British incompetence. As W. Walton Claridge wrote in his monumental *History of the Gold Coast*, echoing the language of the Old Testament, 'the gallant defense of Fort William by its small garrison against the hosts of Ashanti furnishes one of the finest chapters of the history of the English on the Gold Coast.'

After the fighting round Anomabu, we see the emergence of another British imperial cliché, the 'nobility' and 'dignity' of peoples whose first experience of an encounter with Europe was to have their men mown down by modern firearms. The Fante and other coastal peoples, among whom the British traded and lived in conditions of intimacy, and who had long since learned to take cover in the presence of European weapons, were routinely described as 'cowardly.' The Asante, however, whose aggression and slaving were feared by all the neighboring peoples, were quickly elevated in British imperial literature into fearless paragons of knightly virtue, even their festivals of human sacrifices excused. As James Swanzy, Francis's brother, told a parliamentary committee in 1816, 'It is a singular thing that these people, the Ashantee, who had never seen a white man, nor the sea, were the most civil and well-bred people that I have seen in Africa. It is astonishing to see men, with so few opportunities, so well-behaved.' As for the king of Asante, 'of all the native sovereigns of Africa that I have ever read or heard of, he is the man most likely to act in good faith.' As Kipling was to write, catching the attitudes of British soldiers to many African battles that resulted in heaps of dead Africans, from Sudan to Zululand, 'You're a poor benighted heathen, but a first-class fighting man.'

## Prospero's books again

In the records of the long palaver between the British and the Asante that took place in Cape Coast Castle over the following months, we hear the voice of the Asante commander, albeit filtered through British perceptions. Since the British could usually speak Fante, which is mutually comprehensible with the language of Asante, there is no reason to doubt the accuracy of the translation. Although the Asante army had not captured the fort, the commander claimed, they had undoubtedly defeated the Fantes. The king was, therefore, entitled to take their place in all respects, including receiving the payments that the Fantes had previously received from the British:

> The English know, with my own powder, with my own shot,
> I drove the Fantees under their forts, I spread my sword
> over them, they were all killed, and their books from the fort
> are mine. I can do as much for the English as the Fantees,
> they know this well . . . When the King of England takes
> a French town, he says, come this is mine, bring all your
> books, and give me all your pay . . . I must have the books.

Under the local laws and conventions under which the peoples of this region of Africa conducted their wars, he was right. Nor, for all the talk of gallantry, could it be doubted that the British bluff had been called and that their military power was largely a sham. If the Asante army had brought just one of the guns that they captured from the Dutch fort, they would have been able to destroy the most modern fort in Africa. Even without a gun, they could have blown down the walls with a barrel of gunpowder or stormed the walls with ladders. Governor Torrane acknowledged the Asante victory in letters to London and flew a white flag at Cape Coast Castle, but took care not to concede anything in writing. Nor was the lesson lost on the coastal peoples, who could see that the two aggressively imperializing slaving nations, the British and the Asante, which they had sought to keep separated, might prefer to hunt together.

Under a show of parades, presents, ceremonies, and declarations of mutual esteem and friendship the British rushed to give the Asante what was demanded. In accordance with custom and with the agreement, Torrane handed over to their enemies a group of refugees who had sought safety in Cape Coast town expecting to be protected by the Castle, destined, like all the losers, to be either redeemed or sold to slave merchants and eventually sent off the coast. The whole population of Amoku, the town that had invited in the French, were, for example, already among the many thousands enslaved and sold.

But what of the people of Anomabu who had been given refuge by the British in the fort? In modern terms, they were civilian refugees who had been fortunate to survive the disasters that had struck their community and they would have been allowed back to the remains of their homes nearby, homes that had been destroyed a second time within a generation. In slaving era terms, however, they too were spoils of war. After negotiations in which it was accepted that neither the Asantes nor the British had been defeated, Torrane agreed to divide the refugees, half and half, with the Asantes. How the division took place is not recorded, but presumably the Asantes added the men, women, and children that fell to them as their share to the many slaves they already possessed as a result of their invasion. As far as the British share is concerned, according to a testimonial written by Henry Hamilton, governor of Tantam fort, dated September 10, 1807:

> Colonel Torrane made the Ashantees a very considerable
> Present, in the European [unreadable] at Annomaboe,
> sent out of 1,300 Women and children who had received
> Protection of Mr. White, during the Engagement with the
> Ashantees, Colonel Torrane did at night Ship 100 of the
> choicest of them on board the Ship Swift in Payment for
> a Barter with Mr. Thos. Bynon [a merchant on shore] and
> received the Goods for the same.

Slave ships from Britain and many other nations that had flocked to the Gold Coast to fight over what they thought would be their last poor pickings before the British slave trade ended in May 1807 found instead that they were offered an ongoing feast of new disasters. Torrane's first hundred would have brought him £2,500.

But, even for the African Service, Torrane's decision not only

*21. Anomabu fort in 2003, showing the embrasures for the guns, the exposed English red bricks, and the perennial vulture.*

to disobey British law but to sell the refugees of Anomabu was carrying respect for the local laws and customs of war too far. Henry Hamilton, who blew the whistle about what was going on, was summoned to Cape Coast Castle and suspended from duty – he died before he could be dismissed. James Swanzy, governor of Accra fort, whose son Francis had fired 300 musket shots during the attack on the fort at Anomabu, left his sickbed to take the long canoe journey to Cape Coast Castle to protest. As Swanzy had been a colleague of Torrane for nearly twenty years, when he threatened to write to London to demand an inquiry, the governor was persuaded to set the remaining refugees free but not before 'most had disappeared along the paths or under the horizon.'

When Governor Torrane died in the Castle shortly after these events, the excuses and exonerations followed him like the band at his funeral: given the situation he found himself in, he had had no alternative but to yield to the brave Ashantees; in the end what he did was for the best; he saw the big picture; he realized that British interests required good relations; and so on. But a hundred years later, even the great imperialist historian Claridge squirmed. Colonel Torrane may have had to hand over half the refugees, Claridge argued, but 'it was the use the Governor made of those that he had saved that must be cavilled at.'

British romantic writers and artists, following the tradition of the churchmen of the pre-Enlightenment, liked to imagine and present the apocalyptic end that would, they believed, sooner or later engulf modern Britain. For although the slave trade was brought to an end, slavery itself was still in place. A century later Rudyard Kipling was still warning of the judgement to come: 'Far call'd our navies melt away / on dune and headland sinks the fire. / Lo, all our pomp of yesterday / is one with Nineveh and Tyre!' The picturesque ruins of the British slaving fort at Anomabu evoke the unregretted past more vividly than any other monument of the slave trade.

# 8

# The emporium

Neither the governors of Cape Coast Castle nor the slave-ship captains knew where most of the people whom they bought and sold had originally come from. Indeed it was part of their political stance that these were questions that they had no responsibility for inquiring into. They knew, from day-to-day experience, that a minority of the slaves they bought, estimated at about a quarter, came from the coastal states in the immediate hinterland of the Castle and the forts, and that many others came from Asante, marched, already shackled, through the forest paths, and that their first sight of the sea was also their first sight of men with skin color that was not black. They knew too that many of the people whom they bought did not originate from Asante, but came from communities conquered by, and subject to, the Asante empire, or who had been brought to Asante as slaves from further inland. Governor Hippisley, one of the few who took an interest, noticed the variety of mutually incomprehensible languages, the fact that some men and women were decoratively scarified and others not, and that a few were so pale in complexion as to be of North African or Middle Eastern appearance. Hippisley speculated, correctly, that the interior of Africa was not a desert, as some Europeans believed, but luxuriant and well populated, and that the slaves brought to the Castle may have come from the whole of the vast area of sub-Saharan Africa, east as well as west, and even beyond. It was only in the Asante invasion of 1807, during which men literate in Arabic who had seen the Mediterranean were found among the Asante army, that the British in the Castle began to understand.

Modern researchers, notably Akosua Adoma Perbi, have established that there were about thirty inland slave markets in the territory of modern Ghana in addition to the thirty or so on the coast, of which the most active was Salaga in the north – now a site of memory as important as the European castles and forts on the coast. And Salaga was itself linked with a network of markets and routes that exported slaves to the north and east as well as to the south. When, in the mid-nineteenth century, the British authorities in Sierra Leone interviewed slaves freed by the British Navy from captured illegal slave ships, they found that some had come from places a thousand miles from the sea in the area of Lake Chad.

The enslavement of most of those sent off the coast from Cape Coast Castle occurred far from the eyes of any European. Many slaves were said to have been prisoners of war, and the losers in wars were, according to local laws and customs, legitimately enslaved, but, with the exception of the destructive Asante invasion of 1807, there were few wars in the coastal areas during the time when the legal British slave trade boomed, and they were on a small scale. As for the slaves arriving from inland, the British surgeons noticed that few showed any sign of having taken part in fighting, for example by having healed wounds. It is now established that one of the main sources of slaves was slave raiding, which included aggressive wars aimed at obtaining slaves as well as individual kidnappings. Modern research, collected by Sylviane A. Diouf, has identified many forms of defense and resistance adopted by the peoples in the raided areas, such as building refuges in mountain caves or on islands in river estuaries.

## Buying

The British had to pay fees to the local authorities in each of the coastal states and towns where a British fort was located if they wanted to buy slaves, a cost to be taken into account in commercial decisions but also a source of legitimacy. At Whydah in Dahomey, a kingdom with a strong central government that was itself deeply involved in the transatlantic slave trade, the duty was related to the number of masts that a slave vessel carried. According to Surgeon McLeod, the governor of the British fort, like those of the French and Portuguese forts in the same town, paid twenty-one slaves for a three-masted ship, fourteen for a brig or schooner, and seven for a cutter or a sloop, 'being in short seven for each mast.' Elsewhere a duty was payable on each slave. A note that Thomas Miles, governor of the small unfortified factory at Popo, wrote in the inside cover of his trading book mentions the amounts: 'Lattie receives an oz trade [about £4] on every slave sold in this factory except those sold by Quaw. The broker generally takes another oz so that yr trade loses 2 oz [about £8] on a slave.' These payments also appear in the daily buying books, itemized, for example, as 'custom on a slave.' Although the prices paid for men were invariably higher than those for women, at Anomabu the customs duty was the same for both sexes at 0.6 oz (about £2.4) per head. In the later eighteenth century the flow of foreign-exchange equivalent into local exchequers that these payments brought about was far greater than the payments made by the Castle as rents.

Many slaves were bought by the captains direct from local African rulers, dealers, brokers, and individuals, or from a few private British traders established ashore. Between July 1775 and April 1776, for example, Richard Brew, the former African Service officer who had set up as a private trader with his own warehouse in Anomabu, is recorded as having bought and sold 780 slaves. James Lane, another private trader, whose name suggests that he also may have been an expatriate British living ashore, is recorded as selling

*22. Slaves outside the Portuguese fort at Whydah in Dahomey, 1849.*

250 slaves a year to the shipping in Anomabu roads. The following note, of about 1776, was prepared by the governor of that fort for the guidance of his successor:

> Aggah [Egya slave market] and Cormantyn [Kormantse slave market] traders seldom or ever go near the fort, while there's a ship in the road; notwithstanding which, if any of them, such as Tom Coffee, Adwesoe, Ado, or any of the principals should call, treat them kindly and make them believe you like them whether you do or not.

The scale of activity is evident from the letter books and the reports to London. For example, at Cape Coast Castle on July 23, 1751, the governor noted, 'The *Flamborough*, Captain Jepson of New England, 150 slaves going off, The *Gally*, Captain Ellis of

Bristol, 300 slaves almost, The *Keith,* New England, finished, 115 slaves.' But these large figures conceal the fact that most slaves were bought individually, or in ones and twos, over long periods, with the transactions each taking many hours or days to complete.

In some modern writings it is implied that human life was cheap, and in some senses that may have been true. But, in financial terms, a slave who could be sold off the coast was never cheap to buy, and as demand rose, so did prices. The following table, for West Africa as a whole, gives an indication of quite how steep that increase was.

**Estimated slave prices, Atlantic coast of Africa, £ sterling per person bought**

| | |
|---|---|
| First half of eighteenth century | 5 to 6 |
| 1783–87 | 15.6 |
| 1800s immediately before abolition | 33.2 |

I have not found estimates of the prices inland during the eighteenth century. But at Salaga, where slave trading continued until the early twentieth century, there are scattered records of nineteenth-century prices, some less than £1 per person. If, as there is no reason to doubt, inland prices during the slaving era responded to the prices paid by the ultimate buyers, the profits of slave raiding and trading accruing within Africa were large. As for the transatlantic leg of the trade, as a rule of thumb the slaves who were landed in good health in the Americas fetched about double the prices at which they were bought in Africa, a ratio that seems to have been quite stable. As for profitability, at the time when the British abolition bill was going through Parliament, the Liverpool slaving industry compiled an estimate of the losses the city would sustain. They claimed that each year a total of about £2,000,000 was employed, which produced a net return of 15 percent; in other words it was a huge industry but also an extremely costly one to operate, and net profitability was not unusually high.

Although the prices of slaves at the coast were set in direct negotiations between the selling dealers and the buying captains, the local political, religious, and judicial authorities also bargained with the Castle governors:

**October 26, 1777, diary of Cape Coast Castle**
[A]t 8 this morning came into the Castle Amooney
Coomah, the Cudo Pynims [family heads and judges],
and almost every Caboceer [political leader] belonging to
Annamabue to talk with me respecting the Price of Slaves.
[The governor describes the discussion and threats from
both sides, then reports the day's outcome.] . . . agreed that
all should remain quiet untill either the Europeans chuse to
raise the Price, or the Blacks agree the Price now offered . . .

**October 31, 1777, diary of Cape Coast Castle**
[T]his Day Aban, Aggerie, Tom Coffee & sundry others
went on board the Adventure in this road & agreed with
Capt. Muir, at 8½ men & 6½ wom. [Ounces of gold per
person, about £34 for men and £26 for women.] At 1 o'clock
they all came on shore, as did the Capt. to acquaint me
every thing was settled.

As prices rose, the African suppliers increasingly demanded to be paid, in part, in gold, not just in the equivalent in goods, and this affected the behaviour of the buyers.

**May 15, 1773, Daniel McCarthy of the ship *Thomas* to
Richard Miles, governor of Tantam fort**
[W]hat's Goold I have is at yr Service upon your promise of

Annamaboe Fort — 1776.

March 19th

23. *Typical page from the barter book of Richard Miles, when governor of Anomabu fort, 1776. The left-hand column gives the accumulating number of slaves purchased, the next is the amount of gold he paid as part of the transaction, and the right-hand column lists the value of the goods, also measured in gold ounces.*

giving me all the woomen you can, and all the Goold I can
get here after you may depend on only dont menshon my
name in the Goold way for a reason I beleive you may gess,
as to the 24 ounces of Goold you recd before you may send
the Slaves when it is most conveniant to you

To avoid the risks of sending packets of gold dust across the surf, the
Castle provided banking and safe-deposit services to both sellers
and buyers, with a grand reconciliation of mutual liabilities shortly
before a ship sailed, and only very occasional transfers of the metal
itself. Such arrangements also reduced the time-wasting business
of testing the purity of the gold; many inexperienced captains,
particularly Americans, who had no shore facilities, discovered
too late that their gold dust was adulterated with brass filings. By
conducting much of their business with the British in the Castle
on paper credit – 'notes' – the African suppliers of the eighteenth-
century slave trade were already integrated into the international
'gold standard' payments system that lasted until 1914.

More important than gold were the armaments that, like the
other goods imported from the ships, were taken inland along the
forest paths to barter for the slaves brought in the other direction.
In Birmingham, a city in England where armaments were
manufactured, it was said that one musket equaled one slave, and
the tag catches the direct link between the supplying of firearms
from the ships and the use of these arms in Africa to capture slaves
in wars and raids. On the coast, however, even before the steep
rise in the later eighteenth century, the price of buying slaves was
many times higher than the saying implies, as this example from an
account book from Dixcove fort in 1730 shows: 'bartered for 5 men
slaves 25 large, 1 middling, 39 sheets, 3 long ells [cloths], 26 trading
guns, 4 fine guns, 40 pounds gunpowder.'

During the eighteenth century several hundred thousand

European firearms were imported into West Africa every year, many of which made their way inland and some into the hands of slave raiders. Indeed, looking at the complex assortments of goods, gold, and guns that feature in many of the recorded barters, it appears as if the suppliers on their return inland were concerned to take the weaponry to ensure more supplies. In the private barter account-books of Richard Miles, governor of Cape Coast Castle, written in 1778, he notes the accumulating totals of slaves that he has bought, divided into M[en], W[omen], B[oys], and G[irls]. He notes the name of the sellers, and the amount of goods he paid in exchange, mainly cloths, guns, gunpowder, brandy, and small metalwares, which he values in terms of gold ounces. Below are some examples from his barter books written when he was governor of Anomabu fort in 1776:

> bartered for a woman, Kuah's, and a boy, Tikies, at oz 6.15 [about £25 each], [cloths of various kinds,] 6 ankers [barrels of brandy], 1 pan, 1 keg tallow, 2 guns, 1 oz powder [gold ounce worth of gunpowder, around £4], 1 roll tobacco [normally about 6 feet long]
> total oz 14/14 [about £50]
>
> bartered for 3 men, 4 women, and a boy, Amuno's, [cloths of various kinds,] 44 ankers, 24 pans, 6 gallons rum, 1 oz powder . . .

The same names appear regularly: 'bartered for a small girl, Appia's, 2 men, Amuno's, and 2 men, Quashi Kuah's'; 'bartered for a boy, Jemmy Quo's'; 'bartered for a girl, Amuno's'; 'bartered for a small boy, Botty's.' Some slaves are noted as having been bought from 'Stranger,' 'Stranger speaks English,' and 'Stranger (very saucy fellow).' It would be possible to list the names of hundreds of men selling slaves. Although difficult to judge when so many men had the same name, the African sellers, like the European buyers, appear to have operated a network along the same narrow strip of the landward and seaward side of the coast.

The British bought men, women, boys, and girls. They bought more men than women in a changing ratio of about 4 to 3, and the prices they paid for women were always lower, although not in the same proportion. This gender imbalance reflected the wishes of the planters in North America and the West Indies. What the planters wanted were fit young men to do heavy work in gangs in the fields and in the processing industries. But the planters were also trying to improve the rate at which transported slaves produced children, so reducing their dependency on slaves born in Africa whom they had to buy.

Since the slaves bought at the Castle, and elsewhere on the Gold Coast, were reputed to be larger and stronger than those obtainable elsewhere in Africa, they commanded a premium price, but they could normally only be bought in smaller numbers. A round-trip slaving voyage from a slaving port in Britain to the Gold Coast and the West Indies could take fifteen to eighteen months, compared with ten months to slave markets further east in the Niger delta, even although geographically the latter were further away.

By modern standards, however, all the people who were sold, bought, and sent off the coast from the Castle were small, with fully grown men seldom above five feet tall. And many of the 'men' were only teenagers, 'men' being males who had reached the age of puberty. The final customers in the Americas, especially the Jamaican planters, were exact in their specifications. The 'men' they demanded had to be aged between fourteen and twenty to be regarded as 'prime.' Since males who were a little younger, described as 'manboys,' might be accepted as 'men' and fetch the full price when they were sold some months later in the Americas, much effort went into discovering exactly when young males were likely to reach full puberty. According to fort governor Westgate, the captains of Portuguese slave ships licked their faces searching for indications of beard. With female slaves too, the judgement whether a person was a 'womangirl' or a 'woman,' crucial to both the buying and the selling price, sometimes required intimate examination of their bodies. As for the slaves who were undoubtedly still children, they were carefully recorded by height: 'bartered for a girl 4 f[ee]t 1 in[ches],' 'bartered for a boy 3 f[ee]t 6 in[ches],' '2 boys of 4 f[eet]t 2 in[ches],' 'a small girl.' In the 1790s Thomas Miles, a brother of Richard, divided his slave-buying notes into columns for men, manboys, boys, women, womengirls and girls. The boys were listed in nine bands ranging from 4 feet 2 inches to 3 feet 4 inches, the girls in six bands from 4 feet 3 inches to 3 feet 8 inches. Among his purchases in November 1794 was '1 undersized girl,' who presumably was even smaller.

The buyers in the Americas thought they could distinguish different national characteristics among the slaves bought from coastal markets in various parts of Africa. But the slaves they obtained from the Castle were often brought there from forts far along the coast where the local peoples had different customs, languages, diets, and physical characteristics. In October 1730, for example, Accra fort sent 61 men, 23 women, 7 boys, and 6 girls, an operation that would have required a flotilla of canoes on a voyage of two days if they all went together. Occasionally, however, the captains did distinguish slaves by their local origin rather than solely by gender, age, height, and physical condition.

**No date, Captain Dear of the ship *Fly* to a governor onshore**
[A]s the woman you sent me the night before you left is a Benin slave therefore cant think of keeping her as it may

prove to be a great detriment to my average in the West Indies. in case she was taken notice of, hope you have no objection to changing her

**1773, Captain Goodwin to the governor of Tantam fort**
In respect to the women slave I have on board I must have as prime fante women as the Coast can afford

Slaves were transferred along the coast both by land and sea:

**October 20, 1749, William Dacres of Pram Pram fort to the governor of Accra fort**
This goes by the five hand Canoe, by which I send 2 Men Boy Slaves one with a sore toe, and the other I think looks sickly but was obliged to buy him on the lump. I would send the rest by Land tomorrow but don't care to trust the Men without a Collar, so hope you will send it with the Hamockmen. I have now 24 Slaves, (exclusive of the two I now send) all paid for . . .

'Collar' is a slaver's euphemism. All men slaves appear to have been shackled at all times: before their arrival on the coast, when they were sold and bought, when they were in the Castle dungeons, when they were being embarked into the canoes and taken aboard the ships, when they were waiting for the ships to sail, and during the middle passage. The practice of branding slaves like cattle, with the mark of their new owner – well documented for an earlier period when many were branded with the letters 'DY' for the Duke of York, the future James II of England and VII of Scotland – continued. This made it possible to identify and segregate the slaves in the compartments in the Castle dungeons and then, if they had been bought on commission, to identify when they arrived at their destination.

**August 23, 1775, Captain Thomas Gullan of the sneau**
*Roebuck* **to Richard Miles at Anomabu**
Receive by this Canoe Eighty Brass pans. Send of[f] the Marking Irons when you have done with them

**March 23, 1776, the captain of the ship *Sally* to Miles**
Per return of Canoe you'll receive 10 Pair of Irons for the Legs & as many hand Irons – all I have to beg is that you will return the same by return as near as possible.

The slave-ship owners, by making a contract with the Castle governors, were able to order the persons their customers wanted for delivery in the Americas at a specified time and destination, so minimizing the number of months that the slave ships would spend on the triangular oceanic voyage. In much writing on the transatlantic slave trade, the middle passage of five or six weeks with slaves packed on board is understandably seen as central. In commercial terms, however, it was less significant to the slaving industry than the six months to a year that some ships spent cruising or anchored off the African coast. It is now established that more embarked slaves died when the ships were lying off the coast than on the transatlantic passage, but when they did, the empty slots could be filled. Although the slave-ship owners managed to reduce the mortality rate on the middle passage, that was of less commercial importance to them than reducing the number of months the ships spent off the coast of Africa, their hulls and sails rotting in the tropical damp, their crews mutinous, and their embarked slaves an expense, a danger, and – because of deaths and illness – an asset of eroding financial value.

The Castle governors, by being told in advance when the ships of their favored business partners would arrive, could accumulate slaves in the Castle and fort dungeons to await the arrival of their ships. In some cases the governors bought slaves for their partners on commission, so that slaves were already 'owned' by favored planters before they left Africa. In others, the governors were paid a percentage of the net proceeds when the slaves were sold in the Americas. While they were waiting for the ships of their partners to arrive, governors would refuse to sell to other ships whose owners were not in the partnership. Ships in these partnerships arriving on the coast could therefore sell their goods and 'slave up' far more quickly than other ships. Such contracts had penalty clauses that put the financial risk on to the governors if they could not supply the slaves they had contracted to provide on the due dates.

Ordering slaves *à la carte* was explained in a pamphlet of 1772, *A Treatise on the Trade to Great-Britain from Africa*, in which a group of slave-ship owners attacked the African Service for damaging their business by making exclusionary deals with favored partners. Quoted here are the actual figures used. A planter in the West Indies contracts with a governor in Africa for '1,500 slaves deliverable in twelve months, at four different periods, at a stipulated price of 22 sterling for every merchantable negro, two thirds males, one third female.' The specifications were laid down in detail, for example, 'one hundred and twenty prime men, not to exceed 27 years of age, as near as can be judged, eighty boys, four feet, four inches and upward, thirty four boys from three feet ten inches to four feet three inches; seventy women not to exceed 24 years, twenty five women girls, twenty one girls from four feet to four feet three inches.' The partner charged the governor a penalty of £9 for every slave short. The ship is to stay two calendar months if the governor cannot supply in time for which he pays £30 per day demurrage. Both parties give sureties for £5,000.

Since 'a prime man slave' was a currency as immediately

negotiable as gold or gunpowder, we see lending and borrowing, as well as buying and selling, between all three parties involved: the African suppliers, the Castle and fort governors, and the ships' captains. 'Lending' did not mean transferring the actual person in the expectation of getting him or her back, but an obligation by the borrower to provide a person of comparable gender, age, and health at some fixed future date. Occasionally Governor Richard Miles noted some feature that shows how concerned he normally was only to buy people who were both immediately saleable and easily exchangeable: 'a woman (wanting three teeth),' 'a woman wanting a toe,' 'a man, rather elderly.' The grand emporium, besides being a repository where slaves could be temporarily lodged, acted as a multilateral clearance facility, with transactions in and out, as traders and captains tried to meet their commercial aims in rapidly changing situations. A captain keen to fill his last few slots before sailing would pay a premium price to avoid losing time. If a captain intended to stay for some time, he would sell slaves he already had on board, expecting to replace them later at a lower price. For example, a receipt dated December 6 (no year) confirms the sale of 'one Prim[e] Woman Slave from Deck' for goods worth £40.

In the rush to complete a slave cargo before a ship sailed, children were particularly valuable, and since they could be packed on board to run about the decks without being shackled, every extra child loaded at the last minute represented pure profit at the other end of the voyage. In 1776, for example, a ship offered a governor 'three very fine boys at 25 sterling per head.' In 1780 a captain who sold a boy to the Castle in part exchange for a woman was charged £12, another premium price. In Richard Miles's record of child barters for 1791, when he was governor of Accra fort, against each child he has noted 'shipp'd.'

As for the slaves, they might find themselves embarked on one ship and chained there for months, only to be suddenly taken back on shore or moved to another ship. Brothers might be separated, as was reported by Surgeon Falconbridge, and children taken from their mothers. Parentless children, who might have begun to build some attachment with prisoners, could find themselves suddenly separated. And although we see the cruelties of uprooting and separation at the African end of the slave trade with especial vividness, the British slavers were acting in accordance with laws that operated not only in Africa but throughout the areas of the oceanic world under British, and then United States, jurisdiction. The Colonial Debt Act of 1732, which lasted until the end of the legal slave trade, and far later in the United States, made slaves as well as other forms of property liable to be seized as payment for debt, uniformly throughout the British colonies in America and elsewhere. That act was described by the planters as '[t]he English merchants' grand security.' It also applied in and around the grand emporium.

In this market a governor who had difficulties in finding the slaves he had contracted to supply at the due time could be squeezed into paying extremely high prices to avoid incurring the penalties, and the risk of bankruptcy. Besides borrowing slaves from whomever would lend, at exorbitant rates, a governor could send out instructions to his subordinates in the forts to get him slaves at whatever price, and by whatever means, fair or foul. Anthony How, a botanist, who visited the coast on board a British warship in 1785, told the parliamentary inquiry in 1790 of an episode he witnessed:

> When I was at Secundee [Sekondi], an order came from
> Cape Coast Castle, but for what purpose I cannot tell,
> however, the same afternoon between 4 and 5 o clock,
> several parties went out armed and returned the same night
> with a quantity of slaves which were put in the repository
> belonging to the factory. The following morning I saw

several men and women coming to see their friends who
were imprisoned, and requested of Mr. Marsh, the resident
at Secundee, to release some of their children and relations;
some of them were released, and a part of them sent off to
Cape Coast Castle – but on what terms they were released I
cannot say.

When asked about the instruments of coercion, he replied:

> . . . they consisted of different kinds of chains made of iron,
> as likewise an instrument made of wood, about five inches
> long, and an inch in diameter, or less, which I was told by
> Mr. Marsh was thrust into a man's mouth horizontally,
> and tied behind, to prevent him from crying out, when
> transported at night along the country.

The same inquiry asked former governor Richard Miles, already by
then the grand old man of the African Service living off his fortune
in Wallingford in England, the question that must occur to anyone
who knows even a little about the African end of the transatlantic
slave trade. And we not only see him wriggling but, despite having
been governor-in-chief, trying to excuse himself from all responsibility, even to the extent of denying that he had any right to have
an opinion. We also see how, in order to have something to say, he
invoked notions of essential racial difference as justifications for his
cruelty:

> Do you apprehend that the Negroes sent abroad to our
> settlements in the West Indies are more or less attached to
> their wives, families, and relations, than the Europeans are?

> MILES: I do not know if I ever made any particular

observations on that head – If it had been possible to have foreseen that I should have been questioned to that head, there are many other points of information as well as this I should have endeavoured to make myself more master of.

Then can you not give any further answer to this question, having resided there eighteen years?

MILES: I do not believe affection is very predominant in the breast of the Negroes – If I were to give an opinion, I should think it rather otherwise.

Asked about the judicial processes under which men, women, and children were enslaved, he said that they received 'as fair a trial as in any other part of the world.'

## Skin color boundary

When a slave ship ran aground, or was unable to make the oceanic voyage back for some other reason, an auction sale was held in the Castle. On April 14, 1794, for example, 105 slaves from Gabon, far to the south, were sold at an auction among the officers, and presumably later resold to the slave ships. On February 12, 1806, the ship *Mary*, on her way to the Americas, was captured by a French naval squadron and, according to the owners, 'after taking out the principal part of the goods, all the ivory, and all the slaves except a few old ones, she was given up to the crew to bring them to some British port.' When she arrived at the Castle, Governor Torrane sold the fourteen rejected slaves at auction for the benefit of the insurers, including one boy and '1 mulatto slave' at £32 each. (This is one of the few cases I have found of a person of mixed race being sold off the coast. I have found none of whites.)

Although Chaplain Thompson had declared in his book that

the enslavement of Christians, as well as non-Christians, was endorsed by the Bible, and therefore by Christianity, the records show that, with the growing numbers of people of part European/part African descent living near the Castle, the skin color boundary increasingly transcended considerations of education, religion, or culpability. On February 25, 1790, for example, William Fielde, the governor of the Castle, told the Governing Committee in London that Richard Davis, a soldier, reprieved from the gallows, 'has been in the Slave Hole two thirds of the time since his arrival.' The governor recommended that in future the law should take its course 'as it is extremely repugnant and hurtful to our feelings to confine this man almost perpetually in a loathsome dungeon.' Governor Fielde had no legal authority to sell a British expatriate soldier, but neither had he any legal authority to sell Africans, whether slaves or people he caught stealing. His letter shows how 'men of feeling,' more interested in their own tender emotions than in their direct responsibilities for the miseries of others, found a way through the contradictions by developing, or taking a free ride on, notions of inherent racial differences, establishing hierarchies based on skin color that had been largely absent a generation earlier, and then acting upon them administratively as cases arose.

Supporters of the transatlantic slave trade complained that their opponents were guilty of double standards. Why did they fuss about the transportation of African criminals – as Governor Hippisley complained, 'scarce one of them is ever sold, unless for very great crimes' – when British criminals were also transported across the ocean to harsh penal service in North America, and later Australia, with the full authority of British laws and British religions? To an extent this was a debating point – the British criminals sent abroad were never regarded as 'property,' nor did the children of women criminals inherit their slave status. But the main reason why anglophone American plantation owners preferred blacks to whites was that they were better able to survive the climate and therefore to do the work. In the mainland colony of Maryland, for example, between 1767 and 1775, British and Irish convicts were being sold as laborers for about £16 each at a time when Africans ordered *à la carte* from Africa fetched three times this price.

Other slaves could be obtained at the closed sales held in the Castle when a colleague died. At the sale of the effects of John Bartlett, who died in 1785, for example, we see a wide range of prices, all of which the rules of the sale required should be paid in gold:

to John Dowling a man slave £17/17/0
to Thomas Miles a man slave £25
to John Dowling a man slave 'lunatic' £1
to Thomas Miles a boy 4f[ee]t 2 inches £23/5/0
to James Mourgue a boy 3f[ee]t 10 inches, yawed [suffering
    from yaws, a skin disease] £6/10
to James Morgue a girl 4f[ee]t 2 1/2 inches £15/5/0
to John Cleland [not the captain] a boy 3f[ee]t 11 inches,
    yawed, £4/15
to Thomas Miles a woman slave £17
to Philip Quaque a very old woman slave £2/5

(This is the only reference I have found of Chaplain Quaque's participating in a sale of slaves. Since we do not know what happened to the woman, who was unlikely to be saleable to the slave ships, it is impossible to say what his motives may have been.)

The range of buying prices at the sale of the possessions of Joseph Carless, governor of Accra fort, who died in the Castle in 1786, was also wide: 'A man slave £24, a boy £8/5, a man £23/5 to James Morgue, an old woman slave £4, a small boy £4 to Adam Bannerman, a woman £27, a man with one eye £16, a man boy slave £28/15, an old man £4/14.' Most unusually, one record preserves a few names, although the first two slaves have names imputed to them by their British 'owners' from the forts from which they were presumably brought: 'a manboy named Accra £36,' 'a ditto named Prampram £44,' 'a manboy named Quashie £37,' 'a manboy 3 feet 10 inches named Zey, £19/15,' 'a ditto named Ajebrebee, £29.' At the sale of the effects of Joseph Jennings in 1803, 'a woman and 2 children £10/3/0.'

## In the Castle

Given that the capacity of the slave dungeons at the Castle and Anomabu alone was over 2,000 persons, and given what is known about the scale of the trade, the numbers mentioned as being lodged in the Castle during the eighteenth century appear small. Maybe the traffic in and out was so intensive that many slaves were only there for a short time. On July 7, 1753, for example, Governor Roberts wrote to a slave-ship captain:

> . . . your Slaves, 18 in the Castle in Good health, 3 in Town, 2 of them in a bad way, 1 died yesterday. James tells me he wants some Liquor to give them in the morning a Dram and some Pipes and Tobacco waits your orders for that Purpose. Excuse heast Going on board the Flamborough to Dine.

The 1770 rules of the Castle, which were prominently displayed, read: '7th that no sick slave be kept in the fort on any consideration whatever.' They do not say what should be done with them; nor is it recorded how the bodies should be dealt with, although slave-ship captains threw them overboard without ceremony.

A Castle inventory of January 1779 lists as 'slaves for sale': '6 men at £18 each, 4 women at £14 each.' For December 1779 the list of 'slaves for sale' records a larger number at a lower price:'40 men at £17, 19 women at £13.' As part of their response to the charge by the slave-ship owners that the governors were stealing their business, they were instructed to provide the captains with a list of all the slaves they had in the Castle available to be bought. In the same inventory the Company's own 'slaves and pawns' – slaves for sale, not Castle slaves – are included at the same prices: '51 men at £17, 12 women at £13.'

## Embarking

The letters carried by canoe between ship and shore speak for themselves:

### 1773, Captain Goodwin to Richard Miles
. . . I sincearly Congratulate you on your Safe arvell in Africa, Should have stopt with you but have no officer on board and no Water for My Slaves and am mutch out of ardor My Self . . .

### June 10, 1775, Captain Cayzneau at Cape Coast Road
. . . I received yours with five very indifrent Men Slaves I am sorry to send two of them ashor again But Could not take them By No Means there not Such Slaves as I should Got off Mr Trinder [governor of Accra fort, who had recently died] Had a lived. I am sorry to say that I have Ben obloyge to Tak very Bad Slaves . . .

### July 20, 1775, ship *Hector*
Recd by your canoe 2 Men Slaves and two oz Gold with a Letter from Mr. Westgate. All Right

**July 27, 1775, Captain King at Cape Coast roads**
I received your Esteemed favour This Moment which was
Delivered on Board this morning with 10 Slaves, 5 of which
I must return You as they are either old or scorbuticall . . . I
would have Returned the Slaves by this canoe but she is very
Deep with Tobacco and the Sea dangerously High

**August 6, 1775, John Chilcott of the ship *Hector***
I have on board belonging to myself oz 5 Prime Goods &
Oz 2 [abbreviation not read in full] of Gold Youll Oblige me
much by finding me a Prime Woman for the Above. If you
have one in the Fort or Give me an Order on Captain Noble
– I shall sail this Night if we get a Breeze off the land.

**September 1, 1775, Captain Thomas Gullan of the sneau
*Roebuck***
I have returned one of the Men and given Mr. Miles Credit
for three Men and two Women. There is only one prime
Slave amongst the others is but barely passable

**September 21, 1775, Captain Clement Noble of the (soon to
be notorious) ship *Brookes***
 I have recd. 3 Men and one woman the other Six I have
sent back as they are by no means merchantable they being
old, Dropsical, and with swell'd testicles. I shall be obliged
to you to send of[f] my empty Casks and Trunks when you
have any empty Canoes coming of[f] in the road

**December 23, 1776, Captain Clement Noble of the *Brookes***
Pray sir what was your meaning for ordering all the goods
back that were sent ashore.

At the ocean's edge a named individual could suddenly become a nameless interchangeable commodity:

**1798, George Lawson, a slave-ship captain, to Thomas Miles, at Popo fort**
Lattee yesterday talk'd of selling a Man called Quee – Avoursee's Son – ask him if he will sell him . . .

Moreover, in some cases, in addition to taking away names, the slavers employed another dehumanizing and distancing device:

**February 16, 1794, John Lyndall, mate or surgeon on board the ship *Liverpool Hero* in the roads, to Captain Thornborrow, living ashore**
Yours by the Canoe, with 16 Male and 9 female Slaves, I received . . . The Slaves are all in good spirits I always have them shaved when they come on Board, and indeed make a Point of shaving the whole of them, every now and then

## Resistance

As is now well established, there was violent resistance and insurrection by embarked slaves on many slave ships, probably on about 10 percent of all voyages, as well as many instances of suicide, attempted suicide, and forced feeding, both when the ships were at anchor in the roads and during the middle passage. Few of these insurrections were successful in the sense of enabling the slaves to remain in Africa, let alone go free, but ships were often seized, crew members killed, and the ships blown up or run aground.

**August 14, 1771, diary of Cape Coast Castle**
An Insurrection happened on board the Juliet, in this Road;

perceiving some slaves in the water, fired my eighteen
pounder to intimidate them & induce them to return to the
ship; also sent off several canoes to their assistance. Late at
night recd. a letter from Capt. King advising all was quiet &
his Loss only 2 Slaves.

The Liverpool slave-ship captain Hugh Crow noted another episode
in his *Memoirs* (1830):

During the last voyage I was upon the coast I saw a number
of negroes in Cape Coast Castle, some of whom were part
of a cargo of a ship from London, on whose crew they had
risen, and after killing the captain and most of the sailors,
ran the ship on shore, but in endeavouring to make their
escape, most of them were seized by the natives and resold.
Eighteen of these we purchased from Governor Morgue.

If an insurrection occurred in which slaves escaped or were killed or
drowned, the costs and delays involved in obtaining replacements
could affect the commercial viability of the whole voyage. Whether
the slaves who took part in insurrections had any sense that it
was others rather than themselves who might benefit, or whether
they were simply driven beyond the limits of desperation, is hard
to judge. However, David Richardson, an economic historian, has
calculated that the extra costs that the slave-ship owners incurred
in having to employ larger crews and ships with nets to prevent
jumping overboard may, by reducing the average profitability, have
saved many hundreds of thousands of people born in Africa from
being sent to the Americas. The same may have been the case within
Africa, where there is mounting evidence of violent resistance at all
stages, including during the initial enslavement by local political
and religious authorities and warlords, during the march to the

coast, and during the period of waiting while decisions were made whether they were suitable for the long journey across the ocean.

As with slaves who were lost by drowning in the surf before they had been insured by their new owners (see Chapter 1), the slave traders were so inured to thinking of slaves as commodities that they unhypocritically demanded sympathy for their own financial loss.

**November 11, 1776, Riley Clarke, slave-ship captain, to Richard Miles at Anomabu**
My Unhappy Misfortune of haveing an Insorection on board you must of heard before this comes to hand, we lost 34 Men & 2 woman . . . as I have meet with Crewel misfortune of Looseing my men beg you will give me Men for the Order in the roome of woman . . .

## Offshore

The Castle records show the governors buying, selling, and exchanging credits with the Danes and the Dutch, their neighbors on the coast, as well as selling to the French, the Portuguese, the Brazilians, and the Americans, who only had ships. William Wilberforce was advised that, out of a total of about 100,000 slaves exported annually from the African coast as a whole in a typical year, the British sold on over 15,000 out of their total of about 41,000 to other slaving nations. Since trading with foreign countries was illegal, it mostly took place out of sight of land after a ship had sailed, literally an offshore market, with transfers from ship to ship at sea. In addition to the slaves who, because they were physically strong, were snapped up by the captains almost at once and might then spend months chained in a slave ship in the roads before setting off on the transatlantic voyage, there were other unfortunates who, because they were physically weak, were touted for sale to and fro along the coast. It is to these men, women, and children that Governor Hippisley is referring in his 1764 pamphlet on the 'African' trade, explicitly identifying the slaves with livestock:

> It is said at Annamaboe that scarce a sheep, fowl, or duck, is ever offered on shore for sale till it had been the whole round of shipping in the road and brought back sea-sick and half drowned with salt water.

One puzzle is what happened to the slaves who were bought at extremely low prices, persons who would not be accepted by slave-ship captains of any nation. One possibility is that they may have been sold to dealers who took them inland, where they may have had a value among poor communities, or they may have been sold to those rulers who, on occasions, as is well attested, arranged for the ritual putting to death of enslaved criminals as part of religious and funeral ceremonies. 'I cannot answer that question positively,' replied former governor Weuves, when asked about the practice by a parliamentary inquiry, 'but I have every reason to believe that those refused slaves are generally set aside for such sacrifices – I think so.'

## Pawns

Many men, women, and children sold off the coast were not slaves but unredeemed 'pawns.' As with 'pledges,' the Europeans who used the term understood the custom in pawnshop terms, a form of credit used by the poor who have nothing to exchange but the future labor of their bodies. The British were surprised at how lightly some local people pawned themselves, their relatives, and their children, appearing to do so, in some cases, in hopes of being able to turn a quick profit on selling the goods that they obtained by such credit and immediately redeeming themselves. Among the

Castle records can be found such examples as: 'Quashie, pawned by Pettewary for trade'; 'Old Quashie, slaves, bomboy etc and his wife, country woman'; 'Quon alias Endoom, canoeman pawned to DM [Governor David Mill] redeemed by J. B. Weuves with a man slave'; 'pawned for one woman slave 10 oz [about £40] in two instalments'; 'Quamen Abady, this man lost his note and got a new one'; and 'Bynee has this day redeemed this Boy with Oz 1.5 [about £5] gold. [signed] J. B. Weuves [governor].' Some records hint at desperation: 'was brought for a pawn by his father a canoeman born at the Mine named Aninghan about 35 years old.'

A Swiss missionary, Rev. Carl Gilbert Reindorf, records that in a war, whose date he does not give, the people of Accra asked the Danish governor of Christiansborg to supply them with gunpowder, and when he refused, they obtained it by pawning their children to a slave ship. That was evidently an extreme emergency, but the powerless had few means of defending themselves against armed enemies and slave raiders, and defeat could have meant enslavement for the whole community, including the children. In this case Reindorf records that the children were redeemed.

The British in the Castle, determined always to be able to maintain that the slave trade was fully in accordance not only with British but with local African laws, religions, and customs, were uncertain how far their rights to send off the coast extended to pawns. In pawnshop terms, a pledge not redeemed passed into the 'ownership' of the party who accepted it. Did this mean that unredeemed pawns could be treated as owned slaves? Miles advised a fort governor that, under local Fante law, a father could pawn but not sell his child, but that did not provide a bridge across the divide. The outcome of one palaver was that the pawns could 'be redeemed either in gold or a prime man for each . . . and such slaves given in redemption shall be disposed off [*sic*, meaning 'off the coast'] by the Company.'

It may be that the people who pawned themselves or their relatives thought that by handing their children over to the British they were, essentially, putting them into working service in the Castle until they could be redeemed, and pawns in the Castle were regarded as part of the workforce, with the same pay and working conditions as the permanent Castle slaves. But to suggest that local people were unaware of their own best interests would be not only patronizing but untrue – they had seen men, women, and children enter the Castle never to return, for over a century. What the records show, I suggest, is rather a further advance of the Western ideology of 'property' into human and social relationships, and a widening of the gap between the institutions of indigenous slavery, which were cruel enough, and the slavery practiced in the Americas. In their pawn books, the British began to put a limit on the time before redemption. On April 10, 1777, for example, Richard Miles notes that he bartered for goods worth about £37, 'A Pawn of Botty of Aggerie redeemable 3 months or my slave.'

It would be extraordinary if, in such a market, the suppliers did not match the men, women, and children that they brought to the Castle to be sold to the known requirements of the prospective buyers. And there is evidence that this happened. The dealers complain to the governors that they cannot make a living when so many of the slaves they offer are rejected, and demand that they be allowed to sell to the French, but the British, for all their talk of 'free trade,' always insist on maintaining the local monopolies. Instead much of the political, judicial, and religious system in Africa, both on the coast and in the hinterland, was increasingly biased towards supplying exactly the persons wanted by the final buyers in the Americas. The local African system of pawns, for example, suited the British slavers. It put the onus of finding substitutes, often specified as 'prime slaves,' on to the relatives and friends, who would have to find the wherewithal to pay high prices at extremely short notice, maybe by pawning themselves or other relatives. For the slavers, it meant that persons who were not sellable to the ships, being for example too old or too young or not in good health, could be exchanged for persons who were readily saleable. By accepting pawns for goods, Miles wrote, 'some of primest men slaves may be purchased with less money.' For some families, pawning led to a cycle of more borrowing, more pawning, and more transportations.

## Redemption

An episode in the roads at the Castle in April 1802 was recorded by the captain of the slaving ship *Bruce Grove*, when two men brought on board were redeemed by three friends. 'I need not attempt to describe the poor fellows joy on being released from their irons,' he wrote. As Sylviane A. Diouf noted in publishing the passage, not only do we have no record of the attitudes of those who were substituted, but they probably did not know that they were the ransom. Even the innocent had to be redeemed with someone else's sufferings.

> **A receipt given by a slave-ship officer for men sent by the governor from the Castle dungeons**
> Redemption of C[ape] C[oast] Sailors
> Received of John Gordon Esqre. two prime Slaves in lieu of
>      two free Sailors who were caught & sold wrong.
> the Ann[omabo]e palaver 11th June 1791 H. Mullior for Capt
>      R[ober]t Bibby

As the next example shows, redemption was only open to the (outwardly) submissive:

**December 21, 1773, Captain Goodwin to Governor Richard Miles, Cape Coast roads**
Yours with a man Slave I Recd this Instant. I did promase a Black fellow to Redeme the Woman with a Nother Prime Slave & one oz of Gold – But Seein that the Same Woman Being all Most the Ocasion of My Ship Being Cut of By the Slaves on Board. Seein that I am determined she shall Not be Redeemed at any Reat – therefore you will Excuse My Not Complying With your Request

## Criminal and religious offenses

When Surgeon Falconbridge was asked by the 1790 parliamentary inquiry what were the main sources of slaves bought on the African coast, he replied, 'Kidnapping and crimes, I should suppose.' As far as crimes were concerned, the most common offenses were theft and adultery. In such cases the transition from free to slave was decided upon by a local public judicial process, to which the British were admitted as observers if they chose.

Different were what may be called offenses against the local official religions, which included cases where someone had died suddenly – as happened frequently – that were attributed to 'witchcraft.' In these cases the decision appears to have been a summary one taken at night by local religious authorities, and it sometimes attracted the death penalty for the man accused. For religious crimes, whole families were enslaved, and it was often laid down that they were 'not to be redeemed.' Religious crimes therefore provided the British slavers and their clients in the Americas with the women and children that they wanted, as well as an African and a biblical legitimacy for visiting the sins of the fathers upon the sons and daughters. Former governor Weuves told the inquiry of a case of a man condemned for 'witchcraft' in which 'The person convicted was of course executed, he had his head cut off – his father, mother, two wives, and his sister and three children, which were all that remained of the family, were sold to me, on condition that they should never return to that country again.' In cases such as these, the British slavers, secure in the knowledge that the official British Christian line as well as the local religions endorsed the enslavement of children, provided continuing financial incentives to local political and religious leaders to remove whole families of opponents from the locality. And, as in Europe and the colonies in previous centuries, 'witchcraft' was a convenient means of getting rid of members of a community who had, for whatever other reason, become unwelcome, including, as Sarah Bowdich noticed, 'the feeble and wretched, blamed for deaths of children.' As early as 1732 the British slave trader Francis Moore noticed a rise in the number of crimes punishable by enslavement, which brought business to the political and religious authorities who ran the courts. In most societies, caring for those unable to take care of themselves, such as orphans, has been thought of as a family and a public responsibility, an obligation that necessarily reduces the incomes of those who undertake it. In the slaving era there were merchants offering money to take such persons away, no questions asked, with the certainty that they would never return.

Although the slavers took scant interest in how the people they bought came to be enslaved, occasionally in the buying records we see what may be family enslavement for religious crimes. At Tantumquerry fort in 1773, for example, we find the following record: 'bartered for 1 man, 1 woman from Asssiney . . . [next day] bartered for the above woman's mother (Assiney).'

If any 'not-to be-redeemed' conditions were set by the judicial or religious authorities when the sentence of enslavement was passed, they remained attached to the enslaved persons and families, binding anyone who subsequently bought them with the same obligation. In 1799, for example, at the request of the slave seller Botty, Richard Miles redeemed one of four men from a slave-ship captain to whom they had all been sold by his colleague Thomas Westgate. The man was returned from the slave ship to the Castle, but as Miles immediately wrote to Westgate, 'I would not deliver him out until I had writ you, as possibly you may have bought him in terms of his not being redeemed.' The man concerned, having no identity, Miles described as 'the handsome fellow.' Only after Westgate had confirmed by letter that no nonredemption conditions had been set when he bought the four men was the redeemed man released. Ever conscious that the transatlantic slave trade depended upon the successful operation of the African judicial, religious, and enslavement customs that supplied the slaves, the gentlemen of the African Service were scrupulous in upholding them. In this non-condescending policy of noninterference, their attitudes were quite different from those of their successors in colonial times who never hesitated to condemn any local customs they disliked and to seek to change them.

## 'Panyarring'

By kidnapping, Falconbridge meant the seizure of persons for unpaid debt and then selling them. The word used by the slavers was 'panyarring,' another adaptation from the Portuguese, but also a verbal distancing device. In offering his judgement that panyarring was one of the main sources of supply, Falconbridge was not only drawing on his own experience but repeating the opinion of Chaplain Quaque, with whom he had discussed the point when he stayed at the Castle. Imprisonment for debt was, and is, practiced by many societies, including Britain. However, at the Castle the existence of a high-price market for persons in good health of all ages meant that here too the transatlantic slave trade set up incentives. Creditors could turn their bad debts into assets that were worth more than the debt by seizing the debtors and selling them; even, according to some local laws, by seizing a member of the debtor's local community rather than the debtor himself. By the time the prisoner's relatives and friends found out what had happened and gathered the wherewithal to pay the debt, their relative could already be in the Castle dungeons or on board a slave ship riding in the roads. The effect was to set up economic incentives for what was, in essence, commercial kidnapping. As the demand for, and price of, slaves rose, armed gangs roamed the coastal areas looking for opportunities to take prisoners. Two groups of local people were especially at risk: men traveling away from their communities, for example going into the forest to cut trees; and poor families in villages inland who were unable to supervise their children during all the hours of day and night.

One of the advantages that the Castle provided to the British slave traders was that the officers of the African Service knew the local laws and customs. They could be expected to know who might be legitimately sent off the coast and who might not. Since the governors were in constant contact with local leaders, the Castle provided some safeguards. If, as happened from time to time, a slave-ship captain seized the canoemen delivering to the ship, the other canoemen might go on strike, the local people could refuse to supply the castle with food and water, a complaint could be made to the governor, and he could take action. Sometimes the complaints resulted in a measure of redress even if the slave ship was over the horizon. In 1780 Joshua Johnson, captain of the snow *Patty* of Liverpool, was fined by a British court 'for forcibly carrying off 12 free negroes.' The statutory penalty was £100 per head. In some cases, at least, the wrongly enslaved persons were brought back. In 1777 Captain Benjamin Francis of Liverpool was fined £200 for selling at Jamaica 'two free negroes whom you had hired on the coast of Africa to navigate your ship to that island.' One of the men taken, Quamino Amissa of Anomabu, was paid a proportion of the fine and brought back to the Gold Coast by way of England. In this case the Castle arranged for 'Coffee Aboam, son of Quaw, a gold taker at Anomabu' to go to England to make the identification. The Governing Committee was advised by the governor to make sure he too returned for, 'as he is rather unwilling to leave England you will take care he returns home lest his absence should be attended with any bad consequences for the trade.' There are many other references to local African free men being employed by the slave ships not only along the coast but on the transatlantic voyage; one whom Surgeon McLeod met at Whydah had retired there with a fortune.

If the local people had a grievance, they could seize British slave-ship captains or African Service officers, but this was one feature of local law and custom that the British were reluctant to accept, and it is seldom mentioned either in the colonial histories or in modern accounts of the transatlantic slave trade. In 1751, for example, Thomas Derbyshire, captain of the *Jenny* of Liverpool, was seized in his longboat for having allegedly taken free people on board his ship with the intention of transporting and selling them, but in the negotiations for his release it was he who sought atonement. In the report of the palaver he demanded ten slaves and was offered two. Derbyshire then said that if he did not get what he had asked for in three days, he would go down to Anomabu, 'hang the most considerable of his prisoners in sight of their friends; fire a broadside into the town, and go off the coast.' Eventually the governor of the Castle agreed a price of eight men and one woman, the Company of Merchants to pay.

On June 23, 1753, Captain Derbyshire, on his next voyage, was involved in another complex palaver at the Castle that was documented and so preserves a record, albeit mediated, of African voices. Quoted here is a long passage – difficult to follow though it is – to illustrate the day-to-day operation of the slave trade, with its panyarring and counter-panyarring, its open as well as its threatened violence, and how the settlement of every dispute required more people to be transported:

### Captain Derbyshire's palaver, Cape Coast Castle, June 23, 1753, according to the Fanteen relation

Above Three years ago Capt. Derbyshires Long Boat
Going from Cape Coast to Annamaboe robb'd the Blacks
nets of Their fish (Which by their Laws is Death). They
catch'd his people; Carried Them on Board; told their fault,
and the penalty, and made the affair for 10 oz.[about £40]
– Sometime after Capt. Derbyshire had his Boats Sail Stole;
he could not find out by Whom, But at last Discovered part
of the Bolt Rope in a Canoe belonging to His Gold Taker.
He panyared the canoeman. The Gold Taker offered to
forgive him 24 ounces [about £96]. (The Wages then Due
to him by Capt. Derbyshire) Provided he would release
him. This Capt. Derbyshire Absolutely Refused; and he
was killed by ill Usage in his passage to the West Indias as
Captain Derbyshire himself confesed before Mr. Stokes [a
British officer] and Mr. Wm Currantee [a local political
leader] at Annamaboe.

This voyage the Annamaboe People Panyared Captain
Derbyshire going in a Cano from Cape Coast Castle to
Annamaboe; Carried him ashore with a Design to keep him
till his Ship should go off the Coast & then Put him on
Board Some Other in Order to prevent his doing any further
Mischeif. But Released upon a message from this Council
of Cape Coast on his paying 60 oz. [about £240] Slave Price
for the Canoeman. at the time that Capt. Derbyshire had
the Palaver about the Nets Captain Lawson was likewise at

Annamabo who observing that somebody stole his goods
and Suspecting the People ashore went off in the night he
watched and detected a Canno in the fact he fired and killed
the two Canoemen Upon which he determined to take
no further Notice of it as he had Punished the offenders.
But Capt. Derbyshire Perswaded him to Panyar Quassa
(Currantee's Cousin) Peter Clois and Appia. Which Captain
Lawson refused but took and carried off 3 Men and 2
Women Slaves which were carried on board him for sale
for which They Obliged Captain Derbyshire to pay 31 oz.
[about £124] ie 7 oz for men and 5 for women. – This voyage
Capt. Derbyshire took a Pawn from one Quancoom a fantee
for 8 oz; the Pawn died on board and Capt. Derbyshire did
not acquaint his friends therewith but threw him into the
Sea on which they Demanded Payment. he told them he had
lost his Debt which he thought was enough but gave them 3
oz. [£12] to make custom for him . . .

And so on, for many pages, with questions and answers until the
palaver is settled, an act that is then recorded and signed in a book.
Despite the finding of the palaver that Captain Derbyshire had
seized at least thirty-two traders and canoemen in little over a
month, it was agreed that he could resume trading.

In 1812, a few years after the end of the legal slave trade, Henry
Meredith, governor of Winneba fort, having returned to the
coast after recovering from the wounds he received at the siege
of Anomabu fort by the Asante, was seized while on his morning
walk and a ransom demanded. When Hope Smith, the governor of
Tantam fort, arrived, he too was seized and carried into the forest,
but was released after promising to pay 225 gold ounces (about
£1,000) for both. On arriving back at the fort, he started to pay the
ransom, but Meredith, who had been marched barefoot through the

forest in the sun and held for days with his head tied to a stake, as if he were a recalcitrant slave, died on his way back to the fort. The ransom was nevertheless paid in full. In a society in which every person had a market value, a prime white fort governor was about fifteen times more expensive than a prime black laborer.

In his evidence to the 1790 parliamentary inquiry, Surgeon Falconbridge, who spent many months talking with slaves ashore and afloat, reported that onboard ship:

> we had many, both boys and girls, who had not father, or mother, or any relation on board – many of them told me that they had been kidnapped in the neighbourhood of Annamaboe, particularly a little girl of about eight years of age, who told us she had been carried off from her mother by the man who sold her to our ship.

She may be among the 'child barters' in Miles's book. And she may be one of those remembered in the laments for seized children that Akosua Adoma Perbi collected in the traditional folksongs of the peoples of Ghana. And again we have the chance to read what the British slavers had to say when questioned about kidnapping. 'I never heard of such a thing, nor do I conceive that such a thing ever existed on the coast' was the answer of John Fountaine, always anxious to please his employers, when asked about kidnapping. Captain Knox, a slave-ship captain, when asked, 'Do you know of kidnapping slaves or of their being obtained by fraud or deception?' gave the same answer: 'I never knew the practice nor ever heard of the word in that country.' Former governor Richard Miles, whose barter books are full of purchases of men, women, and children, bought individually, no questions asked, when questioned directly, 'Is kidnapping practised there?' also took refuge in literalism:

I do not know I ever heard the word mentioned there or anywhere else but in this country. It cannot be practised on the Gold Coast to any extent without certain detection; for the Natives have one general language, and the Brokers who sell the slaves have daily intercourse with the shipping; if therefore any Slave on board ship felt himself in that predicament, he would communicate it to the Slave Brokers, who, from motives of interest, as well as from regard to their own law, would sift it to the bottom, and the delinquents must be found out.

It may have been the publicizing of such unconvincing replies to criticism that persuaded the slaving industry that they must do something about panyarring, if they were not to lose their political base in Britain and face a complete ban. One of the actions of Governor Colonel Torrane (appointed in 1805) was to concert measures with the Dutch to prevent panyarred persons from being sold off the coast. The officers, before buying any man, woman, or child who was brought to the Castle gate, were instructed to find out how they came to be captive. As Torrane proudly told the Governing Committee, 'six local canoemen who went to buy equipment in Ahanta country were seized and an attempt made to sell them. . . . The man who attempted to sell them is in irons in the Castle – I will make an example of him.' Torrane boasted that his new policy of asking questions, apparently the first time this had ever been done, had saved about 200 innocent people from being panyarred and sent off, and that, taking into account the deterrent effect, the numbers of those saved from illegal panyarring were far larger. The kidnapper concerned appears in an account of sales '(not to be redeemed)' made shortly afterwards by order of the governor and Council: 'one mulatto soldier' £32, and four canoemen who had been caught stealing gunpowder, £26, £32, £32/10, and £20, also 'not to be redeemed.'

## *Military slaves*

One of the largest purchasers of slaves in the final years of the legal British trade was the British government, although this was little known at the time and is still seldom mentioned. From 1793, the beginning of the war with France that was to last, with only one short interlude, until 1815, the British island colonies in the Americas were vulnerable to external attack. Since the British planters feared that the plantation slaves might revolt, there could be no question of raising local defense forces, and the British army, even when it could find the men from jails and debtors' prisons, could not sustain the losses from disease. The solution was to create an army whose rank and file were composed of men who could withstand the climate, men with no possessions, no ties, and no choices. As one officer wrote, it was safer to arm 'the ship Negro' who arrived 'with only a Rag around him.' Between 1795 and 1808 the British government bought 13,400 young males for the West India Regiment at a price of about £1,000,000. This was about 7 percent of the male slaves arriving in the British Caribbean at the time.

The contracts the British government made with the slavers were *à la carte*, usually for 200 to 400 men at a time, to be delivered by a specific date. Many of the men, and perhaps 'menboys,' who were purchased came through the Castle. On their arrival in the West Indies, after a medical examination, they were marched off by a sergeant major, clothed in a scarlet tunic, and given pay. Whether these soldiers were technically slaves or not was left ambiguous for a time, but many were evidently well content to serve in the British army where conditions were far better than on the plantations, and from which they could expect formal freedom in due course. The discovery a few years ago of correspondence between the British government in London and the leaders of Liverpool's slaving industry shows that the government delayed the abolition that came into force on May 1, 1807, to allow the British army to make a large final purchase.

On November 9, 1806, Pudsey Dawson, on behalf of the Liverpool slavers, wrote to the government:

> About 130 sail of Vessels have been fitted out from this port this year for the Coast. The greatest part of them gone to the Bite [of Biafra] and Angola, not above 12 or 14 of them, I should suppose to the Gold Coast. The Gold Coast Negroes only, I presume, are wanted by Government. Calculating 12 Vessels to carry on average 300 Negroes each, the number of able-bodied Men would not exceed one third, or 1,200 in those Ships if so many, allowing for Women & Children & Youths from 12 to 16 years of Age, which from the circumstances of the increased attention to the Cultivation of Coffee have latterly been found to be the most saleable, as better calculated for that purpose & suiting better than full grown men. . . .

Dawson said that if the government would relax the rules that had been introduced in 1780 to limit the number of slaves per ship on the middle passage, he and his colleagues would supply 2,000 'of the Corymantee Tribe, to be delivered at Barbadoes' at £65 to £70 per head. It was probably in fulfilment of such a contract that so many ships are reported as taking on slaves after the legal trade abolition date, a time when (as described in Chapter 7), large numbers were available as a result of the Asante invasion in 1807.

The regiments of the British West India Regiment, consisting initially mainly of men born in Africa, under the command of socially unconnected, disgraced, and misfit British officers, became an imperial army that not only deterred attack on the Caribbean colonies from other countries, but defended the slavery system against internal slave revolts. It was a small step, when the wars ended in 1815, to send one of the regiments to West Africa. It arrived in Sierra Leone in 1819, and was redeployed, in part, to the Gold Coast in 1821. It seems likely that some of the soldiers or noncommissioned officers in that force who came ashore at Cape Coast Castle had passed through the door of no return in the other direction in 1808 and earlier. The West India Regiment, who also recruited men from intercepted slave ships until the 1860s, was to be the main British garrison in the colonial Gold Coast for much of the nineteenth century, one regiment serving in Cape Coast Castle, with another regiment arriving specially from Jamaica at the time of the Asante wars of the 1870s.

## Breaking the silence

Akosua Adoma Perbi in her *History of Indigenous Slavery in Ghana* and Anne C. Bailey in *African Voices of the Atlantic Slave Trade: Beyond the Silence and the Shame* have recently published accounts of oral traditions passed down by storytellers in Ghana. Although, after so long, it is difficult to know how far such oral history preserves historical information, what emerges is a deep sense of shame, which affects both those whose ancestors were enslaved individuals and those who were slavers. There is, both writers notice, a collective wish to preserve a silence that is characteristic, they believe, of societies still traumatized.

Almost all that we can know about the slaves who passed through the Castle is mediated through their later experience, by learning English, by adopting Christianity, and in some cases by becoming educated enough, and well enough integrated into their new society, to write and to publish a book. Of those few who did succeed against these obstacles, almost all were from the tiny minority of slaves who had been taken to Britain as personal servants by their masters, making two legs of the triangular voyage of the slave ships in reverse, from Africa to the West Indies to Britain. There is, as far

24. *Quobna Ottobah Cugoano, renamed John Stuart, the black servant in* Mr. and Mrs. Cosway, 1784, *a fantasy of luxury in a classical Italianate garden.*

as I can discover, only one contemporary autobiographical account that mentions the Castle. Quobna Ottobah Cugoano, who was born around 1757 in the Fante village of Ajumako, was kidnapped at the age of thirteen, sold off the coast, and spent years on a slave gang in Grenada and other places in the West Indies before being taken, renamed John Stuart, to England in 1772. His book, *Thoughts and Sentiments on the Evil and Wicked Traffic of the Slavery and Commerce of the Human Species* (1787), was evidently compiled with the help of others involved in the abolitionist cause, including his friend Equiano, a former slave from the area of modern Nigeria about whose life much is known and who is the subject of a recent biography by Vincent Carretta. In the early part of his book Cugoano tells how his kidnappers persuaded him that he and the other captured children, from whom he was separated, would be taken to a great man who would ensure they would soon be back with their families. He recounts his walk through the forest, the handing over to white men at a fort in exchange for a gun, a piece of cloth, and some lead, and his fears that he might be eaten – the story that the inland Africans practiced cannibalism was a reciprocal myth put about the slavers. From the dates, it is possible that Cugoano may be one of the 'manboys' or boys recorded in Governor Miles's barter books, bought from a stranger, no questions asked. Cugoano was kept in the fort prison for three days, where:

> I heard the groans and cries of many, and saw some of my
> fellow-captives. But when a vessel arrived to conduct us
> away to the ship, it was a most horrible scene; there was
> nothing to be heard but rattling of chains, smacking of
> whips, and groans and cries of our fellow men. Some would
> not stir from the ground, when they were lashed and beat
> in the most horrible manner. I have forgot the name of this
> infernal fort; but we were taken in the ship that came for us,
> to another that was ready to sail from Cape Coast ...

Cugoano tells of his unsuccessful attempts to speak to the African gold takers to try to get a message back to his family, of a failed slave insurrection, and of the sexual abuse of women by the sailors. In London he was employed by Richard Cosway, a court painter, and probably came into direct contact with members of the British royal family. Cugoano was the artist's model for the black servant in 'Mr. and Mrs. Cosway, 1784.' In this picture (page 242), Cugoano's blackness symbolically emphasizes that the wealth of the family within which he lives and which, to an extent, he now shares, is drawn from across the oceans, and therefore from slavery and the slave trade. As it happens, this picture of splendid civilized living

– which could also remind viewers of the divine wrath that had biblically attended luxury – contains the only representation that is known of a person who passed through the dungeons of Cape Coast Castle.

Around 1810, after the last men, women, and children had left the Castle dungeons, the floor was spread with lime and sand as part of the cleansing. It was in the remains of that layer that an archaeological excavation in the mid-twentieth century discovered bones of animals and birds – apparently part of the food given to the prisoners – together with tobacco and clay pipes, which helped 'to drive away melancholy,' as their jailers professed to believe. A few beads of the type worn round the waist, neck, and wrist were also found, probably not possessions that the enslaved individuals had brought with them from their homes but part of the ornaments in which they were decked out for market on their arrival at the coast. That is all that remained in Africa of the lives of those who had worn them, but had lost them, along with their family, friends, language, beliefs, customs, ancestors, and name, on their way to the Americas.

25. *Cape Coast Castle, c. 1805, at the end of the slaving era. The 'door of no return' as it then appeared, before later changes, is at far right.*

# 9

# The wide wide world

In 1807 the British slave trade was booming, with more African men, women, and children being carried across the Atlantic Ocean than ever before. The British naval victory at Trafalgar in 1805 meant that there was no longer much danger to British merchant shipping between the three continents, and large areas of North and South America were not yet converted to plantations. Slave prices were at their highest ever on both sides of the Ocean. David Eltis and other economic historians have shown how the British slaving industry carried more slaves per ton of shipping, more quickly, more cheaply, and with a lower death rate, than any of its rivals. Indeed, with the increasing use of specially designed ships, and British government regulation of the numbers per ton that could legally be carried, the mortality rate fell during the later decades of the legal trade.

Why then did an activity whose legitimacy had scarcely been challenged until less than a generation before suddenly cease to be acceptable in the country that had come to dominate it? Historians have looked for explanations based on long-run changes, for example in changes in the demand for sugar, or the effects of the coming on stream of other sources of supply in Asia. Philosophers and political economists such as Montesquieu, Adam Smith, and

Condorcet offered a critique of American plantation slavery as not only ethically wrong but also less efficient than the cultivation of the land by free employees who were paid normal wages and were at liberty to leave or to change employers if they wished. And there were fierce slave revolts in Jamaica, and especially the violent and successful 1790 uprising in the French colony of Saint-Domingue (modern Haiti), a colony that in 1789 had supplied two thirds of France's overseas trade. For the colonists from Europe, the precariousness of the whole institution of plantation slavery was frighteningly obvious.

However, although it is reasonable to assume that the abolition of the British slave trade must have had deep historical causes, none of the explanations can, by itself, adequately account for the change or for its suddenness. Plantation slavery continued in the southern United States until forcibly brought to an end by the military victory of the North in the Civil War, and there was no slackening of demand or supply. Nor was everyone worried by the cruelty that became harder to deny or shrug off with every inquiry. A look through the biographies of the British leaders at the time of the abolition campaigns shows that, when forced to confront the question, most of them favored a continuation of the slave trade, although with tighter regulation, a middle way for the middle passage.

In these debates, the men from the Castle came across as condescending, shifty, and self-deceiving. Former governor Weuves, now a slave-ship owner, assured a parliamentary inquiry that 'I hardly know a trade that is carried on in a fairer manner.' Former fort governor Norris, also now a slave-ship owner, declared that 'the African slave trade is carried on as much to the ease and comfort of those that are the subjects of it, and also of those who conduct it, as is possible for human ingenuity to devise. . . . Interest is so much blended with Humanity that I conceive every possible Attention Circumstances will permit is paid to them [the slaves].' Indeed, he advised, the slaves 'are in general more happily situated by being brought to the plantations than they were in their own country.' Former governor Dalzel in his *History of Dahomy*, which was partly written in the Castle with the help of John Fountaine, admitted that 'there is no good without some mixture of evil.'

The British slave trade was brought to an end by a series of political campaigns in Britain, led by men and women from outside the main structures of British political and ecclesiastical wealth and power, notably the Quakers. The abolitionists declared that the slave trade was simply wrong and that the Christian tradition to which they too mostly belonged demanded more than an uncritical reliance on ancient biblical texts. They organized petitions, distributed free pamphlets, and threatened sugar boycotts. It was, one might guess, with a sense of contemptuous bravado that the Liverpool and Boston slavers named their ships the *Quaker,* the *Willing Quaker*, the *Accomplished Quaker*, taunting their opponents. Even in the mid-nineteenth century, long after the end of the slave trade, British expatriates in the Gold Coast drank a strong alcoholic punch that they called 'a Quaker.'

## Towards colonialism

But if there was no British slave trade, what was the purpose of Cape Coast Castle and the forts? The decision of 1807 instantly rendered illegal 90 percent of the British commerce with the Gold Coast. One answer was to stop others from taking over the trade, or, as the slaving industry hoped, to keep the way open for a resumption. A report into the future of the Castle and the other British settlements was commissioned in 1811, but nothing much could be done until the European wars ended. By that time, 1815, all northern European countries and the United States had agreed to stop their nationals from trading, a provision that was built into the peace settlement,

*26. Missionaries, with their wives and children, in the forest.*

and Spain, Portugal, and the South American states promised to
phase out at least the transatlantic part of the trade.

One group in Britain argued that the African settlements,
having no further purpose, should simply be abandoned, or rather
returned to the coastal states from whom they had been leased, on
condition that they were not then leased out to some other nation
that was still slaving, such as the Portuguese, or used for illegal
trading by others. However, among the most vocal opponents
of a British withdrawal were the victorious abolitionists, who,
from their knowledge of what had happened in the past, did not
believe that British slave trading would cease unless the British
government itself took direct responsibility for ensuring that it
did. The price of slaves on the African coast fell drastically after
the transatlantic trade was made illegal, but was soon back to pre-
abolition levels. And then there was the problem of the economic
effects on the African governments and peoples who had depended
on the trade for their incomes, both directly and from the huge

local expenditures that the forts and the ships had generated. What were they to do? Zey, the king of Asante, sent a personal letter to the British king in 1817 asking him to allow the slave trade to be renewed.

Instead of withdrawing, the British government decided that it would encourage palm plantations as an economic alternative to slave trading and encourage Christian missionaries to bring European education, combat the power of local religions, and discourage the internal slave trade and indigenous slavery. In 1816 some of the forts were duly abandoned. And, although there was now little for the officers and men of the African Service to do, Parliament voted that their salaries should be doubled. If the slave trade was to be genuinely ended and not just continued under various new pretences, a new type of British public official was required, a civil servant not a trader. Never again would the men in the Castle be allowed to argue that they had been forced into slave trading by the low salaries.

Then, in 1821, by Act of Parliament, the British government took over direct responsibility for the ending of the slave trade for the first time, abolishing the Company of Merchants, who had managed the Castle and forts since 1750, and transferring all the obligations and liabilities to the British Crown, an example of the flag reluctantly following trade, or in this case the ending of trade. At that time the number of forts had been reduced to 6, the number of Europeans employed was 45, and locally employed Africans, mainly Castle slaves, about 450. It was at this time, incidentally, that the archive of papers on which much of this book is based became public property. By its decision, the British government knew that, since the Asantes were likely to invade again, the Castle might, unless more money was spent on its defenses, face a threat from the land for the first time in its history. It was Sir Charles McCarthy, the first official British governor – he arrived from Sierra Leone in 1822 – who, by extensive building works – most of which are still in place – in effect turned the Castle round so as to face the land rather than the sea. However, when McCarthy, with British as well as local troops at his command, responded to a series of hostile acts by the Asante against the local coastal peoples by marching a British force north into the forest, he was catastrophically defeated, losing his own life along with those of about 200 men. The war with the Asante was resumed in 1824, with another invasion from the north, and in 1825 Cape Coast Castle suffered the biggest crisis in its history.

In May 1825 an Asante army of many thousands again invaded the coastal states, and arrived a few miles from the Castle within sight of the lookouts in the newly fortified towers on the outlying hills. The expatriate British, officers and other ranks, including merchants and ships' crews armed for the purpose, numbered in all 360 men, of whom 104 were in hospital. They were allied with local African forces of about 11,000 men, armed with muskets, including a contingent of about 5,000 from Accra. The Danes also sent a small force. The gates of the Castle were opened to let in about 5,000 refugees fleeing from the Asante army, and the men inside were put to work making bullets by breaking up pewter dishes and the Castle's water pipes. It looked for a time as if the Castle was about to sustain its first attack since it was taken by the English in 1664, but smallpox broke out and the Asante withdrew. Many thousands were slaughtered by the coastal armies or were captured and sold to (mainly illegal) slave ships. Famine, disease, and death pervaded the coastal regions, and although peace was patched up at palavers in the Castle, and a treaty signed, with a handing over of pledges, it was soon clear that this invasion was unlikely to be the last. It was as a result of the events of 1825, the first and last time that the Castle had ever been attacked when in British hands, that the Fante, who had hitherto been their landlords, surrendered their books, formally acknowledged British sovereignty, and released the

British occupants of the Castle from their obligation to pay rent. That date can be regarded as the formal beginning of the colonial era, although sovereignty was confined to the area within the walls and an indeterminate area of land nearby.

With the Asante invasion frustrated, at least temporarily, the British government again decided that this was a good time to abandon the Castle and the forts altogether, but again they were persuaded not to do so. With substantial direct legitimate trade with the interior now possible, a committee of British merchants in 1828 was given responsibility for the buildings under a new mixed public/private system, with some similarities to the former Company of Merchants. But after it became clear that Governor Maclean was, in effect, behaving like a direct British ruler, exercising judicial powers over a widening area of the Gold Coast, and imprisoning those convicted of crimes in the former slave dungeons, the British government again reluctantly resumed direct responsibility in 1843.

The later history of Cape Coast Castle is part of the history of the colonial Gold Coast. The policy of encouraging local plantations, mainly of palms, worked by local slaves as well as by waged labor, began to succeed quite soon, to the extent that the Liverpool firms that had led the slave trade adapted their vessels and were able to build successful soap and margarine industries in Britain. The gold mines were reactivated with modern machinery. However, the policy of changing the local religious beliefs and customs took longer. In 1841 the Castle was visited by Rev. James Frederick Schön, a Swiss missionary, and Samuel Crowther, who had been rescued as a boy from a Portuguese slave ship by the British, educated in Sierra Leone, and was later to be the first black bishop of the Anglican Church in West Africa. The visitors admired the schools (for girls as well as boys) and the farms that paid wages that Governor Maclean had encouraged. The Castle now had its

own printing press, symbolic of the progress of European civilization. They admired too the dedication of the missionaries of many
competing denominations who were settling there, although Schön
complained that, to set an example, they ought to keep their gardens
more tidy. But they found it hard to maintain their beliefs. On the
ship, when a heavy lamp fell on his head but only grazed him, Schön
thanked his God for his special care. When his hammock broke in
the night but at the end where his feet were, so that he did not fall
head first onto the deck, he again felt gratitude for the protection
of a benign providence. But, if they hoped that missionaries enjoyed
some special kind of divine protection, they were soon disillusioned.
The first missionaries were wiped out, most soon after their arrival,
by the same remorseless illnesses as had struck down the slavers of
previous generations. Indeed, since they ventured into the forest,
the domain of the tsetse fly, the mortality rate was probably worse.
As Schön wrote, 'almost every vessel carries home mournful tidings
from this coast. How unsearchable are God's ways! The field is
prepared for labour; yet scarcely have His servants entered upon it
before they are called hence.' He tried 'to meditate upon the gain of
the departed,' but admitted to an 'unbelieving heart.'

In 1873 the British and their local coastal allies decided to
mount a full-scale invasion of Asante, as the only way of preventing
invasions, and of suppressing the slave trade. At the time the British
had only 160 officers and soldiers in the whole country, not much
greater than they had had 100 or even 200 years before during the
slaving era. The British troops that were mobilized from Britain and
the West Indies for the invasions began to disembark from the roads
in early morning by moonlight, the boats from the warships being
towed in by steam cutters, to the edge of the surf, and – as is shown
in the contemporary woodcut here – the men were transferred
to canoes. In a few weeks the campaign was over and the British
soldiers back on board, the Asante capital of Kumasi having been

*27. British troops arriving over the surf for the campaign against
Asante, 1874.*

burned down when the king refused to surrender. A huge booty of
gold was seized and a sale held at the Castle, with the result that
the art of Asante has been distributed to many museums in Europe
and North America.

   The Danes withdrew from the Gold Coast in 1850, handing over
the castle of Christiansborg to the British. The Dutch kept Elmina
Castle and some of their other forts until 1872, mainly in order to
recruit soldiers – who were, some said, slaves – for their huge empire
in the East Indies. And in 1877 the British colonial government
moved its headquarters to Christiansborg. It was then that they
discovered, from the records kept over the years, that Cape Coast
Castle was the hottest place on the whole coast. (Christiansborg
Castle remains the seat of the head of state of Ghana.) Since then
Cape Coast Castle, although always in use, has been a provincial
center rather than a headquarters. As the only building in the locality

*28. The West India Regiment parading for a funeral in the Castle, 1874.*

with large public rooms, it was put to a variety of uses, including as a law court and as a school. In the 1950s A. W. Lawrence described as 'disgusting' the temporary buildings made from corrugated iron and tarred paper that he found cluttering the Castle at that time, and in 1955 he persuaded the colonial Works Department to strip them out to reveal the old walls. The Castle as it is presented today is the result of an ambitious restoration project undertaken between 1989 and 1994 by the Ghana Museum and Monuments Board in association with the Smithsonian Institution in Washington.

## Retrospect

The transatlantic slave trade continued long after it was made illegal for British citizens. In order to encourage legitimate trade, ships of any nation were allowed to use the roads at Cape Coast Castle, and American ships flying false flags and fitted out as slavers were soon to be found there. Although the British slave trade did cease

*29. Cape Coast Castle school c. 1900.*

almost entirely, the slaves could be marched or canoed to other coastal markets, notably at Whydah in Dahomey, where the local king wanted it to continue. In the 1820s Sarah Bowdich noted that at every place the vessel in which she went home called along the West African coast, the captains were offered slaves with the expression 'Do you want to buy bulls?' Soon the British Navy was deployed off West Africa, intercepting slave ships of all nations, and releasing the slaves on board mainly in Sierra Leone, but new slaving vessels were built, designed for speed rather than capacity so as to outrun the British naval cruisers, and for some decades the illegal transatlantic trade continued at a level not much less than the legal trade had been. In 1861 the *Clara Windsor* of Baltimore, built in 1851, was intercepted carrying 753 slaves – men, women, boys, and girls – destined for Cuba. Another ship of unknown name in 1861 successfully sold 600 slaves there. The *Fairy Flight*, captured by the British in 1861, contained 143 men, 57 women, 237 boys, and 67 girls. In 1866 a ship about which nothing more is known landed 700 slaves in Cuba. Two other slavers were intercepted with no slaves embarked. The last transatlantic slave voyages recorded in the electronic database show a far higher proportion of children than during the period when slaving was legal. The British colonial authorities did not, however, manage to bring the internal slave trade in what is now Ghana to an end until much later. Formally, the institutions of indigenous slavery, including buying, selling, and pawning, were abolished in 1874, with the consent of the local kings and chiefs, but the law was difficult to enforce. In the 1880s children were still being brought down the Volta river to the coast to be sold to work in the palm plantations. And in 1881 the British discovered an American slaving vessel there, allegedly from Brazil, calling itself provocatively by the contemptuous racist Americanism *The Spade*.

The following tables summarize the latest estimates:

**Persons born in Africa sent as slaves from West Africa**

| | |
|---|---|
| Sixteenth century | 266,000, mainly by the Portuguese |
| 1601–1650 | 503,000, mainly by the Portuguese |
| 1651–1700 | 750,000 |
| 1701–1750 | 2,270,000 |
| 1751–1800 | 3,826,000 |
| 1801–1850 | 3,266,000 |
| 1851–1867 | 180,000 |

**Carriers, percent of the total**

| | |
|---|---|
| Portuguese | 46 |
| British | 28 |
| French | 13 |
| Dutch | 5 |
| Spanish | 5 |
| United States and British Caribbean | 3 |
| Danes, Swedes, and Germans | 1 |

The huge numbers transported by the Portuguese in the first half of the nineteenth century after the ending of the legal trade by the northern nations include American-owned ships flying Portuguese colors. Other slaves continued to reach the plantations of the southern United States from large entrepôt markets such as Havana in Cuba. The British share was heavily concentrated in the second half of the eighteenth century until abolition, after which it seems to have been small. Of the British share about 15 percent of the slaves are thought to have been embarked from the Gold Coast.

Recent work that draws on the database shows the overwhelming role of what the slavers called 'the Brazils,' north and south:

**Destinations of persons sent as slaves from West Africa, percent of the total**

| | |
|---|---|
| Brazil | 41 |
| Jamaica | 11 |
| French Saint Domingue | 8 |
| Spanish Caribbean | 8 |
| Barbados | 5 |
| Spanish American mainland | 5 |
| English-speaking mainland North America | 4 |
| British Windward Islands and Trinidad | 4 |
| Guianas | 4 |
| French Windward Islands | 3 |
| British Leeward Islands | 3 |
| Dutch Caribbean | 1 |
| Elsewhere in Americas, including Danish colonies | 1 |
| Africa | 1 |

Information about the numbers of Africans sent north and east is more speculative, but the latest estimates made by Paul E. Lovejoy suggest the following:

Slave exports, mainly of persons born in sub-Saharan
Africa across the Sahara, Red Sea, and Indian Ocean

|  | *1600–1700* | *1700–1800* |
|---|---|---|
| Sahara | 700,000 | 700,000 |
| Red Sea | 100,000 | 200,000 |
| East Africa | 100,000 | 400,000 |
| Totals | 900,000 | 1,300,000 |

A proportion of the slaves exported through North and East Africa
were taken to plantation colonies in the Indian Ocean and to the
Americas.

## Resistance to illness

It was the ability of Africans to withstand the climate of the
plantation colonies in the Americas that helped to create the demand
for slaves. The following table, simplified, has been taken from the
work of Philip D. Curtin. It concerns a later (but still pre-quinine)
period and covers only a particular group of men. But it shows quite
how dramatically different the mortality rates were:

**Annual deaths per thousand soldiers, 1817–38**
**European soldiers**

| Europe and North America | about 15 |
|---|---|
| India | 40 to 70 |
| West Indies | over 100 |

**British expatriate soldiers in West Africa**

about 500

**British soldiers of African origin in Cape Coast Castle**

about 20

Such figures go a long way to explaining not only the transatlantic slave trade but the eagerness of the main European colonial powers to employ men of African origin in their imperial armies.

## *Effects*

What effect did the annual drain of population have on local African societies? Some scholars, such as David Eltis, have concluded that, large though the numbers were, they were small as a proportion, and that to attribute what happened in a vast continent to the influence of a few Europeans in a handful of flimsy forts on the water's edge is a condescending exaggeration, a modern form of Eurocentrism. Roger S. Gocking's *History of Ghana* (2005) scarcely mentions the transatlantic slave trade. However, Patrick Manning, using computerized models, has come to a different conclusion. In Ghana the rising demand at the coast drew supply from deeper and deeper inland. The average length of the march that an enslaved individual might make to the coast rose from perhaps 60 miles in the seventeenth century to 200 miles in the eighteenth. Slave exports were enough to cause a population decline of between 5 and 10 percent from 1720 to 1780 and, since many more men than women were exported, the imbalance of the sexes was as much as 25 percent. The Castle records suggest also that it was a swathe of the fittest and healthiest young men, women, and children that were sent across the Ocean in every voyage.

Attempts have been made to trace the continuation of African cultures and customs on the American side of the ocean, for example in the Chesapeake area of the United States, the destination of many sent from the Castle. Archaeological excavations of grave goods have shown a continuation of the practices of the peoples of West Central Africa, but the results are meager and uncertain. On the American side, reciprocally with the African, there were consistently more men than women, a gender imbalance that over time affected the nature of sexual practices, family, marriage, inheritance, and property in both African American and European American societies, the results of which continue.

In 1944, before much statistical work had been done, Eric Williams argued in an influential book, *Capitalism and Slavery,* that the British industrial revolution was built on the profits of the transatlantic slave trade. However, not only is it now clear that direct profits could only have provided a small fraction of the capital that was mobilized in Britain, but industrialization was well under way long before the years when the trade reached its height. As Joseph E. Inikori has argued in his recent book *Africans and the Industrial Revolution in England*, the argument was never just that those who made profits from the transatlantic slave trade invested the money in manufacturing industry, but that the large-scale production of agricultural commodities made possible by transported Africans encouraged a growth of British manufactured exports all over the oceanic world; in this respect Britain differed from other countries, including China, where industrialization might have been expected to occur. The slaving industry had itself deployed the argument in a pamphlet of 1772: 'how vast is the importance of our trade to Africa, which is the first principle and foundation of the rest; the main spring of the machine which sets every wheel in motion.' Williams may therefore have been right, at any rate in part. However, looking at the matter from a longer perspective, it is clear that the main reason why a succession of fairly small European nations, Portugal, Holland, and then England and Great Britain, were able to project power all over the oceanic world lay in their technological superiority. It was the fact that these countries were already quite industrialized by about 1700 that enabled them to operate the transatlantic slave trade, not that the slave trade resulted in industrialization.

## *What do we tell our children?*

For most people Cape Coast Castle is not a monument, like the Parthenon or the Taj Mahal, that they feel they already know even if they have never seen it. Cape Coast Castle is a site of memory of one of the most far-reaching events in modern history, whose consequences continue to shape our modern world and, although it cannot be approached without preconceptions, it resists easy interpretation. How should we respond? How can we explain this monument to ourselves and to our children and grandchildren? A memorial tablet, recently installed among the plain walls and the old tombs, is inadequate, limiting, and usurping:

> In everlasting memory / Of the anguish of our ancestors / May those who died rest in peace / May those who return find their roots / May humanity never again perpetrate / Such injustices against humanity / We the living vow to uphold this

To regard the transatlantic slave trade as a 'holocaust,' as some have suggested, does not work well as an analogy, except in one respect: the innumerable barriers, some physical, some linguistic, some based on ignorance, organized fictions, hypocrisies, and self-deceptions, that enabled so many otherwise reasonably decent people to condone, to participate, and to benefit. Nor was it a genocide, although some of the harsh treatment inflicted on the slaves in the plantations and mines of the Americas has some similarities. And, although slave trading and North American slavery became increasingly more racist, at the African end of the trade there is no easy correlation between black/white and victims/oppressors. Nor, however, although there were many others who suffered, can we take refuge in the thought that they were all victims.

Is the Castle of the colonial era symbolic of the tropical British Empire, beautiful to behold, admirable even in many of its aspirations and achievements, but in essentials built on hypocrisy, exploitation, and racism? If the story had ended with Governor Torrane's selling of the Anomabu refugees in 1807, that would have been a credible, though shameful, narrative, but our generation is able to appreciate the real, though necessarily ambiguous, benefits that the colonial period brought to some of the peoples of Ghana. Is the Castle an embodiment of imperialism, including modern neo-colonialism, in which the beneficiaries in the developed world keep their eyes as firmly shut as did Jane Austen's ladies? Or is the Castle rather a monument to the ultimate in laissez-faire free-market capitalism, including especially the steps by which human beings were turned into commodities and the stories that participants, and their political and religious leaders, invented to justify institutionalized, industrialized inhumanity?

Two presidents of the United States, Bill Clinton and George W. Bush, publicly visited the 'House of Slaves' on Gorée Island in present-day Senegal as a political gesture of solidarity with African Americans. As a symbolic site of memory Gorée Island, which lies near the westernmost point in Africa – and therefore the nearest point to the Americas – has strong symbolic claims as the last of Africa. It is easy to imagine the enslaved Africans chained in the ships catching their final glimpse of their native continent before the open ocean. There are stories that people of European descent are not permitted to visit some sites that are regarded as sacred. However, the choice of Gorée Island also shows the risks of symbolism divorced from historicity. Although the island was undoubtedly a place from which slaves were taken to the Americas, slave ships from further south did not hug the coast before turning west near Gorée Island. Nor, with the possible exception of the handful who had lived among Europeans, did the embarked slaves think of themselves as 'Africans.' Until they were introduced to the notion of belonging to a continent or to a racial community when they reached the Americas, their sense of identity was founded on much smaller and more local social groupings within the limits of their knowledge and experience. Furthermore, there is a growing consensus that the 'House of Slaves' may never have been a slave facility at all.

Cape Coast Castle, about whose past so much is known, brings out vividly the tensions inherent in preserving ancient monuments. Is the Castle to be presented as a historical document to help us understand the past, conscious that today's building has more affinity with the colonial period than with the slaving era? This approach, although necessarily a compromise, gives primacy to architectural authenticity, continuity and development, and to explanation. Or is it rather to be regarded primarily as a visitor experience, a place for pilgrimage, mourning, therapy, and other (mainly Judaeo-Christian and modernist) imported approaches to commemorating and ritualizing suffering? Should the Castle be a 'wailing wall for the African holocaust'?

In the Castle African leaders have made public displays of contrition for 'African complicity' in the slave trade. By using such language, however, the leaders imply that the Africans who traded in slaves were behaving in a way that was somehow aberrant from their people's main traditions, or were a minority of collaborators. There have been ceremonies in which the bones of unknown African American slaves have been ceremonially brought back from America through the 'door of no return' and laid to rest in his or her native continent. The Ghanaian poet Kwadwo Opoku-Agyemang scolds his fellow countrymen for their silence: 'Growing out of the rock upon which it stands,' he writes, 'Cape Coast Castle is today a blind permanence, the white-heat centre of a pyre, anguish become a castle, a castle as a sign of the triumph of others over us and of our seemingly rootless grief; rootless because we are so silent. But the world does not listen to silence.'

Some American writers of African descent have suggested that, for the modern world to come to terms with the slave trade, and to understand its many implications, there has to be not just history and monuments, vital though they are, but a reshaping of the world's memory, a re-memory, honestly attempted, the word 're-memory' psychologically linked with re-membering, a putting together of broken members. But, to judge from what visitors say and write, not every person of African descent wishes to regard himself or herself as part of the African diaspora. Some Black British and African American visitors comment, 'I'm sad that my ancestors were enslaved and transported, but look at how much better my life is compared with the lives of the descendants of those who remained in Africa.' Ekow Eshun, a British writer of Ghanaian-born parentage, writes in his autobiography of going to Elmina, only to discover that his respected ancestor, Joseph de Graft, who is described on his tomb as 'Nobleman, Merchant, Warrior, Statesman, Patriot,' was a slave dealer – his name can be found among the 'gold takers' in the records of Cape Coast Castle.

As I sit on the Castle walls, alongside the vultures, I watch the parties of schoolchildren, with their eager but puzzled faces, on an educational visit. Am I right to feel glad that they do not think the Castle has much relevance to their own lives?

# Bibliographical note

## Illustrations

It was in 1806, the year before the British slave trade was legally abolished, that supporters of the continuation of the trade published the most evocative of all the illustrations of Cape Coast Castle (see page 244). One of a set of four beautiful hand-colored aquatint views seen from the sea (Cape Coast Castle, Dutch Elmina, Danish Christiansborg, and the British fort at Dixcove) that were prepared in London from drawings made on a visit by the naval artist George Webster, the picture shows a busy scene of peaceful, serene normality, with goods being traded, British ships and boats, and numerous canoes. The two officers in the governor's barge are shown in some copies in red uniforms (African Service), in others in blue (Royal Navy), presumably differentiated for purchasers. What is most striking is that, neither in this picture nor in any of the other three, is there the smallest hint that the sole purpose of these buildings was to facilitate the export of slaves.

## Manuscripts

The T70 series in the National Archives at Kew, described in the Introduction, contains papers of the Royal African Company and of the Company of Merchants, mainly relating to their activities in Africa, but also in Great Britain and in the colonies in the Americas. The typed finding list at Kew is fuller than the one at present online. An annotated list, appended to the article by Eveline C. Martin, 'The English Settlements on the Gold Coast in the Second Half of the Eighteenth Century' in *Transactions of the Royal Historical Society*, 4th series, V (1922), remains unsuperseded. If anyone wishes to find the source of a particular quotation, I will try to oblige.

Two books by J. J. Crooks, an army major, and colonial secretary in Sierra Leone, *Records Relating to the Gold Coast Settlements from 1750 to 1874* and *Historical Records of the Royal African Corps* (both Dublin, 1923), are based on explorations in the T70 series. A few articles, mainly in the tradition of British local history, printed in the middle years of the twentieth century in the *Transactions of the Gold Coast and Togoland Historical Society* (later the *Historical Society of Ghana*), make selective use of these archives, and are valuable for their transcriptions of documents, notably the articles on Fountaine, Harrington, Quaque, and Swanzy. Margaret Priestley in her book-length work on the Brew family, *West African Trade and Coast Society: A Family Study* (Oxford, 1969), quotes many documents. A few documents are quoted by Ty M. Reese, 'The Drudgery of the Slave Trade, Labor at Cape Coast Castle, 1759–1790,' in Peter A. Coclanis (ed.), *The Atlantic Economy during the Seventeenth and Eighteenth Centuries: Organization, Operation, Practice, and Personnel* (Columbia, SC, 2004). The archives were also used, for their histories of the early centuries, by K. G. Davies, *The Royal African Company* (London, 1957), and Kwame Yeboa Daaku, *Trade and Politics on the Gold Coast 1600–1720* (Oxford, 1970).

Many reports, maps, treaties, and other documents compiled and transcribed for William Wilberforce, one of the leaders of the campaign to abolish the slave trade, are held in the British Library, Egerton MSS 1162 A and B. The letters of Rev. Philip Quaque to the United Society for the Propagation of the Gospel and others are in the Bodleian Library, Rhodes House, Oxford, C/AFW/1, West Africa. (I quote extracts not used by F. L. Bartels, 'Philip Quaque, 1741–1816' in the *Transactions of the Gold Coast and Togoland Historical Society* 1 (5) (1955): 153–77.) The letters of Governor Archibald Dalziel, later Dalzel, are in the Edinburgh University Library Dk 7.52. (I quote extracts not used by A. Akinjogbin, 'Archibald Dalzel: Slave Trader and Historian of Dahomey,' *Journal of African History* 7 (1966).) A few manuscripts in my collection relate to a presentation made in the Castle to a departing governor, 1816.

## *Electronic and Printed*

The electronic database on CD is David Eltis, Stephen D. Behrendt, David Richardson, and Herbert S. Klein (eds.), *The Transatlantic Slave Trade: A Database on CD-ROM* (Cambridge, 1999). The implications for a more complete understanding of the transatlantic slave trade were discussed by Bernard Bailyn and others in a special volume of the *William and Mary Quarterly* 58 (2001).

The phrase 'grand emporium' was used by Governor Maclean, in a letter to the Committee of Merchants in 1837: 'Previous to the year 1807, Cape Coast Castle and its dependencies formed the grand emporium whence the British West Indian Colonies were supplied with Slaves' (George Edgar Metcalfe, *Great Britain and Ghana: Documents of Ghana History 1807–1957* [London, 1964], p. 150). Maclean was remembering and repeating a phrase used by Henry Meredith, an officer during the slaving era, in his book *An Account of the Gold Coast of Africa; With a Brief History of The African Company* (London, 1812): 'The countries from Cape Coast to Accra inclusive formed the grand emporium of that [slave] traffic on the Gold-Coast.'

For the Castle and other buildings, see A. W. Lawrence, *The Trade Castles and Forts of West Africa* (London, 1963) and a shorter revised version, *Fortified Trade-Posts: The English in West Africa, 1645–1822* (London, 1969); Albert van Dantzig, *Forts and Castles of Ghana* (Accra, 1980); Kwesi J. Anquandah, *Castles and Forts of Ghana* (Atalante, 1999). For the relations between the early Europeans seeking coastal settlements and the local rulers in the building of the forts, see Yann Deffontaine, *Guerre et société au royaume de Fetu* [Efutu]: *Des débuts du commerce atlantique à la constitution de la fédération fanti (Ghana, Cote de l'Or, 1471–1720)* (Ibadan, 1993). Some details of an attempt by the Dutch to take over the Castle from the Danes are in the report of a trial, [Isaac Coymans], *Brieven, confessie; mitsgaders, advisen van verscheyden rechtsgeleerden in de saeck van Isaac Coymans gegeven: als mede de sententie daar op gevolgt* (Rotterdam [1662]). The last part was published as a broadside. For the history of Cape Coast (town as well as castle), see J. Erskine Graham Jnr, *Cape Coast in History* (Cape Coast, 1994).

The life and career of Sarah Bowdich, later Lee, are summarized in the *Oxford Dictionary of National Biography*, as are those of her first husband, Thomas Edward Bowdich. Although many of her publications that refer to the Castle are in the form of novels or short stories, she claims that they are drawn from direct experience: 'Every production, every character is true; and most of the circumstances are drawn from the personal experience of the Author or her friends' (from the Preface to *The African Wanderers* [London, 1847], reprinted in the United States as *The African Crusoes* [New York, 1870s]). Particularly valuable are the diary entries and factual notes in *Stories of Strange Lands and Fragments from the Notes of a Traveller* (London, 1835), which brought together (and added to) the short pieces about Africa and elsewhere published separately in the annuals *Forget Me Not* and *Friendship's Offering* in the 1820s and 1830s. Many of her later works, such as *Anecdotes of Animals* (London, 1853), include occasional passages about her life in the Castle. See also *Sir Thomas; or the Adventures of a Cornish*

*Baronet in North-Western Africa* (London, 1855), reprinted in the United States as *Adventures in Fanti-Land* (New York, 1870s).

Among the many accounts by European travelers and traders during the slaving era, some reprinted in modern editions and translations, see Pieter de Marees, *Description and historical account of the Gold Kingdom of Guinea (1602)*, trans. from the Dutch and ed. Albert van Dantzig and Adam Jones (Oxford, 1987); Erick Tilleman, *A Short and Simple Account of the Country Guinea and Its Nature: En kort og enfoldig beretning om det landskab Guinea og dets beskaffenhed* (1697), trans. from the Danish and ed. by Selena Axelrod Winsnes (Madison, WI, 1994); William Bosman, *A New and Accurate Description of the Coast of Guinea* (1705), reprinted with notes by J. D. Fage and R. E. Bradbury (New York, 1967); Jean Barbot, *Barbot on Guinea: The writings of Jean Barbot on West Africa, 1678–1712*, ed. by P. E. H. Hair, Adam Jones, and Robin Law (London, Hakluyt Society, 1992); William Snelgrave, *A New Account of Guinea* (London, 1734); John Atkins, *A Voyage to Guinea, Brasil, and the West-Indies* (London, 1935; 2nd edn., 1737); Thomas Phillips, 'A Journal of a Voyage Made in 1693 from England to Africa,' in *A Collection of Voyages and Travels* (London, 1746); Ludwig Rømer, *A Reliable Account of the Coast of Guinea* (1760), ed. by Selena Axelrod Winsnes (Oxford, 2000); Paul Erdmann Isert, *Letters on West Africa and the Slave Trade* (1788), trans. from the German and ed. by Selena Axelrod Winsnes (Oxford, 1992); and William Smith, *A New Voyage to Guinea* (London, 1744). Some of the early printed accounts first published in German are included in *German Sources for West African History, 1599–1669*, comp. and ed. by Adam Jones (Wiesbaden, 1983). Extracts from some of the early and later travelers are collected in Freda Wolfson, *Pageant of Ghana* (London, 1958).

Printed accounts were the main source for the early chapters of W. Walton Claridge's massive colonial history, *History of the Gold Coast and Ashanti* (London, 1915): he made no use of the archives. W. E. F. Ward, *A History of the Gold Coast* (London, 1948; revised 1969) remains useful. There is much primary material about the Castle in Mary McCarthy, *Social Change and the Growth of British Power in the Gold Coast, The Fante States 1807–1874* (Lanham, MD, 1983). Modern histories of Ghana tend to say little about the Castle or the slave trade.

The local, mainly commercial, correspondence of the Royal African Company was printed by Robin Law, *The English in West Africa 1681–1699* (Oxford, 1997, 2001). This is a different body of archives from the main T70 series at Kew. For *Robinson Crusoe*, see the text and accompanying essays in the Norton Critical Edition, ed. Michael Shinagel (2nd edn., 1994). For the many reprints after 1774 when changes in intellectual property practice drastically reduced the price and increased the readership of *Robinson Crusoe* and other early eighteenth-century texts, with figures, see William St Clair, *The Reading Nation in the Romantic Period* (Cambridge, 2004).

Many of the officers of the African Service wrote, or contributed to, books and pamphlets, some as part of the British slaving industry's political defense against calls for abolition. See, for example, John Hippisley, *Essays: I. On the Populousness of Africa. II. On the Trade at the Forts on the Gold Coast. III. On the Necessity of Erecting a Fort at Cape Appolonia* (London, 1764); Rev. T. Thompson, *An Account of Two Missionary Voyages . . . to the coast of Guiney* (London, 1758) and *The African Trade for Negro Slaves Shown to be Consistent with the Principles of Humanity and with the Laws of Revealed Religion* (Canterbury, 1772). Unfortunately I have not traced Thompson's book on the catechism and Thirty-Nine articles that is referred to in some accounts. See also Rowland Cotton, *Extracts from an Account of the State of the British Forts on the Gold Coast of Africa . . . to which are added, Observations by John Roberts, Governor of Cape Coast Castle, etc.* (London, 1778); Archibald Dalzel, *A History of Dahomy* (London, 1793) – this book contains a printed subscription list that includes the names of prominent individuals and firms connected with the slave trade, as well as others; T. Edward Bowdich, *Mission from Cape Coast Castle to Ashantee* (Edinburgh, 1820; repub. with more material, 1873); W. Hutton, *A Voyage to Africa* (London, 1821); Henry Meredith, *An Account of the Gold Coast of Africa; With a Brief History of The African Company* (London, 1812); Brodie Cruikshank, *Eighteen Years on the Gold Coast of Africa* (London, 1853). The anonymous work by many hands *A Treatise on the Trade from Great-Britain to Africa . . . by an African Merchant*, ed. J. F. Demarin (London, 1772), is unusual in containing much directly reported information about actual conditions in the Castle. No list has yet been compiled of the local African rulers in whose territories the Castle and the forts were established. The records of the names of European governors, although fragmentary for the first decades of the Castle's existence, are reasonably complete from the early eighteenth century, although not yet collected. The lists on websites, complete from 1750, mainly derive from that in Claridge (1915).

Among the books by slave-ship captains and surgeons, see particularly Alexander Falconbridge, *Narrative of Two Voyages to the River Sierra Leone During the Years 1791–1792–1793* and *Account of the Slave Trade on the Coast of Africa* (rep. Liverpool, 2000); James Field Stanfield, *Observations on a Guinea Voyage* (London, 1788); and Hugh Crow, *Memoirs* (London, 1830).

For the printed books found in the Castle, most of my information is from the T70 archives. For the books at Charleston, see James Raven, *London Booksellers and American Customers* (Columbia, SC, 2002). For Barbados, *Barbadoes: A Catalogue of Books, to be Sold by Mr. Zouch, in the Town of St. Michael, alias Bridge-Town, in the said Island* (no date, apparently printed in London in the 1740s), Wren Library, Trinity College, Cambridge.

For what was known about the Castle and its activities in Britain, vols. 68, 72, 73, and 82 of the *House of Commons Sessional Papers of the Eighteenth Century*, ed. by Sheila Lambert (Wilmington, DE, 1975 and later), contain the questioning of the Castle governors and other officers of the African Service. Of the many later official reports, particularly relevant are the *Report of the Select Committee on Papers Relating to the African Forts* (1816), and the *Report from the Select Committee on the West Coast of Africa* (1842). According to James Swanzy, governor of four forts between 1789 and 1799, who was questioned by the 1816 parliamentary inquiry, the Castle dungeons housed two types of prisoner – firstly persons who had already been enslaved and sold to the Europeans, and secondly local Africans accused of crimes who were remanded there awaiting trial at the request of local African authorities.

The early attempts by the European slaving nations to change the religious beliefs of the peoples of Africa are related by Joseph Kenny, *The Catholic Church in Tropical Africa, 1445–1850* (Ibadan, 1982), available to be read on the Internet at time of writing. For (former Dutch slave) Capitein and a translation into English of his defense of slavery, see *The Agony of Asar: A Thesis on Slavery by the Former Slave, Jacobus Elisa Johannes Capitein, 1717–1747*, trans. with commentary by Grant Parker (Princeton, NJ, 2001). For the proposed new role for the Castle after the end of the slave trade, and some information on how it stood at that time, see *West-African Sketches, Compiled from the Reports of Sir G. R. Collier, Sir Charles Maccarthy, and Other Official Sources* (London, 1824). Among accounts of the Victorian missionaries who visited the Castle, I quote from S. A. Crowther and J. F. Schön, *Journal of an Expedition up the Niger in 1841* (London, 1843); Rev. Carl Gilbert Reindorf, *History of the Gold Coast and Asante* (Basel, 1889); Rev. Dennis Kemp, *Nine Years at the Gold Coast* (London, 1898); and Friedrich August Ramseyer and Johannes Kühne, *Four Years in Ashantee / by the missionaries Ramseyer and Kühne; edited by Mrs. Weitbrecht* (London, 1875).

For indigenous slavery and the slave trade within Ghana, including local oral traditions, I draw on the work by Akosua Adoma Perbi, *A History of Indigenous Slavery in Ghana* (Accra, 2004). Also S. D. Fomin, *A Comparative Study of Societal Influences on Indigenous Slavery in Two Types of Slavery in Africa* (New York and Queenston, 2002). For recent work on African perspectives that uses African oral sources, see Anne C. Bailey, *African Voices of the Atlantic Slave Trade: Beyond the Silence and the Shame* (Boston, 2003); Sylviane A. Diouf (ed.), *Fighting the Slave Trade: West African Strategies* (Athens, OH, 2003). For evidence from archaeology, see Christopher R. DeCorse, *An Archaeology of Elmina: Africans and Europeans on the Gold Coast, 1400–1900* (Washington, DC, 2001) and *West Africa during the Atlantic Slave Trade: Archaeological Perspectives*, ed. by Christopher R. DeCorse (Leicester, 2001). For slave trading in, and raiding for, markets to the north and east, see Humphrey J. Fisher, *Slavery in the History of Muslim Black Africa* (London, 2001), which includes an account of the graphic reports and illustrations by Gustav Nachtigal in his *Reisen in der Sahara und im Sudan* (Leipzig, 1887).

For military and naval forces, see Paul Mmegha Mbaeyi, *British Military and Naval Forces in West African History 1807–1874* (Lagos and London, 1978) and Roger Norman Buckley, *Slaves in Red Coats: The British West India Regiments, 1795–1815* (New Haven, CT, 1979). For the effects of the exchanges of pathogens and the mortality rates of European forces in the various regions of the tropical world settled by Europeans, see the many writings of Philip D. Curtin, notably *Death by Migration: Europe's Encounter with the Tropical World in the Nineteenth Century* (Cambridge, 1989) and *Disease and Empire: The Health of European Troops in the Conquest of Africa* (Cambridge, 1998).

For the discussions of the slave trade in Britain, selections of printed writings are reprinted by Kenneth Morgan et al. (eds.), *The British Transatlantic Slave Trade*, 4 vols. (London, 2003), and Peter J. Kitson et al. (eds.), *Slavery, Abolition, and Emancipation: Writings in the British Romantic Period*, 8 vols. (London, 1999); the latter includes the pamphlet by Quobna Ottobah Cugoano. The recent biography of Equiano by Vincent Carretta, *Equiano the African: Biography of a Self-Made Man* (Athens, GA, 2005), adds much to previous work, notably on the role of former slaves in the abolition campaign in Britain. Among much other writing of all kinds on slavery and the British slave trade, I commend Gad Heuman and James Walvin (eds.), *The Slavery Reader* (London, 2003), Kenneth Morgan, *Bristol and the Atlantic Trade in the Eighteenth Century* (Cambridge, 1993), and Adam Hochschild, *Bury the Chains* (Boston, 2004), although I know of none that makes use of the Castle archives. For the British policies of persuading other countries to stop trading, a useful factual summary is James Bandinel, *Some Account of the Trade in Slaves from Africa as Connected with Europe and America* (London, 1842).

For George Maclean, see George Edgar Metcalfe, *Maclean of the Gold Coast* (Oxford, 1962) and the previously mentioned *Great Britain and Ghana: Documents of Ghana History, 1807–1957*. For Letitia Elizabeth Landon, most of the sources are collected by F. J. Sypher, *Letters by Letitia Elizabeth Landon* (Ann Arbor, MI *c*.2001) and *Letitia Elizabeth Landon: A Biography* (Ann Arbor, MI, 2004). The article by Cynthia Lawford, with its revelations and documentary records of Landon's children, which is not given due weight in Sypher's biography, was printed in the *London Review of Books*, vol. 22, no. 18 (September 21, 2000). See also Kwadwo Opoku-Agyemang's collection of poems *Cape Coast Castle* (Accra, 1996).

Among the many Victorian visitors to the Castle who wrote of their experiences, especially relevant are Henry Huntley, *Seven Years' Service on the Slave Coast of Western Africa* (London, 1860); Richard Burton, *Wanderings in West Africa* (London, 1863); A. B. Ellis, *West African Sketches* (London, 1881) and, with an account of his landing his troops across the surf, *Land of Fetish* (London, 1883); Mary H. Kingsley, *West African Studies* (London, 1899) and *Travels in West Africa* (London, 1900); George Macdonald, *The Gold Coast* (London, 1900); Garnet Wolseley, *The Story of a Soldier's Life* (London, 1903); and Decima Moore and Major F. G. Guggisberg, *We Two in West Africa* (London, 1909).

For recent research on the transatlantic slave trade, including statistics and economic analysis, I have used Patrick Manning, *Slavery and African Life* (Cambridge, 1990); Herbert S. Klein, *The Atlantic Slave Trade* (Cambridge, 1999); Barbara L. Solow (ed.), *Slavery and the Rise of the Atlantic System* (Cambridge, 1991); Paul E. Lovejoy, *Transformations of Slavery* (Cambridge, 2000); David Eltis, *The Rise of African Slavery in the Americas* (Cambridge, 2000); Robin Law (ed.), *From Slave Trade to Legitimate Commerce: The Commercial Transition in Nineteenth-Century West Africa* (Cambridge, 1995); and Joseph E. Inikori, *Africans and the Industrial Revolution in England* (Cambridge, 2002).

For the debates about the modern purpose of the Castle as a monument, see Anthony Hyland, 'Monuments Conservation Practice in Ghana: Issues of Policy and Management,' *Journal of Architectual Conservation*, 2 (1995), and Brempong Osei-Tutu, 'African American reactions to the restoration of Ghana's "slave castles",' *Public Archaeology* 3/4, 2004. For so-called roots tourism at the Castle, see Cheryl Finley, 'Authenticating Dungeons, Whitewashing Castles: The Former Sites of the Slave Trade on the Ghanaian Coast,' in *Architecture and tourism: perception, performance and place*, ed. by D. Medina Lasansky and Brian McLaren (Oxford 2004).

For a modern response, see Ekow Eshun, *Black Gold of the Sun* (London, 2005). Many others are available to be read on the Internet.

# List of illustration

# Index

Goodwin, slave ship captain 221, 229
Gorée island 2, 262–3
Governing Committee 44, 58, 62,
    108–9, 125, 143
'Grain Coast' 10
Greenhill, Henry, governor 60, 273
Greer, Germaine 171
Grossle, John, governor 51, 60, 147
Guggisberg, Sir Gordon, colonial
    governor 20, 91, 176
Guiana 15, 181, 257
guineas 92, 116
gun salutes 17–18
Guy, Thomas, beneficiary of South
    Sea bubble 85

**H**
Hamilton, Henry, fort governor, his
    protest 197–8
Harrington, Edward, American sea
    captain 167–8
Hazlitt, William 121
health and illness 2, 47–8, 98–105,
    112–13, 149, 160, 184;
    death rate 99–102, 252, 258–9;
    effects of quinine 168, 259
Hippisley, John, governor 58, 118,
    147–8, 151–2, 200–201, 218, 225
Holmes, Robert, captures the Castle
    32
How, Anthony, botanist 80–81
Huntley, Henry, naval officer, spoils
    his white trousers 26
Hutton, William, officer 48–9, 73
Hyland Anthony 274

**I**
India, goods from 15, 70–72
Inikori, Joseph E. 260
illness *see* health
Isert, Paul, Danish scientist 12
ivory 37, 92–3

**J**
Jamah, wife of Governor Miles
    148–9
Jamaica 3, 15, 93, 133, 164, 209, 233,
    246, 257
James II and VII, British king,
    investor 85, 182, 211
Jerdan, William editor 170–71

**K**
Kemp, Dennis, Christian missionary
    91, 98, 167
King, slave ship captain 23, 190, 221
Kingsley, Mary 6, 49, 80
Kipling, Rudyard 195, 199
Koelle, S. W. 138
Komenda fort 16, 17, 41, 82
Korante, Eno Basi 182–3
Kormantse fort 192, 203
Kumasi 48, 192, 252
Kwekwi *see* Quaque

**L**
Lacey, William, officer, his final
    sufferings relieved by religious
    rites 119–20
Landon, Letitia Elizabeth 64,
    169–80
Lattie, slave seller 202, 222
Lawford, Cynthia 171, 273
Lawrence, A. W. archaeologist, 5–6,
    29, 36, 80, 185, 254
Lawrence, T. E. 5
Lévi-Strauss, Claude 69
literacy and orality 68–70 *see also*
    palavers
Liverpool, slaving port 18, 85, 86, 186,
    204–5
Lovejoy, Paul E. 140, 256

**M**
McCarthy, Charles, military officer
    and governor, 249–50

# Acknowledgements

I should like to record my thanks to the members of staff of the British Library; Cambridge University Library; Cape Coast Castle; Guildhall Library, London; London Library; Bodleian Library (Rhodes House), Oxford; Edinburgh University Library; Ghana National Archives, Accra; National Archives, Kew; National Portrait Gallery; Library of Trinity College, Cambridge; and the Schomburg Center, New York Public Library. Without exception, they have been welcoming, knowledgeable, and helpful, and have made my work a pleasure.

Among the many friends and colleagues who have encouraged and helped me in researching, writing, and revising the book I should like to record my particular gratitude to Annika Bautz, Mary Beard, Peter Carson, Penny Daniel, Heather Ewing, Andrew Franklin, Kevin Gray, Jan-Erik Guerth, Richard Holmes, Anna Joy, Ruth Killick, Peter Kin, Sue Lamble, Deirdre le Faye, John Lonsdale, Nana Nyarkua Ocran, Augustine Kofi Mensah, David Parrott, Caroline Pretty, Barbara Ravelhofer, Emma Rothschild, Leigh Shaw-Taylor, Nicola Taplin, and Frances Wilson.

WStC